W9-DFC-922

SIGNIFICANT CSIS ISSUES SERIES

KOREA 2010

THE CHALLENGES OF
THE NEW MILLENNIUM

PAUL F. CHAMBERLIN

KOREA 2010
THE CHALLENGES OF
THE NEW MILLENNIUM

Significant Issues Series
Timely books presenting current CSIS research and analysis of interest to the academic, business, government, and policy communities.
Managing editor: Roberta L. Howard

■ ■ ■

For four decades, the **Center for Strategic and International Studies (CSIS)** has been dedicated to providing world leaders with strategic insights on—and policy solutions to—current and emerging global issues.

CSIS is led by John J. Hamre, formerly deputy secretary of defense, who has been president and CEO since April 2000. It is guided by a board of trustees chaired by former senator Sam Nunn and consisting of prominent individuals from both the public and private sectors.

The CSIS staff of 190 researchers and support staff focus primarily on three subject areas. First, CSIS addresses the full spectrum of new challenges to national and international security. Second, it maintains resident experts on all of the world's major geographical regions. Third, it is committed to helping to develop new methods of governance for the global age; to this end, CSIS has programs on technology and public policy, international trade and finance, and energy.

Headquartered in Washington, D.C., CSIS is private, bipartisan, and tax-exempt. CSIS does not take specific policy positions; accordingly, all views expressed herein should be understood to be solely those of the author.

The CSIS Press
Center for Strategic and International Studies
1800 K Street, N.W., Washington, D.C. 20006
Tel: (202) 887-3119
Fax: (202) 775-3199
E-mail: books@csis.org
Web site: http://www.csis.org/

KOREA 2010

THE CHALLENGES OF
THE NEW MILLENNIUM

PAUL F. CHAMBERLIN

Foreword by Kim Kihwan

THE CSIS PRESS

Center for Strategic
and International Studies
Washington, D.C.

HARVARD-YENCHING LIBRARY
HARVARD UNIVERSITY
2 DIVINITY AVENUE
CAMBRIDGE, MA 02138
12/10/2001

The CSIS Press, Washington, D.C. 20006
© 2001 by the Center for Strategic and International Studies
All rights reserved.
Printed on recycled paper in the United States of America
05   04   03   02   01   5   4   3   2   1

ISSN 0736-7136
ISBN 0-89206-390-4

Cover design by Robert L. Wiser, Archetype Press, Washington, D.C.
Cover photo, flag of the Republic of Korea, © CORBIS

Library of Congress Cataloging-in-Publication Data
Chamberlin, Paul F.
   Korea 2010 : the challenges of the new millennium / Paul F.
Chamberlin; foreword by Kim Kihwan.
      p. cm. -- (Significant issues series, ISSN 0736-7136; v. 23, no. 2)
   Includes bibliographical references and index.
   ISBN 0-89206-390-4
   1. Korea (South)--Forecasting. I. Title. II. Series.
DS902.C48 2001
303.495195--dc21
                                        2001003117

Contents

Figures

Acknowledgments

I WISH TO THANK THE KOREA FOUNDATION for its foresight in encouraging and supporting a comprehensive, interdisciplinary assessment of the challenges Korea faces in the coming decade. I appreciate Dr. William J. Taylor, former senior vice president of CSIS, for inviting me to write *Korea 2010* and my colleagues in International Technology and Trade Associates, Inc. (ITTA), whose support reflects their appreciation of Korea's importance.

I take full responsibility for the work, while deeply appreciating the strong support provided by friends who conducted extensive research or took precious time to review the drafts: Bill Taylor; Sukwoo Kim, senior visiting fellow at CSIS; Mike Mazarr, president and CEO of the Henry L. Stimson Center; Peter Paraschos, ITTA; and Dennis J. Blasko. *Korea 2010* could not have been written without the help of Kyunghwan "Kevin" Jung and Hyun-Yong "Leo" Kim, who were graduate students at George Washington University's Elliott School of International Affairs, and Ian Woodcroft of CSIS. They assisted in the basic research for *Korea 2010*, helping to make it a resource for years to come.

I also thank my dear wife, Kay, and my family, including my late father, for their steadfast support through the many weekends, holidays, and evenings that I took from them to write this book.

Foreword

PAUL F. CHAMBERLIN BEGINS his *Korea 2010: The Challenges of the New Millennium* with an important observation: South Korea has already embarked on a course to becoming a prosperous knowledge-era democracy. He notes, however, that success is not a foregone conclusion. Thus the central question for our consideration is whether Korea, an industrial nation, will make a successful transition to a knowledge-based economy over the next 10 years. This is, of course, an important question not only to policymakers but also to all who care about Korea's future. Chamberlin should be complimented for having placed this question at the heart of his book.

To answer this question as objectively and as thoroughly as possible, the author makes use of the six major trends of development in the world today, trends that were identified in an earlier CSIS study entitled *Global Trends 2005—An Owner's Manual for the Next Decade* by Michael J. Mazarr. Chamberlin, in effect, translates these trends into tests for assessing Korea's transition to a knowledge-era democracy.

Test One concerns Korea's initial conditions. Chamberlin examines whether Korea's demographic structure, natural resource endowment, and cultural foundation are adequate for the nation to become a prosperous knowledge-era democracy. Test Two relates to Korea's ability to undertake broad social and political reforms that are crucial for dealing successfully with the unprecedented challenges brought on by the information technology (IT) revolution and globalization. Test Three has to do with the key element in the success of any society in making the transition to the knowledge era, namely the human resources base. Test Four looks at Korea's ability to overcome the unavoidable tension between globalism on one hand and tribalism on the other. Test Five concerns Korea's capability to devise a new set of institutions and social practices that can command sufficient respect and authority to replace the current ones, including the Korea Inc. business model, political parties, and Confucian ethics that are in rapid decline in terms of influence. Finally, Test Six examines Korea's capacity to cope with the rising level of anxiety and psychological stress the nation will continue to experience as it makes the historical transition from the industrial age to the knowledge age.

On the basis of these six tests, the author postulates four scenarios for Korea's future. These scenarios are not meant to be forecasts. Rather, they serve as a framework for analyzing different paths to the future as well as the policy implications of each. Scenario One envisions a successful and relatively timely transition to a knowledge era, enabling Korea to win a proud place among the family of knowledge-era democracies by 2010. The final outcome of this scenario critically depends on the successful completion of the financial, corporate, labor, and public sector reforms currently in progress. Scenario Two projects a much slower transition to knowledge-era democracy because Korea fails to fully implement the current four-sector reform package.

Scenario Three assumes a situation in which the governments that succeed the Kim Dae-jung administration will reverse the direction of current reforms. This course is likely to reduce Korea's competitiveness in the global markets, thus consigning Korea to the ranks of the also-ran.

Scenario Four projects an outcome much worse than Scenario Three. If the direction of the current reform is reversed, one cannot rule out a further reduction of Korea's international competitiveness along with widespread corruption, serious social disorder, and a dangerous decline in the ability of civil authorities to govern. This could well bring about a military coup d'état.

Of the four scenarios, Scenario Two is the most likely. Scenario Four is most unlikely, but we cannot rule it out in view of Korea's history.

Korea 2010 has many merits for all of us concerned about Korea's future. It is a book written by an American who is thoroughly familiar with Korean people and their culture. It provides many useful insights into Korea, the country, and what makes Koreans tick. In addition, thanks to the author's methodology, the book is full of information on not only the Korean culture and body politic but also the important changes the world is undergoing as globalization and the IT revolution accelerate. Furthermore, the author addresses a large number of the specific policy issues Koreans themselves need to address if they want to make their nation a fully mature and prosperous democracy in the knowledge era.

Thus by addressing those issues yet to be addressed by Korean intellectuals, Chamberlin has done a great favor for his Korean friends. What's more, the author does not hesitate to examine the "unthinkable"—the possibility of yet another military coup d'état in Korea. No doubt this will come as a shock to many Koreans who either are too complacent about the future of their country or have been too preoccupied with short-term issues to notice the true state of democracy in their own land absent economic prosperity. For these reasons and more, *Korea 2010* is well worth a serious reading by all those both inside and outside Korea who are concerned with its future.

KIM KIHWAN

Dr. Kim is International Adviser, Goldman-Sachs (Seoul); Chairman, Korean National Committee for the Pacific Economic Cooperation Council; and Chairman, Society for Unification Studies.

Introduction

Chagun kochu ga mwep da. (The little pepper is the hot one!)

—Korean proverb

South Korea has embarked on a course to become a prosperous knowledge-era democracy. Its success is largely dependent on how it manages the journey into the knowledge era—that time when knowledge, not manufactured goods, become the central product and the core around which society is organized. Success will empower its diligent, educated, energetic people to reach new heights. Success is not a foregone conclusion, however. Failure to complete the transition could consign this advanced industrialized nation to the ranks of the also-ran, not a supplier but a consumer of new technologies and services that are supplied by societies that successfully transition to the knowledge era.

A host of questions arise about Korea's prospects in this, the first decade of the third millennium. Will it successfully implement the four-sector reforms prompted by the 1997 financial crisis and become one of the world's leading economies? Can South Korean companies emerge from the legacies of Korea Inc. to compete successfully—without government protection and subsidies—against the world's major firms? Will South Korea and North Korea become a unified state, forming one market and an economic powerhouse? Will South Koreans continue to regard the United States as a long-term friend and ally, turn to others, or pursue a wholly independent course?

The answers to such questions lie in understanding the factors affecting South Korean individual and institutional decisionmaking, especially Korea's culture and domestic concerns. The foundations of South Korea's ancient culture are trembling as Koreans access the knowledge era, which is transforming Korean values and decisionmaking parameters.

The five Confucian relationships that underpin Korean society enabled Korea's rapid industrialization from the 1960s to the 1990s; this was the first wave of modernization, and it greatly affected Korean society. However, some of these Confucian relationships are ill-suited to the demands of the knowledge era—the second wave of modernization—with its stress on individualism.

Koreans want their country to be a prosperous, knowledge-era democracy. To achieve that goal, they are accepting economic and political principles rooted in Western concepts of the role of the individual, the rule of law, and the necessity of institutional checks and balances. Some of these concepts conflict with Confucian values as practiced in Korea, producing turmoil and anxiety.

Korea 2010: The Challenges of the New Millennium reviews the changes under way in South Korea, their implications, and their challenges. This is the second country study in CSIS's Global Trends project, and it applies a paradigm established in *Global Trends 2005: An Owner's Manual for the Next Decade,* by Michael J. Mazarr.[1] *Global Trends 2005* examined a number of societies in transition to the knowledge era and identified six trends:

Trend one is the foundation for change, specifically demographics, environment, indigenous natural resources, and the ways in which members of the society relate to one another and to others—in short: culture.

Trend two addresses the engines of change. These include developments in science and technology as well as social and psychological processes. The engines of change usually promote liberalization, democracy, and international interdependence.

Trend three is the importance of establishing a human resources economy, as knowledge-era societies focus on discovering, creating, applying, and distributing knowledge. The distinguishing feature of knowledge-era economies is empowered human resources, not machines, which were a distinguishing feature of the industrial age.

Societies that suppress their human resources find it difficult to embrace the concepts and practices required to encourage, inspire, and empower their employees, and they pay the price in lost competitiveness until they change.

Trend four is the relationship between pluralism and tribalism, including nationalism. Societies may seek the benefits of globalization, which promotes pluralism, while they try to retain local nationalistic practices.

Trend five is the collapse of old authorities and the rise of new ones. As a society moves deeper into the knowledge era, some old authorities become unable to provide solutions. People look to new authorities inherent in the new technologies and concepts; this creates immense tension and turmoil throughout the society as old authorities struggle to retain power. Empowered citizens find liberal, pluralistic democracy and free-enterprise, market economics to be the systems best suited to meet their needs.

Trend six is the test of human psychology. The transition to the knowledge era is turbulent, as cultural points of reference lose relevance and both individuals and institutions struggle with changing realities. The transition severely tests the human psyche due to ever-increasing anxiety that can lead to alienation and highly dysfunctional behavior. If the test is too severe, it can dissuade the society from proceeding in its transition.

Korea 2010 in chapters 1–6 applies each trend to Korea and in chapter 7 posits four representative scenarios that Koreans could follow en route to 2010. The purpose of these scenarios is to apply the trends and indicators identified to be driving change to Korea's future, *not* to forecast Korea's future per se but to furnish a range of outcomes that could develop as Koreans negotiate their way to the knowledge era.

In applying the Global Trends paradigm to *Korea 2010,* I relied heavily on Mike Mazarr's contributions and my own understandings reinforced by research to determine how each trend is playing out in Korea. Each trend chapter comprises two major sections. The introductory section describes the trend as it is manifested globally; this provides a foundation for understanding its application in Korea. Recognizing the excellence of Mike Mazarr's description of each trend in the first country study, *Mexico 2005,*[2] I updated and used it in similar fashion in *Korea 2010* with permission of the Center for Strategic and International Studies (CSIS). The second major section in chapters 1–6 focuses on how the trend is playing out in South Korea, its implications, and challenges for the future. Readers might be tempted to begin their review in this second section, but taking this course may deprive them of the fullest understanding of the global trend as laid out in the introductory section.

Korea's future is in the hands of South Koreans and their institutions. *Korea 2010: The Challenges of the New Millennium* is offered to promote understanding of the changes under way in South Korea and their implications.

Notes

1. Michael J. Mazarr, *Global Trends 2005: An Owner's Manual for the Next Decade* (New York: St. Martin's/CSIS, 1999).

2. Michael J. Mazarr, *Mexico 2005: The Challenges of the New Millennium* (Washington, D.C.: CSIS, 1999).

1 ■

Trend One: The Foundations

D EMOGRAPHIC, ENVIRONMENTAL, natural resource, and cultural factors establish the context in which trends unfold.[1] During the first decade of the twenty-first century, these factors should remain relatively constant; that is, prices should be more or less stable and no major global discontinuities should occur although forecasting prices of highly volatile energy resources is admittedly problematic. Despite this expectation of general stability, two overarching issues are paramount. One is a growing need for long-range planning to address needs that, although they may not mature in the first decade of the century, nonetheless demand action during this period. The second is the risk that a combination of factors—regarding energy resources, for example—will conspire to produce a series of recurrent and unpredictable price spikes amid generally sufficient supply in major categories of natural resources.

On the issues of demographics, the environment, natural resources, and cultural values, trend one illuminates the intense combination of challenges and opportunities embodied in South Korea's future, which at some distant point must become part of a unified Korea. Lacking significant natural resources but with a well-educated, diligent, talented, and energetic population, Korea could adopt the technologies and habits of the knowledge era to achieve sustainable—and sustained—growth. Taking advantage of opportunities requires the right political decisions, and Korea must yet prove it can step up to this requirement.

A Story of Two Worlds

Both demography and the environment reveal sharp distinctions between the industrial and developing worlds. The demographic situation is simple: the developing world's population is growing fast, while the population of the industrial world is stagnant and aging. Worldwide population is growing at a staggering rate. After taking almost two millennia to produce its first one billion people, the human race added a second billion in just a century and its most recent billion in little more than a decade. The world is now accommodating a growth in population equal to a new Pittsburgh or a Boston every two days, a new Korea approximately every eight months and very nearly a new India every decade.[2] And yet because of global forces such as modernization, education, and the expansion of women's rights—all of which tend to suppress fertility—the world's population growth rate is actually declining. World population growth is not out of control, and in the course of the next half century it is expected to level off and perhaps even begin to decline to a level somewhere between 8 and 12 billion people (see figure 1).

From 1995 to 2005, world population will continue to grow at its highest annual rate in history, increasing by roughly 800 to 900 million people to reach a total of about 6.6 billion.[3] This means, first, that massive population growth will occur in the developing world. Between 1990 and 1995, 95 percent of population growth occurred in developing countries, and that percentage will inch higher between 1999 and 2015 when developed countries increase by 29 million compared with 1.147 billion in less-developed countries.[4] Most growth will take place in the few countries in the "arc of crisis" that stretches from sub-Saharan Africa through North Africa and the Middle East into South Asia.

Population growth will inaugurate rapid urbanization in the developing world. Fully 90 percent of growth in urban populations during the decade will take place in developing nations—bringing explosive ramifications that include problems of waste, water supply, air pollution, and alienation, especially among youth.[5] By 2005 almost 60 developing countries, including two dozen states in sub-Saharan Africa as well as important Middle Eastern states such as

Figure 1
World Population Growth, 1950–2050

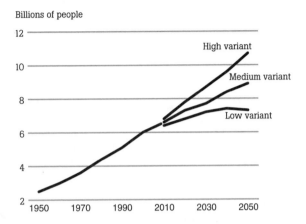

Billions of people

Source: World Population Prospects: The 1998 Revision, Vol. 1: Comprehensive Tables, UN Sales No. E.99.X111.9 (New York: United Nations Population Division, 1999). Reprinted with permission.

Egypt, Iran, and Iraq, will show "youth bulges"—20 percent or more of their populations will be in the 15- to 24-year-old age range.

If soaring populations have ominous implications for developing countries, slowing population growth in industrialized nations is equally disturbing—the industrial world is growing older.

Low birth rates and longer life spans, especially for the massive post–World War II population and the more slowly growing successor generations, mean that most industrial world populations are made up of older inhabitants. In most industrial countries, including Korea,[6] the number of retirees (over 65 years of age) will rise 60 percent by 2025.

The industrial and developing worlds see environmental issues differently also. In the industrial world, although total levels of pollution, greenhouse-gas emissions, and other forms of environmental damage continue to rise, pollution has been declining as a per-dollar-of-gross-national-product ratio and often also in per capita terms. This reflects an important trend: a knowledge economy is better for the environment than an industrial-era economy because

Figure 2
Growth of World Grain Production, 1971–2015

Note: The base year is 1971; total growth and growth per capita are shown as percentages of 1971.

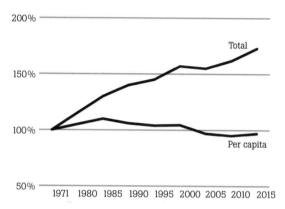

Source: "Global Trends 2015: A Dialogue about the Future with Nongovernment Experts" (Washington, D.C.: Central Intelligence Agency, 2000), www.cia.gov/cia/publications/globaltrends2015/3735781.gif, accessed February 5, 2001.

a knowledge economy pollutes less and uses fewer resources. At the beginning of the twenty-first century, the world is at the start of a radical transition to a social and industrial mode of production based on clean technology. Reflecting this new promise is the emerging field of industrial ecology that focuses on reconciling economic growth and environmental health.

But this transition will be fully under way only in the 2011–2020 decade. In the meantime, pollution from the developing world is growing dramatically. By 1992 developing nations had overtaken the industrial world in terms of the levels of emission of carbon dioxide. Carbon emissions of developing nations are expanding three times faster than those of industrial nations. China alone, if its current growth continues, will emit more greenhouse gases by 2025 than the United States, Japan, and Canada combined.

A Price-Spike Economy

Just as they are environmentally more benign than industrial economies, knowledge-era economies are also less dependent on natural resources. Creating knowledge demands fewer natural resources than manufacturing does. Nonetheless, population growth and economic growth will put new pressure on certain categories of resources in selected areas. Combined with just-in-time delivery techniques, the result may be recurring price spikes amid generally stable resource prices.

World food output, for example, more than doubled in the last three decades of the twentieth century and is expected to continue to expand in the foreseeable future. Food supplies per capita grew by 25 percent, including in many areas of the developing world where the quality of diets continues to improve; in addition the real cost of many food items has declined.[7] Globally, however, reasons for concern persist as grain production declines on a per capita basis and continued yield increases must be developed with further research. Even more alarming, a dramatic exception to the rule of ample food supplies will occur in the arc of crisis, where exploding populations and continuing poverty will make food shortages a way of life and create the need for intervention by numerous outside aid missions (see figure 2 on page 4 for world grain production).

Growing worldwide population will also put new pressure on world water supplies. Eighty countries, most in the arc of crisis, already face life-threatening water shortages. By 2025 the amount of water available to those countries will have fallen by 80 percent.[8] South Korea, in fact, anticipates a possible water shortage by 2006.

More people at a higher standard of living will use more energy (figure 3). Perhaps the greatest part of this increase will not take place in the industrial world, where knowledge-era economies are more efficient in their use of energy, but in developing countries. In the United States, for example, energy use per dollar of gross national product (GNP) declined almost 30 percent between 1980 and 2000. Oil prices, however, are likely to remain highly volatile for the foreseeable future despite abundant energy resources.[9]

Hydrocarbon-based fuels, especially oil, have proved indispensable to the industrial age. Because these are finite resources, a key

Figure 3
World Oil Prices, 1970–2020

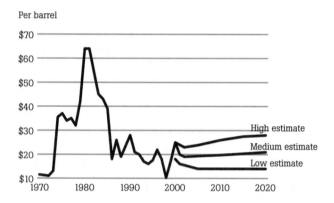

Source: "International Energy Outlook 2000," report no. DOE/EIA-0484 (Washington, D.C.: U.S. Energy Information Administration, 2000), fig. 40, www.eia.doe.gov/oiaf/archive/ieo00/pdf/0484(2000).pdf, accessed July 9, 2001.

concern has been that future time when they cannot be accessed and supplied cost-effectively. Analysis since the mid-1990s has suggested that global oil production could peak by 2015 and taper off by approximately 2050 although new technologies might postpone the peak production date by several years. This conclusion implies an urgent need for research and development (R&D) to produce alternative energy technologies, including renewable sources like solar, wind, and biomass.

Discoveries of new sources of oil and other hydrocarbon fuels naturally would prolong their availability over the long term. In April 2000, in 12 scenarios, the U.S. Energy Information Administration presented peak production estimates that indicate global peak oil production could occur at some point in a 90-year window between 2021 and the second decade of the twenty-second century, 2112 to be precise.[10] Discoveries of new deposits and the emergence of improved enhanced oil recovery (EOR) technology that would permit the cost-effective extraction of more oil given market conditions would postpone the date of peak global production.[11]

Supply interruptions and price spikes could still occur, and energy consumers should not be complacent about their cost-effective access to hydrocarbon-based energy supplies, especially oil. Rapid economic growth in developing nations will place greater demand on oil supplies and contribute to their exhaustion. Price manipulation will affect cost: supplier increases in the cost of oil to a post–Gulf War high of $37.50 per barrel in September 2000 make the point. Although Saudi Arabia, the leading member of the Organization of Petroleum Exporting Countries (OPEC), wants to keep the cost of oil in the range of $22–$28 per barrel, events of late summer 2000 demonstrate the difficulty of achieving this objective. Therefore, governments and industries that want cost-effective fuel might be inspired to increase R&D for alternative energy technologies.

As a result, the 2011–2020 decade may witness the beginning—the real beginning, after decades of fits and starts—of the age of renewable energy. After natural gas, renewables will probably be the fastest growing energy source during 2011–2020. Technological advances could soon make easily usable renewable energy sources (such as photovoltaic cells) cost competitive with traditional energy sources.

The Foundation of Human Perception: Culture

A final foundation of trends in the next decade is culture—that amorphous combination of values, habits, religion, language, and other factors that differentiates one group of people from another. In the simplest terms, the application of culture to the trends examined here involves appreciating the basic insight of sociology. Peter Berger, in his classic *Invitation to Sociology*, wrote that people are not "also" social beings but are "social in every aspect of [their] being that is open to empirical investigation . . .. The structures of society become the structures of our own consciousness."[12] This connection between national culture and national success establishes a baseline for many national forecasts offered later in this study. Some cultures are clearly better equipped than others to succeed in the fast-paced, decentralized, flexible world of the knowledge era. Culture also has profound effects on relations among countries and other large groups and institutions.

Figure 4
Age Groups in South Korea, est., 2010

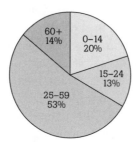

Source: "International Database," U.S. Census Bureau, www.census.gov/ipc/www/idbagg.html, accessed September 20, 2000.

Thus culture will be important to world trends—socially, economically, politically, militarily—during the next decade. Developments can be bent or skewed in one direction or another by cultural proclivities, practices, or preconceptions. But cultural identity emphatically is not a static, predictable, unchanging influence on members of society. In fact, the engines of history outlined in chapter 2 are reshaping world cultures perhaps more profoundly and more rapidly than at any other time.

Applying the Trends to Korea

Demography

Korea joined the Organization for Economic Cooperation and Development (OECD) in 1996, becoming only the second Asian member after Japan. By extending membership, the world's leading industrial nations in the OECD acknowledged Korea's economic accomplishments and transition to industrialized state status. Aside from economic performance, Korea manifests demographic traits that align it more closely with the OECD industrialized nations than with developing nations; for example, Korea has an aging soci-

Figure 5
Percentage of Population Older than 60 Years of Age,
South Korea, est., 2000–2050

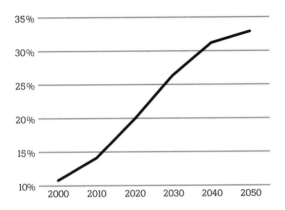

Source: "International Database," U.S. Census Bureau, www.census.gov/ipc/www/ idbagg.html, accessed September 20, 2000.

ety, declining birth rates, increasing per capita income, smaller families, and, unfortunately, an increasing divorce rate.

South Korea's population in 2010 is expected to exceed 51 million people, a 7.6 percent increase over the 2000 number of 47.4 million.[13] This expected growth reflects a continued decline in Korea's population growth rate as the country's median age continues to increase consistently with other OECD countries. By 2030, more than 25 percent of Koreans will be eligible to retire while youths under 15 years of age will constitute less than 15 percent of the general population. These developments and the greatly reduced size of Korean families will present future questions regarding elder care and employment opportunities.

A snapshot of population projections for 2010 (figure 4) shows that 10.2 million Koreans will be under age 15 while 7.2 million will be 60 or older, with more than 2.8 million eligible under current policies to receive government retirement benefits from the National Pension Corporation, up 200 percent from 630,000 in 2000.[14] The remaining 33.7 million will be aged 15–59.

Figure 6
Median Age and Percentage of Population under Age 15, South Korea, est., 2000–2050

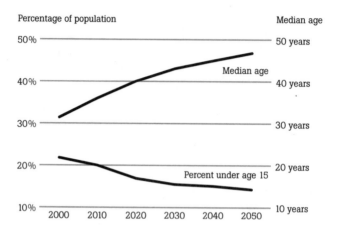

Percentage of population

Median age

Source: "International Database," U.S. Census Bureau, www.census.gov/ipc/www/idbagg.html, accessed September 20, 2000.

Koreans turned their attention to nation building after the signing of an armistice agreement on July 27, 1953, ending 37 months of bloody combat during the ruinous Korean War. As a result of the ensuing baby boom, Korea's population doubled between 1950 and 1990. By 2000, the median age of the population was 31.4, approximately three and one-half years younger than that of Korea's fellow OECD members, with about 80 percent of Korea's population under age 50.[15] The average life expectancy for men was roughly 70 years and that for women was 78. If current demographic trends hold, South Korea's median age is projected to increase from 31 in 2000 to 36 in 2010 and will approach 47 in 2050. Slightly more than 1 in 10 Koreans were 60 years of age or older in 2000. In 2010, this elderly group will make up 14 percent of the population and is expected to constitute more than 25 percent of the population in 2030 (figure 5 on page 9). In comparison, approximately one in five (21.8 percent) Koreans were under 15 years of age in

Figure 7
Population of South Korea, est., 1950–2050

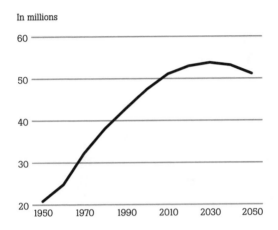

In millions

Source: "International Database," U.S. Census Bureau, www.census.gov/ipc/www/ idbagg.html, accessed September 20, 2000.

2000. This percentage is expected to drop to 20 percent in 2010 and 14 percent in 2050 (figure 6).

South Korea's population growth rate surged through 1970 and then began to decline. The population increased almost 19 percent from 1950 to 1960 and 30 percent in the decade ending in 1970. Since 1970, population growth for 10-year increments was approximately 18 percent when measured in 1980, 12.5 percent in 1990, and 10.7 percent in 2000. Population growth is projected to decline to 7.6 percent between 2000 and 2010, 3.7 percent between 2010 and 2020, and 1.5 percent in the 10 years ending in 2030. In 2040, population growth is expected to be negative (-1.05 percent), declining further to -3.8 percent in 2050 (figure 7).

These data reflect a continuing decline in the fertility rate, from 1.73 in 1996, to 1.72 in 2000, and an expectation of 1.70 by 2040 (figure 8). Between 2000 and 2010, the annual growth rate is expected to drop from 0.93 percent in 2000 to 0.54 percent in 2010, for an annual average of 0.72 percent.[16] Consequently, during 1970–

Figure 8
Fertility Rate, South Korea, est., 1996–2050

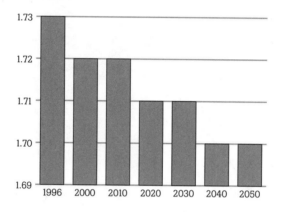

Source: "International Database," U.S. Census Bureau, www.census.gov/ipc/www/idbagg.html, accessed September 20, 2000.

2000, Korea's traditionally large families became nuclear families comprising parents and one or two children (figure 9).

Korea's demographic trends track with those of other leading industrial nations and OECD member nations. From 1990 to 1998, for example, a decreasing population growth rate of 2.3 percent in Korea corresponds with growth rates in industrial nations such as Ireland (2.2 percent) and Australia (1.6 percent), while OECD member Turkey's growth rate was 3.3 percent.[17] Furthermore, over the same period, when Korea's total fertility rate of 1.7 percent is compared with fertility rates in China (1.9 percent), Mexico (2.8 percent), and Malaysia (3.2 percent), it appears that Korea is leading the thrust of developing nations towards parity.[18]

The age range of Korea's economically active population[19] is in transition because Korea's retirement age will change from 60 to 65 by 2033.[20] While some retirement-eligible persons are likely to continue working, the economically active population is assumed to comprise the 18–59 age group. In 2000, this group contained slightly fewer than 32 million people, roughly two-thirds of the general population. By 2030, it is projected to drop to 58 percent of the

Figure 9
Annual Population Growth Rate, South Korea, est.,
2000–2010

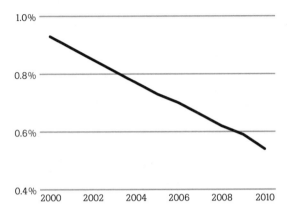

Source: "International Database," U.S. Census Bureau, www.census.gov/ipc/www/
idbagg.html, accessed September 20, 2000.

general population. As a practical matter, however, compulsory military service for men plus the large number of Korean men and women in the 15–24 age bracket who attend college reduce the number of potential workers. The group of Koreans aged 15–24 is expected to decline from 7.7 million in 2000 to 6.7 million in 2010. Applying the compulsory military and college attendance exclusions could yield adjusted economically active populations of approximately 51 percent in 2000 and 53 percent in 2010 (figure 10).

In 2010, there will be 40 percent more Koreans aged 60 or over than in 2000[21] but only 5.2 percent more people in the 15–59 age group—the economically active population. Korea therefore will face a challenge in generating sufficient tax revenue to fund the National Pension Corporation and other government programs. The government established the National Pension Corporation in 1988 and currently intends to pay basic benefits amounting to 60 percent of the retiree's average income.[22] The aging-population situation suggests this is likely to be a challenge whether the retirement age is 65 or 60.

Figure 10
Population by Age Group, South Korea, est., 2000 and 2010

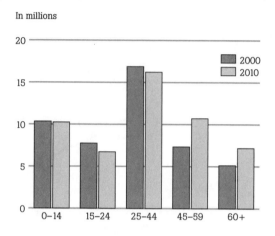

Source: "International Database," U.S. Census Bureau, www.census.gov/ipc/www/idbagg.html, accessed September 20, 2000.

The scope of the problem will become clearer in 2008, the first year Koreans will become eligible for financial benefits from the National Pension Corporation. In August 2000, the fund held 64 trillion won ($57 billion; the symbol for won is W). However, the requisite funds may not be available over the long term. Some analysts estimate that with current funding the National Pension Corporation will be depleted by 2040.[23]

Can Korea create the requisite high-paying jobs required to provide a satisfactory quality of life for most Koreans as well as tax revenue to fund retirement pensions, elder care, and other social programs? Is it the government's or the private sector's responsibility to create jobs? The first question depends on economic growth. The second question remains to be answered.

Koreans since 1962 have looked to their government to take the lead in directing and managing the economy, and one cannot argue with the success of the Korean model from the 1960s into the 1990s. However, in 1997 objective observers saw that the economy had become too large for management by other than free-market principles in a regulated fair competitive environment.

A major financial crisis in 1997 revealed significant structural weaknesses in the Korean model. The crisis came to a head in the weeks before a presidential election, seriously damaging the ruling party candidate, and that December Koreans for the first time in their history rejected the ruling party candidate and elected as president an opposition candidate, Kim Dae-jung, by 1.6 percentage points. The severity of the crisis also prompted the ROK government to request financial assistance from the International Monetary Fund (IMF) and other international financial institutions, and in late December 1997 the IMF approved a $57 billion bailout loan with the proviso that Korea would implement major structural reforms. The appeal for massive international financial assistance was a bitter pill for many Koreans, especially in light of their recent accession to the exclusive OECD family of advanced industrial states.

In 1998, the new ROK government under President Kim Dae-jung immediately began to implement major reforms to change the role of government in the economy and institute free-market, capitalist principles with respect to labor, corporate governance, the financial sector, and the public sector, including state-owned enterprises. Powerful vested interests in these and allied political sectors resisted the reform process, however, which raised questions about the future.

In March 1998, unemployment surpassed 8 percent and averaged 6.8 percent for the year, a stunning increase from 1997's 2.6 percent unemployment. Since 1998, unemployment has slowly dropped; in spring 2000 it was below 4 percent. Koreans consider even this rate to be high, however, because annual unemployment during the preceding decade was well below 3 percent. To help reduce unemployment, the ROK government has created jobs consistent with its historically active role in the economy.

In March 1999, for example, the Ministry of Culture and Tourism announced its intention to invest W 50 billion and create 22,000 new jobs in culture-related industries by the end of 2003. By the end of 2000, 14,000 new positions were to be created.[24] In August 2000, the ROK minister of education announced that fewer than 46 percent of graduates from regional universities were able to find employment, an inflated figure that includes graduates moving on for postgraduate schooling as well as beginning their compulsory military service. Eliminating postgraduates and draftees reduced the percentage of college graduates who could find employment to fewer than 30 percent.[25] Thus, despite an official unemployment rate near 4 percent at the end of 2000, generating employment for younger Koreans was a significant if understated problem.

Owing to the 1997 financial crisis, per capita income dropped from $11,380 in 1996 to $6,723 in 1998. It rose to $9,628 in 2000,[26] and the ROK government envisions it reaching $20,000 after 2010,[27] an assessment that assumes a 9 percent growth in gross domestic product (GDP) in 1999 and steady expansion thereafter. In short, the ROK government assumes that per capita income will increase in excess of 100 percent by 2010.

Is this reasonable? Although the Korean per capita income expanded 220 percent between 1987 and 1997, rising from $3,201 to $10,307,[28] the relatively more modest income growth of 139 percent in 2001–2010 could prove to be an ambitious objective in light of the structural weaknesses and slowing pace of accompanying reform measures. Actual GDP growth in 2000 was approximately 8.8 percent, but some economists in February 2001 forecast that it would drop below 5 percent growth in 2001 and 6 percent growth in 2002.[29] The government's per capita income projection is not a certainty.

In summary, Korea's population is aging while large, traditional families are becoming small, nuclear families. A major challenge facing all Koreans is caring for the elderly and providing sufficient satisfactory jobs to meet the needs of the knowledge era.

Environment

South Korea is a densely populated peninsular country of approximately 99,000 square kilometers, slightly larger than the state of Indiana in the United States and slightly smaller than Iceland; almost two-thirds is forests and mountains. This helps make South Korea one of the most densely populated countries on earth, with 467 Koreans per square kilometer in 1998.[30] More than 81 percent lived in urban areas in 1995, and the United Nations (UN) estimates that more than 92 percent of the population will live in urban areas by 2015.[31] Although natural resources supplied sufficient water to meet the country's needs during the twentieth century, Korea lacks significant energy resources. To fuel the industrialization process and meet the needs of its growing population, which purchased approximately 3,488 new cars daily in 1999,[32] South Korea depends heavily on foreign energy sources. More than 97 percent of Korea's energy needs are supplied by imports.[33]

To escape densely populated neighborhoods, crowded streets, and the pressures of daily life, many Koreans enjoy mountain climbing. The abundance of mountains, even in downtown Seoul, provides readily available resources for Koreans seeking to commune with nature although even hikers cannot quickly escape the negative impacts of Korea's hasty industrialization and growing population. Polluted streams and views obscured by smog provide reminders that the cost of Korea's industrialization during the last 40 years of the twentieth century includes environmental damage. A hiker may take satisfaction knowing that key problems have been identified, but solving them is like climbing the mountain: difficult at the beginning with the hope of healthy rewards at the end.

Water. Korea anticipates a water shortage by 2006,[34] despite ample annual rainfall and the presence of more than 30,000 kilometers of rivers and streams and 18,800 lakes. Rain is concentrated in the summer months and a significant amount of water is lost through runoff, evaporation, excessive usage, and an inefficient distribution system. Much available surface water is polluted and requires treatment.[35]

Most water pollution is attributed to urban nonpoint sources—sewage overflows and water runoff from developed areas. In the late 1990s, most pollutants (approximately 58 percent) comprised household wastes, including rubbish, feces, and detergents. Industrial wastes, including acid and alkali, asbestos, and oil spills, were about 41 percent of the total, and agricultural wastes from insecticides, fertilizers, and livestock contributed about 0.5 percent. Most pollutants drain into Korea's four main rivers—the Han, Naktong, Kum, and Youngsan—that provide 68 percent of Korea's drinking water. Water quality of these rivers varied greatly in the 1980s and 1990s.[36]

One of the best measurements of water quality is the level of biochemical oxygen demand (BOD)—the amount of oxygen that bacteria and other microorganisms use to decompose organic waste. The higher the BOD measurement, the less suitable the water is for drinking. Korea classifies its waters on a scale of 1–5; grade 1 is good and grades 2 and 3 are acceptable if the water is treated prior to consumption.[37]

With BOD as an indicator of water quality, only the Han River consistently supplied acceptable grade 2 water from 1985 through 1998. In 1998 the Kum and the Naktong also achieved grade 2 quality, according to ROK Ministry of Environment data through 1998.[38] The Youngsan River, in southwest Korea, was classified as a grade 3 river in 1998.

Koreans have become better aware of the environmental damage caused by industrialization and population increases. The government has enacted legislation to protect the environment and has developed a strategic vision, "Korea's Green Vision 21," that comprises a number of initiatives to improve the water supply:[39]

- complete eight multipurpose dams by 2001, and increase the waterworks supply ratio from 81 percent to 95 percent;
- achieve a threefold improvement in drinking water standards by 2005; and
- increase the number of environmental facilities—for treatment of sewage and wastewater, for example—through 2005.

Air. Korea's air quality has been poor for a number of years, largely due to industrialization and automotive emissions. To reduce smog during the 1988 Olympics, for example, the government decreed that drivers could operate cars with license plates ending in an even number only on even dates and with odd numbers only on odd dates. However, some athletes complained about the air quality, and Koreans took note. Seoul plans to be better prepared for the 2002 World Cup, which Korea plans to cohost with Japan.

Since 1988, Korea has tightened environmental standards and enforcement to reduce industrial pollutants such as sulfur dioxide and total suspended particulates. Because of an exponential increase in automobile use, however, automotive exhaust has replaced industrial emissions as the primary source of poor urban air quality. Automobiles produce 1.6 million metric tons of pollutants annually, 80 percent in urban areas. Of this pollution, 40 percent is caused by 4 percent of the nation's vehicles, specifically diesel buses and trucks.[40]

The government plans to rectify the air pollution problem by bringing automotive emissions standards in line with OECD standards, increasing the frequency of auto inspections, promoting the use of small fuel-efficient cars, and developing electric vehicles. To discourage indiscriminate vehicle use, the government plans to collect tolls on high-traffic roads and increase the cost for parking in downtown areas. The government also plans to replace 20,000 diesel buses with compressed natural gas (CNG) buses by 2007. When the World Cup starts in 2002, Korea plans to have 5,000 CNG buses in place in the 10 host cities.[41]

Greenhouse gases. In 1998, Korea was the ninth largest emitter of carbon dioxide, mostly owing to the high concentration of passenger cars and commercial vehicles and weak emissions controls standards.[42] Seoul is part of the United Nations Framework Convention on Climate Change (UNFCC) and endorses the objectives of the Kyoto Protocol to reduce certain greenhouse gases. However, South Korea is not obligated by the protocol to lower its greenhouse gases. Nevertheless, Seoul has declared its goal is to "render its best efforts to mitigate global warming within its . . . capabilities," which include applying

- import surcharges on petroleum and liquefied natural gas (LNG);
- sales surcharge on kerosene; and
- safety management surcharges on LNG and liquefied petroleum gas (LPG).

Revenue from these taxes will be used to promote LNG, energy conservation, energy technology R&D, and the development of new and renewable sources of energy.[43]

Energy

Oil. South Korea lacks indigenous access to most of the raw energy resources required to operate an industrial society. The country imports more than 97 percent of its energy resources, including all of its crude oil and LNG and most of its coal.[44] The country, therefore, is vulnerable to both supply disruptions and price spikes in the cost of foreign energy resources, particularly oil and LNG. To lessen dependence on foreign energy sources, the ROK government has implemented a long-range energy strategy that includes LNG and nuclear power as the major energy sources for residential and commercial users.

LNG. Korea was the second largest importer of LNG in the world as of September 2000 although it may become a minor producer by 2002. Annual imports increased 140 percent from 1993 through 1997, dropped by 9 percent in 1998, and increased 24 percent in 1999.[45]

Nuclear power. Korea is one of the top producers of nuclear power in the world. In 1999, nuclear power plants supplied 43 percent of Korea's electricity, and, as of mid-2000, South Korea operated 16 plants and had plans to construct 12 new ones by 2015. As a result, Korea was able to reduce carbon emissions from industrial facilities during the 1990s. The ROK government, with the Kyoto Protocol in mind, is promoting the country as an "excellent CDM (clean development mechanism) partner."[46]

The overall energy picture. Densely populated Korea, highly dependent on foreign energy sources, has achieved remarkable progress in building an industrialized society as well as producing environmental damage as a by-product. The country seeks to improve its environment and energy security through increasingly strict environmental protection laws, conservation, the use of the relatively clean technologies of nuclear energy and LNG, and the development of new technologies for renewable sources of energy. Until such strategies reduce Korea's heavy dependence on foreign energy sources, Korea will remain vulnerable to price spikes.

The more Korea moves into the knowledge era—which uses fewer natural resources than industrializing economies—the more likely it is to reduce its vulnerability to energy price spikes. Korea lacks many natural energy resources, but it possesses the one resource that is crucial to success: intelligent, motivated, and cooperative people who can figure out ways to succeed once empowered to do so. Thus Koreans' perceptions and interactions with one another and the outside world may assume even greater importance as the knowledge era begins in Korea. It is to such cultural factors that we now turn.

The Role of Culture

> *Ha myun dwen da!* (If you try, you can do!)
> —Korean proverb

Korea is an ancient land. It charts its history from 2333 B.C. although there is evidence of ancestors in the sixth millennium B.C.[47] Koreans and foreigners often consider the Korean culture to be a prime example of modern Confucianism and, to be sure, the Confucian philosophy is deeply rooted in the "land of morning calm." Confucian virtues of respect for elders, education, and government service, for example, are readily apparent throughout the society. Other philosophies and religions as well as experiences with foreigners have also had their impact on Koreans' perceptions and interactions with one another and with outsiders.

Confucianism

Confucius (551–479 B.C.) envisioned a society that worked like a good family. The foundation for leadership comprised one's personal abilities and a high moral code of conduct. Heredity itself was not an adequate basis for leadership. Just as children were expected to obey their parents, followers of Confucianism obey their leaders until the leaders lose their mandate of heaven—their moral right to lead.

For centuries, Koreans have followed Confucius and agreed that a society could achieve harmony if its members exercised loyalty, filial piety, righteousness, and good faith through five essential personal relationships: father–son, emperor–subject, husband–wife, elder brother–younger brother, and friend–friend. Strict adherence to the first four relationships produces a very hierarchical society in which each person has relatively formal and vertical relationships with all but a small circle of close friends, who comprise the more informal fifth relationship. Confucius did not prescribe any relationship between an individual and strangers.

To establish the terms of a new relationship, Koreans who meet for the first time traditionally engage in a conversation to determine quickly who is the elder. The parties then assume their culturally prescribed roles as the senior who merits respect, loyalty, and obedience and the junior who complies. Koreans typically address each other formally by professional title or social position—company president, supervisor, elder brother—rather than informally by name. Friends typically share the same age and experiences—as school classmates, for example—and treat each other as equals although their friendship structure could be based on other factors. Overall, these personal relationships establish a culture in which loyalty, respect for elders, obedience, courtesy, and social harmony have been very highly valued. The transition to the knowledge era is promoting unsettling change in these relationships.

Other Influences

A number of other key philosophies and religions, many imported, have contributed to the development of Korea's unique and religiously pluralistic culture. Shamanism, the oldest religion, is rooted in prehistory when Koreans understood the world to comprise a number of spirits that merited careful attention. Buddhism and Taoism entered from China from the fourth through the seventh centuries. The Korean government in the fifteenth century increasingly promoted Confucianism to diminish the Buddhist influence. By the end of the twentieth century, about half of the Korean population believed in a religion. Roughly 47 percent of Korean believers claimed to be Buddhists.

Roman Catholic missionaries took the Christian message to Korea in the late eighteenth century; although they were followed by Protestant missionaries in the nineteenth century, the message was not widely accepted until the twentieth century. At the end of the twentieth century, however, Christianity was the fastest growing religion in Korea and comprised approximately 48 percent of Korean believers.

In the nineteenth century, new indigenous religions built on the Korean value of individual self-worth and blended values from other religions and philosophies, including Confucianism, Buddhism, and Taoism.[48] Ch'ondogyo, established in the mid-nineteenth century, is representative of these indigenous religions in several respects.[49]

Ch'ondogyo, like many of the other so-called new religions, emphasized key themes of the essential quality of mutual respect regardless of social position, optimism, a belief in a better future, and the concept that all persons contain divinity. To realize divinity and salvation, each person must concentrate on achieving self-perfection.[50] Like Christianity, Ch'ondogyo was particularly attractive to the weaker members of the society and was a concern to the ruling classes. Scholars credit Ch'ondogyo with positively influencing the development of democracy and antiauthoritarianism in Korea, as when Ch'ondogyo and Christian leaders collaborated to resist Japanese colonial rule between 1910 and 1945.[51]

Invaders and the threat of invasion also powerfully influenced Korean culture. Over the centuries, foreign armies have crossed and occupied the strategically located Korean peninsula often enough to make Koreans wary of foreigners. Koreans' ability to protect the unique features of their culture despite lengthy periods of subjugation or suzerain relationships with foreign powers including Mongolia, China, and Japan demonstrates Koreans' resilient character.

Core Values

The Korean national flag provides insight into core Korean values. The flag has a white background with distinctive black markings in the four corners and a circle in the center, which is red on top and blue on the bottom.

The red and blue center circle is divided to represent ancient yin and yang symbols of the balanced, harmonized universe of offsetting opposites such as fire and water, day and night, dark and light, male and female. The black bars in the four corners reinforce this message. The solid bars at the top left represent heaven, and the broken bars at the lower right represent earth. The bars at the bottom left represent fire while those at the top right symbolize water. The flag's white background represents the purity and harmony of the Korean nation, a sense of harmony that could well be difficult to sustain as Korea transitions to a knowledge-era society characterized by increased pluralism, liberal democracy, decentralized government, increased alienation, and a greatly heightened role for empowered individuals.

Together these philosophical, religious, and historical influences combine to produce a unique culture with certain traits that at times appear contradictory to foreigners. For example, Koreans have been described as both reclusive members of the "hermit kingdom" and the gregarious "Irish of the Orient." Some traits are particularly germane to contemporary affairs and Korea's transition to the knowledge era:

- a vigorous can-do spirit;
- strong desire for social harmony and fundamental respect for the five major relationships inherent in Confucianism;
- filial piety, righteousness, and good faith;
- strong sense of loyalty and trust in family, government, known elders, and friends, but not necessarily those outside these relationships although foreigners can become good friends over time;[52]
- sincerity;
- strong respect for education;
- strong expectations for social justice, which can produce outrage when injustice persists;
- strong sense of individuality that often strains for expression within the society's relatively formal relationships;
- strong sense of nationalism that can tend toward behavior to resist foreign influence; and
- tendency to blame foreigners for domestic problems.

Challenges

Many of these traits are admirable and probably will attend Korea's transition to the knowledge era. Some, however, are incompatible with globalization and the leveling influences of the information age with its high premium on individuality and ability to interact effectively with people from an array of cultures.

Absent from the cultural values is the concept of institutional checks and balances that is so crucial to democracies, corporate governance, market economies, and the effective functioning of a broad range of social institutions.

Checks and balances are in a sense incompatible with the virtues of trust and righteousness that are inherent in at least four of the five important Korean personal relationships. Stronger checks and balances, for example, might have eliminated or at least mitigated the "crony capitalism" that many argue was the root of the 1997 financial crisis. As Korea moves into the knowledge era, an important question is the extent to which traditional values are likely to survive the major transition and generation shift that is under way.

As the knowledge era unfolds in Korea and especially since the 1997 financial crisis, some younger Koreans are embracing the empowering aspects of political and corporate reform. Senior managers in the hierarchical and bureaucratic Korean business conglomerates (*chaebol*) have been encountering difficulty retaining bright workers of the younger generation. Younger workers are attracted to the opportunities for empowerment, advancement, and personal gain that exist in small and medium enterprises with their less formal corporate cultures.[53] Opportunities of the knowledge era will be more available to Koreans who are confident and equipped to realize their potential through their own efforts, those who accept the empowerment tools in the knowledge era.

Korea's core cultural values have served it well through the ages, and Koreans are likely to adapt their cultural values to cope with the stresses of the knowledge age. However, increased transparency—inherent in the knowledge era with its multiple sources of information—and the increasing availability of personal lifestyle options will dramatically affect Korean perceptions of the role of government, other social institutions, and the five relationships based on Confucianism that have been fundamental to how Korea works.

On the other hand, if elements of national culture change at all, they do so very slowly. The future of Korea's success lies in Koreans' ability to sort through their social institutions and develop new ones that will enable them to ride the crest of the powerful new waves that are propelling all cultures into the knowledge era of the twenty-first century.

Korea's greatest challenge may be the reconciliation of its Confucian vertical social structure with the knowledge-era horizontal structure of advanced societies.

Ha myun dwen da! (If you try, you can do!)—Koreans can be expected to prove again the validity of this proverb. With time and enduring attention paid to becoming a prosperous democracy, they will be able to succeed in making the transition to the knowledge era. The costs remain to be seen.

Notes

1. The introductory section to this chapter as well as introductory sections of chapters 2 through 7 borrow heavily from the first country study in the CSIS Global Trends series by Michael J. Mazarr, *Mexico 2005: The Challenges of the New Millennium* (Washington, D.C.: CSIS, 1999).

2. Korea's population in 2000 was 47,470,969, and the world's population grew in 2000 by 77,472,824; see "International Data Base," U.S. Census Bureau, www.census.gov/ipc/www/idbnew.html, accessed September 20, 2000.

3. *Population Trends Over the Coming Decade—Global Impacts* (Washington, D.C.: U.S. Department of State, 1994), 1.

4. *World Population Prospects: The 1998 Revision;* vol. 1, *Comprehensive Tables,* Sales no. E.99.XIII.9 (New York: United Nations, 1999).

5. World Resources Institute, UN Environment Program, UN Development Program, and World Bank, *World Resources 1996–1997: A Guide to the Global Environment* (New York: Oxford University Press, 1996), 174–175.

6. Korea is considered an advanced industrial economy by the International Monetary Fund (IMF).

7. Donella H. Meadows, Dennis L. Meadows, and Jorgen Randers, *Beyond the Limits* (Post Mills, Vt.: Chelsea Green Publishing Company, 1992),

42–52; Paul E. Waggoner, "How Much Land Can Be Spared for Nature?" *Daedalus* 125, no. 3 (1996): 87; and Robert J. Samuelson, "A Coming Food Crisis? Unlikely," *Washington Post,* August 22, 1996, p. A31.

8. Robert Engelman and Pamela LeRoy, *Sustaining Water: Population and the Future of Renewable Water Supplies* (Washington, D.C.: Population Action International, 1993).

9. Volatility and shortages at the pump will probably be caused by rising demand coupled with both upstream and downstream production constraints—refineries operating at full capacity, for example.

10. Jay Hakes, "Long Term World Oil Supply: A Resource Base/Production Path Analysis" (presentation by the U.S. Energy Information Administration to the American Association of Petroleum Geologists, New Orleans, La., April 18, 2000), www.eia.doe.gov/pub/oil_gas/petroleum/presentations/2000/long_term_supply/index.htm, accessed June 2, 2001.

11. This book differs from the two initial volumes of the CSIS Global Trends series that posited oil resources were likely to be depleted in the middle of the twenty-first century after they peak around the year 2015.

12. Peter L. Berger, *Invitation to Sociology: A Humanistic Perspective* (Garden City, N.J.: Anchor Books, 1963), 106, 121.

13. "International Data Base," U.S. Census Bureau, www.census.gov/ipc/www/idbnew.html, is the source for this discussion of Korean demographics.

14. Information paper, ROK National Pension Corporation, www.npc.or.kr, accessed July 23, 2001 (translated by Jung Kyunghwan).

15. The median age of the aggregated populations of South Korea's fellow OECD members was 35.4 years as of September 2000; see "International Data Base," U.S. Census Bureau, www.census.gov/ipc/www/idbnew.html.

16. Calculated by averaging the annual growth rates from 2001–2010 and dividing by 10 years. The source for the annual growth rates was "International Data Base," U.S. Census Bureau, www.census.gov/ipc/www/idbnew.html.

17. "Entering the 21st Century; World Development Report 1999/2000," World Bank Group, www.worldbank.org/wdr/2000/pdfs/engtable3.pdf, accessed February 6, 2001.

18. Ibid.

19. In theory the economically active population encompasses all people wishing to work. Assessing the size of this group is difficult due to the lack of information regarding who actually wishes to work.

20. "Coverage," *ROK National Pension Scheme,* ROK Ministry of Health and Welfare, www.mohw.go.kr/hp/owa/ha003.general_count, accessed September 26, 2000 (in Korean).

21. In 2000, 5,143,263 Koreans were 60 years of age or older; in 2010, 7,188,068 Koreans are expected to be 60 or older; see "International Data Base," U.S. Census Bureau, www.census.gov/ipc/www/idbnew.html.

22. Charles S. Lee, "The Waiting Game," *Far Eastern Economic Review*, August 17, 2000, p. 48.

23. Ibid.

24. Young-shik Choe, "22,000 Jobs to Be Created in Culture, Tourism This Year," *Korea Times*, March 22, 1999, www.hankookilbo.co.kr/14_6/199903t465195.htm, accessed October 1, 2000.

25. "The Death of Local Communities," *Chosun Ilbo*, August 4, 2000.

26. James M. Lister, ed., "Leading Economic Indicators," *Korea Economy 2001*, vol. 17 (Washington, D.C.: Korea Economic Institute of America and Korea Institute of International Economic Policy, 2001).

27. *Korea's Efforts to Harmonize Energy, Economy, and Environment* (Seoul: ROK Ministry of Commerce, Industry, and Energy, January 2000), 2.

28. ROK National Statistical Office, www.nso.go.kr/cgi_bin/sws_999.cgi?ID=DT-1co/88IDTYPE=3, accessed October 10, 2000.

29. Tom Holland, "South Korea Reform Deficit," *Far Eastern Economic Review*, February 1, 2001, p. 56.

30. *Korea's Efforts to Harmonize Energy, Economy, and Environment*, 2.

31. "Growing Urbanization," UN Human Development Report, www.undp.org/hdro/urban.htm, accessed October 1, 2000.

32. "Statistics," Korea Automotive Manufacturers Association, www.kama.or.kr/eng/ds.htm, accessed October 11, 2000.

33. *Korea's Efforts to Harmonize Energy, Economy, and Environment*, 1.

34. "Water Conservation Measures Focusing on Demand Management," in *Goals and Strategies for Providing Clean Water*, ROK Ministry of Environment, www.me.go.kr/english/tit14/Goals.htm, accessed September 22, 2000.

35. Im-sung Shim, "Deterioration of Kum River Water Quality," *Digital Chosun Ilbo*, July 26, 2000, www.chosunilbo.com/w21data/html/news/200007/20000726008.html, accessed October 3, 2000.

36. "Implementation of Water Quality Management Measures for the Four Main Rivers," in *Goals and Strategies for Providing Clean Water*, ROK Ministry of Environment, www.me.go.kr/english/tit14/Goals.htm, accessed September 28, 2000.

37. Lee Boug Young, an economist with the Korea Water Resources Corporation, maintains a Web site (http://my.netian.com/~watopia/quality.html) with this information. The Web site of the Korea Water Resources Corporation is www.kowaco.or.kr/english/english.htm (in English) or www.kowaco.or.kr (in Korean).

38. "Implementation of Water Quality Management Measures for the Four Main Rivers."

39. "Korea's Green Vision 21," in *Green Vision for the Sustainable Society of the 21ˢᵗ Century*, ROK Ministry of Environment, www.moenv.go.kr/english/tit00/eng10.html, accessed September 25, 2000.

40. *South Korea*, U.S. Energy Information Administration, September 2000, www.eia.doe.gov/emeu/cabs/skorea.html, accessed September 28, 2000.

41. "World Cup 2002 and the Environment in Korea," Special Report, ROK Ministry of Environment, www.moenv.go.kr/english/tit14/Special%20Reports.htm, accessed June 2, 2001.

42. *South Korea: Environmental Issues*, U.S. Energy Information Administration, March 2000, www.eia.doe.gov/emeu/cabs/skoren.html, accessed June 2, 2001.

43. *Korea's Efforts to Harmonize Energy, Economy, and Environment*, 5–7.

44. *Korea's Energy Policy 1999* (Seoul: ROK Ministry of Commerce, Industry, and Energy, 1999) and *Korea's Efforts to Harmonize Energy, Economy, and Environment*, 1.

45. *South Korea*, U.S. Energy Information Administration.

46. *Korea's Efforts to Harmonize Energy, Economy, and Environment*, 1.

47. *A Handbook of Korea* (Seoul: ROK Ministry of Culture and Tourism, 1983), 70–75.

48. Donald M. Seekins, "The Society and Its Environment," in *South Korea, A Country Study*, ed. Frederica M. Bunge, 3rd ed., doc. no. 550-41 (Washington, D.C.: Department of the Army, 1982), 98–100.

49. "Religions," *Facts About Korea* (Seoul: ROK Overseas Information Service, 1993), 138; *A Handbook of Korea*, 5th ed. (Seoul: Ministry of Culture and Information, Korean Overseas Information Service, 1983), 194.

50. *A Handbook of Korea*, 5th ed., 209.

51. Seekins, "The Society and Its Environment."

52. This strong sense of loyalty has led to great confidence that elders and leaders can chart a course of action, and followers often accept leadership without critical analysis.

53. Peter M. Beck, "Korea's Embattled *Chaebol*, Are They Serious about Restructuring?" in *The Two Koreas in 2000: Sustaining Recovery and Seeking Reconciliation* (Washington, D.C.: Korea Economic Institute of America, 2000), 23; and Peter Köllner, "Coping with the Legacy of Unbalanced Development," *The Two Koreas in 2000*, p. 10, www.keia.org/mill-content.pdf, accessed June 2, 2001; and Lee Jeong-il, *The Digital Revolution and Changes in Korean Companies' Human Resources Strategies*, Issue Report, Samsung Economic Research Institute, February 26, 2000, http://seriecon.seri.org/, accessed October 28, 2000.

2 ■
Trend Two: The Engines of History

THE FORCES LIKELY TO DRIVE global transition through 2010 are the engines of history, propelled by science and technology as well as by social and psychological processes. These engines are sure to leave instability in their wake, especially where governments and societies fail to anticipate the inexorable forces bearing down on them. Authoritarian governments (China, Cuba, Vietnam), closed markets and statist economies (Japan, Western Europe), and unreformed corporations are remains of the past that face a particularly precarious decade. Korea, too, could find itself among those left behind if it fails to harness the forces of change and shed the vestiges of the discredited "Korea Inc." development model that threaten to block Korea's emergence as a full-fledged, knowledge-based economy.

The Fuels: Science and Technology

Science and technology are perhaps the fundamental fuels of knowledge-era history. Three areas of scientific advance are especially important: biotechnology, renewable energy, and information technology (IT).

The announcement in February 1997 that scientists in Scotland had successfully cloned an adult sheep was just a marker on a path of unprecedented biotechnological research and discovery that is transforming the human environment. Two years later, a Korean research team announced it had successfully cloned a dairy cow.[1] The Human Genome Project, jointly sponsored by the U.S. Department of Energy and the National Institutes of Health, is scheduled to complete its map of the entire human genetic code before the year 2003. Key to this is "catalyzing the multibillion-dollar U.S. biotechnology industry and fostering the development of new medical applications."[2] Such resources, combined with the rapidly developing capability to manipulate human and animal genetic codes, will allow researchers to identify genetic sources of illness and, eventually, engineer genetic cures. U.S. companies are now seeking approval for some 350 biotech pharmaceuticals, some of which offer treatments or cures for such diseases as Huntington's, Alzheimer's, and Parkinson's; AIDS; multiple sclerosis; and various forms of cancer.[3] Genetically engineered animals—the primary goal of the sheep-cloning experiment—will yield medicines such as insulin and even replacement organs for humans. The U.S. Department of Commerce estimates that "life patents" will be worth $60 billion by 2010; and biotechnology offers promise in fields from agriculture to environmental cleanup.

The second area of technology likely to grow during the coming decade is renewable energy. Its actual role in power generation over the 2001–2010 decade will remain modest; the U.S. Department of Energy forecasts that renewables will make up only 14 percent of global nonoil energy production by the year 2010, or only 8 percent of the total energy sources. Although it may not witness the complete maturation of renewable energy, the second decade of the twenty-first century could easily set the stage for developments that make such a transition inevitable.[4] Before 2010, supplies of major fossil fuels should remain relatively plentiful—natural gas should be especially available—forestalling any major shift in favor of renewables. But renewable energy technology must be stressed because, first, it is nearly a foregone conclusion that it will eventually emerge as the world's dominant energy source; second, the 2001–2010 decade will represent the beginning (just the beginning) of this process; and third, renewables are now sufficiently close to being cost competitive that a major breakthrough—a sudden technological leap to improve the efficiency of solar collectors, for example—could set renewables at the forefront of worldwide energy policy.

The final and, in terms of economic and popular impact, dominant area of technological advance over the next decade will be information technology.

Massive supercomputers of unparalleled power will come into service during the twenty-first century's first decade. Other developments in IT—miniaturization, better wireless communications, natural synergies between what are now different forms of information processing—will produce what can be called a pervasive knowledge network. By the year 2010, if not well before, the majority of people in developed nations will have access anytime, and from anywhere, to voice or video communications, the Internet or other networked computer systems, and an immense variety of entertainment options. Information channels that are now separate will merge, creating powerful and pervasive new information networks. This process will get a strong boost from a proliferating number of new global satellite networks. The Teal Group estimates that 2,145 satellites will be launched from 2000 to 2009, quite an increase compared with the 656 estimated launches from 1993 to 2002. Approximately two-thirds of these satellites will be commercial and carry television, wireless, telephone, and Internet signals into the next generation of communications.[5]

The Fuels: Social and Psychological Processes

The decade leading up to 2010 will also be influenced by social and psychological forces that will continue to recast the character of governments and societies around the world. These include socioeconomic modernization, human needs, and social construction.

One driver of historical change that is a direct product of technological advance is socioeconomic modernization: the slow convergence of social and economic structures toward modern, technological, open societies. To become or remain prosperous and economically competitive, states usually move toward free markets and democratic governments. In the process, human societies around the world are beginning to embrace certain common values that promote cross-cultural understanding and cooperation. But the course is hardly straightforward or predictable because progress always has its doubters and victims and major social transformations often generate instability and alienation and foster reactionary movements. In some cases, gaps between neighbors like South Korea and North Korea are likely to require more time to bridge than gaps between other countries such as the United States and Mexico. The next decade will witness major counteractions to the cross-boundary, cross-cultural requirements for modernization and reform.

Another fuel of historical change is human nature—the needs, desires, and aspirations of human beings. Classical theories of international relations and history have generally relied on simplistic formulas of human nature: humans are either aggressive or peaceful, warlike or cooperative. A more sophisticated view of history, however, is available in the form of human needs theory, which looks at how fundamental human needs—security, relationships, and identity—influence history in both positive and negative ways. In particular, the human need for identity or recognition and the instinct to seek security and a sense of belonging to groups have been behind some of history's greatest mischief, such as Nazi Germany's pursuit of national community (*volksgemeinshaft*), which became "a symbol of transformed consciousness."[6]

Yet another fuel of historical change is social construction. Human beings are social animals and exist within the contexts of societies. The insight of social construction theory is that our understanding of ideas and events is shaped by social context. If we are raised in the United States, we are taught that liberty is a good thing and thus are more likely to believe it than would a Chinese citizen raised in China. Human beings and human institutions such as governments experience the world, draw conclusions from it, and modify their perceptions accordingly; in short, they learn. The speed with which this process takes place is strikingly manifest today in the European Union, a testimony to the lesson that peoples and governments have learned from a series of wars about the need for stronger shared norms and institutions.

Where Are the Engines Taking Us?

The engines of history are pulling us toward liberalization, democracy, and international interdependence.

Figure 11
Economic Freedom, World Average, 1975–1997

Note: Perfect freedom is 10 on this scale.

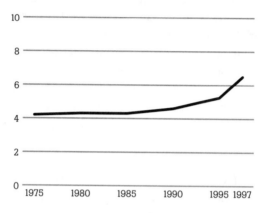

Sources: For 1975 through to 1995, James Gwartney, Robert Lawson, and Walter Block, *Economic Freedom of the World, 1975–1995* (Vancouver, B.C.: The Fraser Institute; 1996); for 1997, *Economic Freedom of the World 2000 Annual Report, 2000* (Vancouver, B.C.: The Fraser Institute), www.fraserinstitute.ca/publications/ books/econ_free_2000/section_07.html (accessed February 8, 2001).

Fueled by science, technology, and social and psychological processes, today's world is moving away from state-planned economies toward free-market, open, liberalized systems (figure 11). The last decade of the twentieth century represented an immense step in this direction: the collapse of the Soviet Union and sweeping reforms in Latin America and elsewhere thrust billions of people into capitalist economies in just a handful of years. This process will continue, albeit at a slower pace, during the first decade of the twenty-first century. In some places this process involves the rejection of whole social systems; in others a more gradual approach to reform clears away barriers to development and competition erected by slow-moving, bureaucratic state structures. Despite the magnitude of forces pressing for liberalization, it will be achieved only at immense cost: social and political discord, psychological stress, and angry or anxious people expressing their cultural identity in the face of onrushing globalism. These countervailing forces are likely to be

Figure 12
Advance of Democracy, 1700s–2005

Note: Number of nations that are free or partly free.

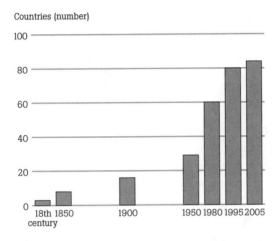

Source: Michael J. Mazarr, *Global Trends 2005: An Owner's Manual for the Next Decade* (New York: St. Martin's/CSIS, 1999), Figure 7.3.

so great that, along with socioeconomic inequities, "counterglobalism" will be a theme of the period.

The engines of history also tug the world farther along the path of freedom and democracy (figure 12). Expanded freedom is partly a product of economic liberalization: economic development and free markets generally produce free polities. But in his instant classic, *The End of History and the Last Man,* Francis Fukuyama argues that a highly successful technological society need not be democratic. "The progressive unfolding of modern natural science," Fukuyama writes, "could just as well lead us to Max Weber's nightmare of a rational and bureaucratized tyranny, rather than to an open, creative, and liberal society." The mechanism of history, then, "needs to be extended." So Fukuyama draws on elements of human needs theory as first articulated by the German philosopher Georg Hegel, who wrote that human beings seek above all "to be wanted by others or to be recognized." The human animal "was from the start a social being: his own sense of self-worth and identity is inti-mately connected with the value that other people place on him."[7] Thus in modern times the ultimate source of recognition—the po-litical system that best allows individuals to seek recognition—is democracy.

Socioeconomic convergence makes war less likely. In a world of free-market economies, free trade will generally prevail; and in a world of free trade, many of the things that nations desire—pros-perity, goods, capital—can be acquired without resorting to force.

The expansion of democracy usually has the same result. By ad-dressing peoples' needs for recognition without relying on external conquest, democracies often reduce the incentives for war. Democ-racies seldom, if ever, war with other democracies. The human in-stinct to create reciprocal cooperative agreements to preserve secu-rity—the instinct that underlies the social contract within nations—can be extended to a lesser degree among them. Although it does not end war or international violence, an emerging global social contract can create new mechanisms of harmony for dealing with violence.

Where Are the Engines Taking Korea?

Koreans energetically mobilized national resources to acquire and apply the engines of science and technology in the post–Korean War period. Within two generations, they transformed Korea from an agrarian Third World economy to the second Asian member of the OECD, and per capita income expanded from $67 in 1953 to more than $10,000 in 1995. To achieve such results, the Koreans blended the strengths of government and large industrial *chaebol* to form what some foreigners called Korea Inc. As the twentieth cen-tury came to an end, Koreans realized the time had come to reform a number of economic and political policies and practices that had promoted rapid industrialization but thwarted the development of democracy and business enterprises capable of competing effectively in open markets domestically and abroad.

At the beginning of the twenty-first century, the engines of his-tory are pulling Koreans into a new age that challenges yesterday's political, economic, business, and social mores. To understand how the engines of history are changing Korea, a brief review of salient developments in modern Korean history is appropriate.

The Legacy of Yesterday

Before 1945, Korean heavy industry was located primarily in the northern part of the Korean peninsula and the agricultural sector was primarily in the South. The peninsula was a colony of Japan from 1910 until August 1945 when Korea was liberated from Japanese rule. After liberation, the peninsula promptly divided as the bipolar Cold War world took shape. South Korea, with its democratically elected government with Syngman Rhee as president, became part of the free world and declared its independence as the Republic of Korea (ROK) in August 1948.[8] North Korea was incorporated into the totalitarian camp headed by the Soviet Union and established itself as the Democratic People's Republic of Korea (DPRK or North Korea) in September 1948.

A Rocky Beginning

South Korea's nation-building efforts halted in June 1950 when the DPRK launched a massive surprise attack to reunify the Korean peninsula by force. The United States led the UN to call on member states to help South Korea survive and to form a UN military command to fight there. After more than three years of brutal combat that touched virtually every part of the Korean peninsula, the ROK's northern border was stabilized by a demilitarized zone (DMZ) that brings to mind the line between yin and yang in the Korean national flag as it segments the peninsula. As soon as the military commanders of the North Korean People's Army, Chinese People's Volunteers, and UN Command signed an armistice agreement on July 27, 1953, South Koreans focused on rebuilding their shattered nation although they still felt threatened by another highly destructive war.

To deter foreign aggression against the ROK, the United States and the ROK became treaty allies in 1953, and the United States has stationed troops in South Korea ever since at the request of the

ROK government. The ever-present threat of war has nonetheless influenced South Korea strongly during the ensuing years.

Nation building in the 1950s was difficult. The war had destroyed most production facilities. Infrastructure, industrial expertise, and capital were limited, especially given the requirement to maintain a large standing military. The primary economic sector was agriculture—75 percent of the population lived in rural areas and only 7.3 percent lived in Seoul in 1955.[9]

To build up the economy, the Syngman Rhee government focused on power generation, textile and cement manufacturing, and import substitution policies for fertilizer and steel, for example. Hyundai, Samsung, and other companies seized business opportunities and grew. GNP increased 5.5 percent on average from 1954 to 1958, with industrial production growing by 14 percent annually. However, economic growth began to decline in 1958 owing to the phaseout of the UN Korean Reconstruction Agency, a reduction in U.S. direct aid, and tightened ROK fiscal and monetary policies. By the end of the decade, South Korean per capita income had risen only $15, from $67 in 1953 to $82 in 1961.[10]

The 1960s did not begin auspiciously. ROK government plans to implement a new seven-year development plan were shelved in April 1960 when a nationwide student revolt protesting election fraud in March caused President Rhee to resign. Prime Minister Chang Myon and a parliamentary cabinet system with a ceremonial president (President Yun Bo-sun) replaced President Rhee and the presidential system in August. This proved to be a weak solution and the ship of state was essentially without an effective captain until May 16, 1961, when the ROK military conducted a coup d'état and installed the army major general, Park Chung-hee, as president.[11]

"Military Government" and Korea Inc.

President Park and his administration brought military authority, discipline, and organization to the ROK government and established policies and practices that powerfully affected Korea for the rest of the twentieth century. For example, the new government amended the constitution to establish a strong presidential system and crafted a managed-economy development model that retains influence although it has long outlived its utility.

To legitimize his rule, President Park set about to improve the quality of life in South Korea by focusing on industrial development. He believed that the government's ability to set industrial development priorities and allocate resources combined with private companies' capacity to manufacture and export products would facilitate rapid modernization and improve the Korean quality of life. He did not intend to develop a free-market capitalist system with its inherent checks and balances. The focus was on guided capitalism[12] through policies to establish a managed economy. In the summer of 1961, the new government issued its first five-year industrial development plan and the following principle:

> Throughout the plan period, the economic system will be a form of "guided capitalism," in which the principle of free enterprise and respect for the freedom and initiative of free enterprise will be observed, but in which the government will either directly participate or indirectly render guidance to the basic industries and other important fields.[13]

With such a vision, Park Chung-hee established the Third Republic. He staffed his government with technocrats who could orchestrate the development of an industrial society. He designated certain companies to be the growth engines for an export-oriented economy and supplied them with such requisite resources as capital through policy loans; labor through promotion of lifelong employment, limits on labor unions, a willingness to break strikes; and promotion of exports and barriers to imports.

Thus was born the system known domestically as the "developmental state" and abroad as Korea Inc. Hyundai, Samsung, Daewoo, LG (formerly Lucky Goldstar), SK (formerly Sunkyong), Hanjin, Ssangyong, Hanwha, Kumho, Dongah, and other *chaebol,* as well as well-known state-owned enterprises such as POSCO (Pohang Iron and Steel Company) emerged over the years as firms favored by the government to industrialize Korea and make it an exporting powerhouse. Not all of these firms are in business at the beginning of the twenty-first century in part because they lost government support for various reasons.

The government over time also undertook major responsibilities for R&D. For example, it invested approximately $10.4 billion in R&D projects between 1988 and 1996. It also provided a number of incentives for firms conducting R&D, especially on such government-sanctioned projects as those under the Highly Advanced Nation (HAN) program[14] and the strategic national R&D program.[15] A primary objective was to help Korean companies develop products that they could export to earn foreign currency and help Korea become less reliant on foreign aid and less subject to foreign influence.[16] This R&D effort has not been particularly effective for industry, however.[17] Nor has it promoted an international reputation for Korea as a recognized source of highly innovative research or product development.

The firm leadership, mobilization of national resources, and import barriers provided by President Park and his successors launched and sustained Korea's economic development. Within roughly 35 years, Korea transformed itself from a very poor agrarian economy to the 11th largest economy in the world, with annual per capita income exceeding $10,000. Such accomplishments accorded well with most Korean personal aspirations for a better life style.

The de facto social contract that emerged comprised the government's obligation to steadily improve the quality of life for all Koreans as well as the people's support for the government and its authoritarian practices. This social contract is largely still in place.[18]

Problems. President Park used Korea's implicit social contract to retain power. He suppressed the democratic process in 1972 when he imposed the Yushin Constitution that made him president for life. He suppressed normal democratic liberties and oppressed opponents. Kim Dae-jung, a dissident politician who won 46 percent of the vote in the 1971 presidential election to threaten Park's presidency, was kidnapped by ROK government agents in Japan on August 8, 1973, and almost killed. Only U.S. intervention persuaded Park to call off the execution.[19] Park and his successor, Chun Doo-hwan, subsequently harassed, imprisoned, exiled, and threatened Kim Dae-jung with death into the 1980s.[20]

Thus President Park established the statist Korea Inc. political–economic model and set the precedent of serving as de facto chairman of an implicit board of directors that included various government officials—especially in the economic planning, financial, and trade sectors—and *chaebol* leaders. Park's successors sustained it, enabling Korea to achieve notable accomplishments and become the second Asian member of the OECD.

These accomplishments, however, were achieved while Korea was perpetuating ultimately self-defeating practices and structural weaknesses in the financial sector, labor markets, public sector, and *chaebol* corporate governance; failing to develop a balanced economy among large, small, and medium enterprises; ignoring basic R&D;[21] and damaging the development of democratic institutions.

Extensive government favoritism toward the giant *chaebol* and use of state-allocated capital thwarted the development of modern market-oriented financial institutions, regulatory institutions, and small and medium enterprises that could compete effectively in open markets. The small and medium enterprises, which historically have employed most Koreans (74 percent in 1997[22] and 75 percent in 1998[23]), were acutely affected as they could not easily acquire the capital to expand their businesses. As a result of government support, 30 *chaebol* were the largest contributors to Korea's GDP. The top 10 *chaebol* have generated 20 percent of GDP since 1981[24] while the more than 2 million smaller enterprises generate approximately 50 percent.

Financial institutions that were directed by the government supplied capital primarily to the *chaebol;* other financial institutions lent to the *chaebol* because they believed the government would pay all nonperforming loans, not because they assessed the envisioned *chaebol* projects to be creditworthy. The cozy mutual dependence of the government–business culture that characterized Korea Inc. constituted an environment known to economists as moral hazard, an environment lacking institutional oversight mechanisms and permitting corruption to thrive while key business skills such as risk assessment remain underdeveloped.[25]

Koreans began to insist on political liberalization in the late 1980s, and Korea today may be one of the most democratic countries in Asia. However, President Park's Korea Inc. development model lived on into the 1990s. As the twentieth century came to an end, Koreans wrestled with the question of whether to divest Korea Inc. and, if so, how. Such conundrums are not unique to Korea; globally, the engines of history inexorably pull a society toward liberalization, democracy, and international interdependence.

Political–Economic Liberalization

Three major events since the mid-1980s demonstrate growing liberalization in Korea: the presidential elections of 1987 and 1997 and the National Assembly election of 2000. The presidential election of 1992 was important but not of the same magnitude.

In June 1987, Koreans took a decisive step in a dangerous environment to insist on an open democratic process to elect their president after 26 years of military government. What made these Koreans courageous was their civil disobedience despite bitter memories of the government's brutal suppression of antigovernment demonstrators in Kwangju just seven years earlier.

Creeping coup and Kwangju. Prime Minister Choi Kyu-hah briefly succeeded President Park following Park's assassination in October 1979, but the power behind his throne was Chun Doohwan. In a "creeping coup" that he initiated in December 1979, Major General Chun solidified his position as the de facto national leader. College students—commonly considered the voice of Korea's conscience—became so alarmed by the creeping coup in late winter and early spring of 1980 that they began to voice their concerns through nationwide demonstrations.

Demonstrations in the southwestern city of Kwangju in mid-May provided impetus for the government to impose full martial law on May 18, 1980.[26] ROK military forces, under ROK government instruction and ignoring U.S. protestations, brutally suppressed the Kwangju demonstrations. Official ROK government estimates state that 240 people were killed, but most Koreans believe that thousands of innocent civilians lost their lives.[27] The government also closed the National Assembly and arrested major opposition political leaders, including two future presidents—Kim Young-sam and Kim Dae-jung. Kim Dae-jung was sentenced to death but gained a reprieve when, for the second time, the United States intervened to save his life.

General Chun completed the transfer of power and became president on August 27, 1980, following his election by the National Conference for Unification.[28] On October 27, the Chun administration promulgated a new constitution that established the president's term of office for a single seven-year term, which was changed to a single five-year term before the presidential election of 1987.

President Chun, who had much less legitimacy than President Park when he took power, concluded that Park's social contract with the Korean people had to be his as well. To rectify recognized problems and improve the economy, the Chun government developed new policies to reduce some trade barriers, liberalize the financial sector, and reduce direct government control of banks and nonfinancial institutions.[29] The envisioned reforms were not fully implemented, however, because of the murder of several cabinet members and key economic planners at the hands of North Korean commandos in Rangoon, Burma, on October 9, 1983. Korea Inc. remained in business; and cronyism, corruption, and a state of moral hazard persisted during the 1980s.[30]

Era of the ordinary person, 1987–1992. On June 10, 1987, President Chun named retired army general Roh Tae-woo to be his successor, indicating that the National Conference for Unification—not the Korean people—would ultimately elect the next president later in the year. Koreans of all ages and occupations—not just students—objected; they demanded a free election. Students, businesspeople, shop owners, housewives, people from all segments of the population rose up in protest across the country. The government responded by employing combat police units to control the demonstrations, but they were ineffective. The government did not employ military units as it had in Kwangju, perhaps because

- Roh Tae-woo and the military had no taste for it in light of the Kwangju backlash;
- Chun was concerned that the International Olympic Committee would not permit the 1988 Olympics to be held in Seoul; and
- the United States issued strong warnings against the use of military force.

On June 29, 1987, candidate Roh Tae-woo declared the election should be decided by popular vote. He also lifted political bans on opposition politicians, including Kim Dae-jung, and indicated his presidency would be the ordinary man's era (*botong shidae*). The so-called June 29 announcement calmed the public, and elections were held without incident in December. Koreans had taken a major first step to liberalize their political process.

Candidate Roh defeated four other major candidates, including Kim Young-sam and Kim Dae-jung, and became the first popularly elected president since 1971, despite his military background. His inauguration in February 1988 ended Korea's quarter century of military government but not the legacy of its political–economic model with its highly managed economy.

Labor was a primary beneficiary of Roh's June 29 declaration and presidency. The Chun administration had suppressed labor and its demands for wage increases, creating hardships and resentment. Within days of Roh's declaration, discontented workers across the country struck illegally against their firms. These strikes affected approximately 32 percent of all manufacturing firms that employed 300 or more workers and more than two-thirds of large factories with more than 1,000 workers. In July, August, and September of 1987, more than 1.2 million workers went on strike. The waning Chun administration did not crush the strikes, and candidate Roh Tae-woo courted the labor vote.[31] Koreans tasted the peaceful transfer of power in a democratic environment in the latter half of 1987 and liked it.

Wages, industrial output, and GDP growth soared. By the end of 1987, per capita income had risen to $3,201 from $1,532 in 1980. It rose to $4,268 in 1988, $5,185 in 1989, and $7,182 in 1992.[32] These overdue adjustments made it increasingly difficult for Korea to compete globally on the basis of low wages. Korea Inc. needed to move into higher-value-added products and services to compete in the increasingly global marketplace, especially in light of the implications of the Uruguay Round of the General Agreement on Tariffs and Trade (GATT) and the emerging World Trade Organization (WTO).

Few Koreans realized at the time that, despite the surge in economic performance, the Korea Inc. managed-economy model had outlived its usefulness. Korea needed to embrace a bold new political–economic paradigm that would permit market factors to guide the economy and transform the government role from active participant to referee. Korea was not yet ready for the new model, but it did take incremental steps under Kim Young-sam's vision of a New Korea.

New Korea and the Beginning of Korea's Information Age, 1993–1997

In 1992, Koreans elected Kim Young-sam their president, the first elected civilian president in more than 30 years. Kim, a longtime opposition politician, had joined the ruling party during President Roh's administration, enhancing Roh's ability to govern and Kim's chances to become president. Inaugurated in February 1993, Kim used his presidency to shape a New Korea. Building on some initiatives in the Roh administration, he implemented a number of political and economic reforms.

Kim's goals were to improve democracy, make Korea "the most attractive place" in the world to do business, lay the foundation for Korea to become a member of the OECD, and make the transition to a knowledge-based society. Political reforms included measures to "civilianize" the government and increase local autonomy. Citizens elected mayors and other local officials in 1995 for the first time since the Syngman Rhee administration, although even in 2001 Seoul continued to control funding for local budgets. Political–economic reforms required government officials to disclose their financial records, which led to some officials being imprisoned. One of the more controversial financial-sector reforms was the Real Name Policy that required depositors to deposit funds only in their own names. President Kim also implemented a new economic plan to enable Korea to compete in the global economy. Although these measures liberalized the political and economic sectors to some degree, they did not challenge the underlying concepts of Korea Inc.

Understanding the potential of IT and the necessity that Korea not be left behind, the Kim administration built on the Roh administration's Korea Backbone Computer Network project and called for the establishment between 1995 and 2010 of the Korea

Information Infrastructure. Goals were the education of public school students in information age topics and the expansion of access to computers and the Internet, among other measures. As a result, Korea is well on its way to becoming a knowledge-based society.

By the end of 2000, more than 19 million Koreans used the Internet, up 90 percent over the 10 million users at the end of 1999.[33] Among all households, it was estimated that 64 percent had a personal computer and 45 percent had Internet access accounts[34]—all this in a population of 47 million.

The Potential of Today

The Kim Dae-jung Era—Crisis and Reform

In December 1997 Koreans rejected the ruling party candidate for the first time in ROK history and in a three-way race elected an opposition candidate, Kim Dae-jung, to be their president. The election came a month after the beginning of a major economic crisis that threatened to bring the Korean economy to its knees.

1997 financial crisis. In November 1997 foreign creditors and investors—already alarmed by financial crises elsewhere in Asia and aware of the Kim Young-sam administration's decisions not to bail out two highly leveraged *chaebol* (Hanbo and Kia) earlier in the year—perceived their Korean loans and investments to be at risk. Creditor and investor concerns grew as they more closely examined the creditworthiness of Korea Inc. and realized the extent of Korea's structural economic weaknesses.[35] On December 3, 1997, the ROK government and the IMF reached an agreement under which the IMF would lend South Korea up to $57 billion to meet its financial obligations, provided the ROK implemented major structural reforms.[36]

> [Korea's] eroding international competitiveness and dismal corporate performance, proliferation of nonperforming loans and paralysis in the banking and financial sector, economic mismanagement of the government, mounting foreign debts and an acute

liquidity crisis, regional contagion effects, and the panic behavior of international lenders drove the South Korean economy to the brink of default and collapse.[37]

The financial crisis pointed out that the Korean economy had reached a size and level of sophistication that greatly exceeded the management capabilities of the highly statist, Korea Inc. political–economic development model. President Park's 1960s strategy of jump-starting industrial development had become an anachronism by the 1980s, but the Chun, Roh, and Kim Young-sam administrations had not reformed it, possibly not wanting to disrupt the social contract established during the Park Chung-hee era and implying the absence of a vision of a practical alternative. The crisis also demonstrated the importance of objective, independent institutional checks and balances throughout the economic and political systems. The government's close involvement in the economy argued for major reforms.

Thus the stage was set for Korea's December 1997 presidential election, a timely opportunity for Korea to redress the structural weaknesses inherent in Korea Inc. The financial crisis had made the previously impossible now possible. Koreans elected opposition candidate Kim Dae-jung to the presidency with a 1.6 percent margin over the ruling party candidate, Lee Hoi-chang, on December 18, 1997.

Kim Dae-jung's vision. In his victory speech on December 19, 1997, President-elect Kim Dae-jung committed himself to open a "new era in which democracy and economic development will go together shoulder to shoulder." He described a new democratic Korea that would practice "market economics—fully and thoroughly," a country in which only the businesses that could adjust to a market economy and international competition would survive. He outlined the twenty-first century as one for small and medium enterprises, the engines of "new economic development" that his government would nurture. In closing, he promised a transparent government and his commitment to "sweep away corruption and sever the knot of political–economic collusion forever."[38] Translating such a bold new vision to reality across the board has proved difficult although successes have been encouraging.

With the support of President Kim Young-sam, President-elect Kim Dae-jung immediately implemented reform measures (referred to here as the 1998 reforms, four-sector reforms, or KDJ reforms) that addressed structural problems in the financial sector, labor sector, public sector, and corporate *chaebol* sector.

Financial sector reform. Financial sector reforms focused on four objectives:

- establishing credible financial institutions by eliminating those that were insolvent and recapitalizing those that were viable;
- reforming the regulatory environment to ensure sound management and transparency;
- further deregulating and liberalizing capital markets; and
- developing institutions to sustain the reforms.

Because of the reform program, by mid-1999 a number of financial sector firms were out of business—approximately 30 percent of commercial banks, 63 percent of merchant banks, and 11 percent of the remaining financial sector firms (securities firms, credit unions, investment trust companies, and others). By early 2000, the government had spent almost W 80 trillion—16 percent of 1999 GDP[39]—to purchase nonperforming loans, recapitalize financial institutions, and pay deposits in failed institutions; the total cost might exceed W 150 trillion. The National Assembly passed necessary laws, including the establishment of the Financial Supervisory Commission and other institutions, to accomplish and institutionalize financial-sector reform. The financial sector had stabilized by 2000, but in December 2000 Moody's Investors Services rated the financial strength of Korea's banks below those of Mexico and as weak as China's. On a scale of "A" through "E," with "A" being exceptional financial strength and "E" being weak, Korea was E+.[40] Additional reform, including privatization of Korea's banks, was still required.

Korea implemented its second round of financial restructuring in the fourth quarter of 2000. The objectives were to strengthen the competitiveness of the financial industry, establish the basic framework for market-oriented restructuring, prevent nonperforming loans by improving the financial system, and enhance asset quality by promptly eliminating potential loss factors.[41] On November 3, 2000,

21 banks named 52 troubled companies they planned to liquidate immediately, put into court receivership, or sell off. Such actions were expected to increase unemployment by up to 100,000 people by the end of 2000. The Kim Dae-jung administration's decision to implement the restructuring plan demonstrates its sincerity in making fundamental changes in Korea's financial system. Another positive step would be to privatize the banks.

Labor sector reform. A major objective of labor reform was to permit companies to adjust their workforces as economic conditions required. In March 1997 the National Assembly enacted reforms that were subsequently shown to be inadequate for the challenges presented later in the year. In January 1998, President-elect Kim Dae-jung formed a tripartite commission comprising representatives from labor, government, and the *chaebol* to develop new reforms. Labor ultimately agreed to more liberal conditions for layoffs in exchange for government pledges to improve labor rights, reduce unemployment, and reform corporate governance. As a practical matter, however, companies found it very difficult to lay off workers through late 2000.

Nevertheless, the attitude toward labor became more flexible. Korean firms implemented such flexible wage systems as performance-based compensation. In a major change, the government recognized labor's right to organize and be politically active. To improve the social safety net and expand the scope of unemployment insurance—other government objectives—official Seoul in 1999 increased budgetary resources for the unemployed by more than 68 percent.[42] More increases were expected.

Public sector reforms. The ROK government instituted reforms to downsize and reorganize government organizations, privatize and improve the management of state-owned enterprises, and eliminate thousands of government regulations. To downsize itself, the government closed a number of its offices to eliminate more than 60,000 positions by the end of 2001; 25,000 were to come from the central government and the remaining 35,000 from local government. By August 31, 1999, the government had released 32,000 employees of state-owned enterprises, approximately 80 percent of the total identified for reduction by end 2001. The government also abolished almost 50 percent of the 11,125 regulations reviewed in 1998.[43]

In August 1998, the ROK government announced a plan to privatize or restructure Korea's 108 state-owned enterprises, which employed 210,000 workers. The government soon privatized the five enterprises identified for privatization by the end of 2000; these were the National Textbook Corporation, Korea Technology Banking Corporation, POSCO, Korea General Chemical Corporation, and Korea Heavy Industries Corporation.[44] By the end of 2000, the government had also made progress in gaining National Assembly approval to begin privatizing the Korea Electric Power Corporation (KEPCO) in 2001; in this the government overcame significant labor opposition and a pro-labor National Assembly.

Corporate sector and *chaebol* reform. *Chaebol* reform was an important Kim Dae-jung goal that rivaled only financial reform for top priority. *Chaebol* had played a major role in Korea's industrialization since the 1960s, but they had become anachronisms by the 1990s. *Chaebol* behavior typified the major shortcomings of the Korea Inc. model; and many Koreans considered the *chaebol* (which did not focus on becoming profitable but concentrated instead on irresponsible expansion with the use of money borrowed in an environment of moral hazard) the primary reason for the 1997 financial crisis. *Chaebol* also dominated the economy, and their business management practices lacked transparency.

The government, envisioning the use of financial and market levers to force compliance, ultimately identified 12 areas for corporate reform:

■ Improve corporate management transparency by

   ■ increasing the presence of outside directors for *chaebol* from 25 percent of the board of directors to 50 percent,
   ■ requiring *chaebol* to establish an internal audit committee with outside directors comprising two-thirds of the membership, and
   ■ strengthening the rights of minority shareholders, for example, by simplifying procedures for class-action lawsuits against managers;

- Abolish cross-debt guarantees among *chaebol* affiliates by March 2000;
- Restructure corporate capital structure by reducing each *chaebol*'s debt–equity ratio to 200 percent by the end of 1999 and restricting a company's ability to borrow funds or issue securities should the debt–equity ratio exceed 200 percent;
- Encourage corporations to concentrate on core businesses by divesting noncore businesses;
- Enforce responsibility of managers and large shareholders of failed companies and set up the legal foundation to punish those responsible for ailing financial institutions;
- Separate the financial industry from other service and manufacturing industries by

  - enforcing firewalls between the affiliates of a financial institution and its corporate shareholders,
  - improving the governance structure of financial institutions owned by *chaebol*, and
  - strengthening the legal responsibilities of senior managers of ailing financial institutions;

- Eliminate financial connections among *chaebol* affiliates by April 2001;
- Stop the ad hoc inheritance of stocks, and thereby inhibit *chaebol* owners from willing their ownership to family members;
- Establish profit-oriented management practices;
- Revise procedures to close hopeless, nonviable companies;
- Establish management systems that hold managers accountable for operating and financial results; and
- Establish a virtuous growth cycle among small and medium-sized venture companies and large companies.[45]

Some *chaebol* reform was accomplished by the end of 2000 but significant challenges persisted. Cross-debt guarantees were abolished but not completely eliminated. *Chaebol* reduced the number of affiliates by about 28 percent between April 1997 and the end of 1999. Most *chaebol* also reduced their debt–equity ratios to the 200 percent target established for the end of 1999. Of the top five *chaebol*,

Hyundai, Samsung, LG, and SK met the 200 percent goal; Daewoo did not and declared bankruptcy, sending a signal that even the large *chaebol* were not too big to fail.

Strategies to reduce debt–equity ratios included issuing new shares and revaluing existing assets, a subjective process that raised questions about the accuracy of the revised ratios. *Chaebol* efforts to resist government direction and oversight regarding outside directors, transparency, and shareholder representation could be seen in some new *chaebol* practices: the *chaebol* were ostensibly using outside directors in late 2000, but in some cases the outside directors were from government organizations, including financial supervisory organizations, which raised questions about the ability of such outside directors to represent shareholders. Such practices also presented ethical concerns regarding a company's relationship with the government organizations represented.[46]

Press reports in the latter half of 2000 suggested that some *chaebol*—especially those with foreign shareholders—were taking to heart the calls to be profit oriented and organized according to international standards. Stories in such respected newspapers as the *Joongang Ilbo* and *Chosun Ilbo* highlighted the realization among *chaebol* managers that they could not rely on affiliates to rescue them if they were to encounter financial difficulty. Reinforcing such assessments were the declining share prices of firms perceived to be insincere about reform. For example, investor concerns over transparency at LG Chemical were cited as a key reason for a 48 percent drop in the firm's stock despite the company's strong cash flow.[47]

The North Korean Angle

One of Kim Dae-jung's priorities was to improve relations with North Korea through a new, constructive-engagement, "sunshine" foreign policy that he initiated after his inauguration in February 1998. North Korea finally responded favorably in the spring of 2000, leading to a historic June 13–15 summit meeting in Pyongyang with the DPRK National Defense Commission chairman Kim Jong-il. This unprecedented summit laid a foundation to improve South–North relations. The Nobel committee awarded Kim Dae-jung a Nobel Peace Prize in October 2000 for his reconciliation efforts.

The ROK government faced a dilemma, however, in promoting economic relations with the DPRK while simultaneously trying to extricate itself from direct participation in its own economy. For example, Hyundai was a leading investor in North Korean projects that were unprofitable. From November 1998 through the end of 2000, Hyundai Asan Corporation spent $612 million on its DPRK-approved tourism project at Mount Kumgang but earned only $233 million from the project, leaving a deficit of $379 million.[48] It will be difficult for the ROK government to avoid using public funds to subsidize Hyundai and other South Korean firms engaged in projects closely associated with the ROK government's foreign policy objectives to improve North Korea's economy and South–North relations.

The Reform Outlook

The ROK government's commitment and ability to replace the Korea Inc. managed-economy model with market economy principles and practices remained a question in late 2000. Impediments included lack of consensus on how to handle enormous *chaebol* debt, which in the case of Daewoo Corporation appeared to be a staggering $73 billion in October 1999. Also, mustering the will to sell domestic firms to foreign buyers became a problem in a number of high-profile cases including the nationalized Korea First Bank and Seoul National Bank and such private firms as Kia Motors, Daewoo Motors, and Jinro Coors. Implementing reliably transparent accounting practices throughout the economy has also been difficult and has deterred foreign buyers.[49] President Park's Korea Inc. legacy remains difficult to dismantle, but as of 2000 increased transparency and the broad deployment of information technology are producing changes.

National Assembly Election of 2000

The 16th general election for representatives to the National Assembly was conducted in April 2000 with encouraging implications for citizens empowered with Internet technology. On January 12, 2000, South Koreans privately formed 150 joint citizen groups to defeat the election of 89 candidates they deemed unfit for public office. Approximately 938,000 people accessed the groups' Internet home pages and 300,000 participated in a signature campaign. In the end, 59 of the named candidates were not elected.[50]

It is admittedly difficult to prove conclusively the technology–politics link—that these 59 candidates were defeated solely because of the Internet-based grassroots movement. Some government officials later claimed the candidates were not competitive and their defeat was inevitable. The key point, however, is that information age technology and Kim Dae-jung's supportive efforts to promote liberal democracy empowered private citizens to take action to further liberalize their political process and set a higher standard for their elected representatives. Such a development implies Koreans are moving steadily into the knowledge age, an age that places a high premium on empowered individuals charting their personal courses through life.

Notes

1. Tai-joon Mo, "SNU Clones First Dairy Cow," *Digital Chosun Ilbo,* February 19, 1999, www.chosunilbo.com, accessed October 5, 2000.

2. U.S. Department of Energy, Human Genome Project, www.ornl.gov/TechResources/Human_Genome/hg5yp/hlight.htm, accessed June 2, 2001.

3. "Guide to Biotechnology," Biotechnology Industry Organization, 1999, www.bio.org/aboutbio/guide2000/guide00_toc.html, accessed July 10, 2001.

4. *Energy Outlook 1995* (Washington, D.C.: U.S. Department of Energy, 1995); William Hoagland, "Solar Energy," *Scientific American,* September 1995, p. 170–173; and Robert W. Righter, *Wind Energy in America: A History* (Norman, Okla.: University of Oklahoma Press, 1996), chap. 12.

5. "Analysts Count 2,147 Satellites to Launch This Decade," *SpaceViews 2000,* April 3, 2000, www.spaceviews.com/2000/04/03b.html, accessed July 10, 2001.

6. Ian Kershaw, *The Nazi Dictatorship: Problems and Perspectives of Interpretation* (Baltimore, Md.: E. Arnold, 1985), 140–142; additional comments by William J. Taylor Jr.

7. Francis Fukuyama, *The End of History and the Last Man* (New York: Free Press, 1992), 202, 206–207.

8. The heavily contested 1948 presidential election is considered to be the first democratic presidential election in the ROK although Syngman Rhee

who was elected in 1948 was subsequently criticized for being an autocrat in charge of a corrupt government.

9. Seekins, "The Society and Its Environment," 61.

10. For per capita income in 1953, see *U.S.–AEP (United States–Asia Environmental Partnership) Country Assessment: Republic of Korea,* www.usaep.org, accessed October 11, 2000; for per capita income in 1961, see *A Handbook of Korea,* 5th ed., 475; for additional background, see Chong-sik Lee, "Historical Setting," in *South Korea, A Country Study,* 3rd ed., 31; and Mark L. Clifford, *Troubled Tiger: Businessmen, Bureaucrats, and Generals in South Korea* (Armonk, N.Y.: M. E. Sharpe, 1994), 115, 317.

11. This discussion draws on Lee, Ibid., and Clifford, Ibid.

12. Clifford, Ibid., 49; and Don Oberdorfer, *The Two Koreas: A Contemporary History* (Reading, Mass.: Addison-Wesley, 1997), 34.

13. Clifford, Ibid., 49.

14. Han is a value-laden nationalist term, part of the Korean phrase for the ROK, which is Tae Han Min Kuk.

15. Paul F. Chamberlin, *High Technology Development in Korea* (Washington, D.C.: International Security Program, CSIS, October 1998), 8–9; and "Science and Technology in Korea," (Seoul: ROK Ministry of Science and Technology, 1994) and "Support Measures and Incentive Systems for Technology Innovation," ROK Ministry of Science and Technology, www.most. go.kr, accessed October 11, 2000.

16. Clifford, *Troubled Tiger,* 54–55.

17. "Long-Term Plan for Science and Technology Development to Be Developed," ROK Ministry of Science and Technology, April 9, 1999, www.most.go.kr, accessed October 19, 2000.

18. By the 1990s, many Koreans recognized the declining utility of the developmental state paradigm that placed the government at the center of economic decisionmaking and resource allocation. Following a major economic crisis in November 1997 and the presidential election in December 1997, the new president, Kim Dae-jung, in 1998 immediately began to lay the foundation for a new paradigm based on market economics, representative democracy, and a correspondingly less intrusive government role in the economy. However, building consensus and implementing the new model is a slow painful process, as it requires virtually all Koreans to change long-established practices in business and governance.

19. Doug Struck, "S. Korea's Kim Wins Peace Prize," *Washington Post,* October 14, 2000, p. A-1.

20. Oberdorfer, *The Two Koreas,* 42–43.

21. Marcus Noland, *Avoiding the Apocalypse—The Future of the Two Koreas* (Washington, D.C.: Institute for International Economics, June 2000), 6;

also Köllner, "Coping with the Legacy of Unbalanced Development," *The Two Koreas in 2000*, p. 10, www.keia.org/mill-content.pdf.

22. Köllner, Ibid., 9; also "Chapter 4: Building a More Market Oriented Economy," *OECD Economic Surveys, 1999–2000: Korea* (Paris: Organization for Economic Cooperation and Development, September 2000), 146.

23. ROK Small and Medium Business Administration, www.smba.go.kr, accessed November 18, 2000.

24. Noland, *Avoiding the Apocalypse*, 21.

25. Moral hazard refers in general to the presence of incentives that cause individuals to act in ways that could incur costs that they themselves do not have to bear. In the case of Korea, for example, bank owners were not required to account for bad loans they made to the *chaebol* because they knew the ROK government would bail them out in any case. Banks, without concern for the loans' viability, lent money without regard for transparent, capitalist principles—a situation that cannot continue in a knowledge-era society.

26. "United States Government Statement on the Events in Kwangju, Republic of Korea, in May 1980," U.S. Department of State, Washington, D.C., June 19, 1989.

27. Mary Jordan, "Seeking Justice in Kwangju," *Washington Post*, December 7, 1995; also Oberdorfer, *The Two Koreas*, 355.

28. President Park Chung-hee established the National Conference for Unification, similar to the U.S. electoral college, under the 1972 Yushin Constitution. The conference's primary responsibility was to elect the president's chosen people to the National Assembly; they constituted one-third of the National Assembly.

29. The Chun administration, in one way a harbinger of the information society, also stated it envisioned at least one personal computer in every home.

30. Noland, *Avoiding the Apocalypse*, 23.

31. Clifford, *Troubled Tiger*, 276.

32. "Comparison of North and South Korea GNP and Per Capita GNP Growth," in *Handbook on Korean–U.S. Relations: Centennial Edition*, ed. Yong Soon Yim (New York: Asia Society, 1985), 403; and ROK National Statistical Office, www.nso.or.kr/, accessed October 10, 2000.

33. "Analysis of Factors Leading to Sharp Increase in Internet Users in Korea," Korea Network Information Center, http://stat.nic.or.kr/, accessed June 25, 2001.

34. By comparison, 53 percent of U.S. households had Internet access accounts as of September, 2000, www.nua.ie/surveys/how_many_online/n_america.html, accessed October 20, 2000.

35. For contemporary accounts, see Chung-in Moon and Jongryn Mo, *Economic Crisis and Structural Reforms in South Korea: Assessments and Impli-*

cations (Washington, D.C.: Economic Strategy Institute, 2000), www.econstrat. org/ECONSTRAT/skorea.htm, accessed July 10, 2001; and Noland, *Avoiding the Apocalypse.*

36. Noland, *Avoiding the Apocalypse,* 212-213; and Sohn Jie-ae, "IMF, G-7 to speed up loans for South Korea: President makes reform pledge," CNN Interactive, December 24, 1997, http://europe.cnn.com/WORLD/9712/24/imf.s.korea/, accessed July 17, 2001.

37. Moon and Mo, *Economic Crisis and Structural Reforms in South Korea,* 1.

38. Kim Dae-jung, press conference, December 19, 1997.

39. *OECD Economic Surveys, 1999–2000: Korea,* 182.

40. According to an executive of Moody's Investors Service, there is little analytical distinction between the strength of Chinese and Korean banks in general; see also *Bank and Sovereign Credit Comments* (New York: Moody's Corporation, January 2001), 22. The assessment here also draws on Moon and Mo, *Economic Crisis and Structural Reforms in South Korea,* 27–28; and Kim Kyeong-won, ed., *Two Years after the IMF Bailout: A Review of the Korean Economy's Transformation* (Seoul: Samsung Economic Research Institute, March 2000), 67–77, www.koreaeconomy.org/file/rpt/20000823133250 IMF.pdf.

41. *The Second Round Financial Restructuring Plan* (Seoul: Financial Supervisory Commission, International Cooperation Division, September 25, 2000).

42. This assessment draws on Moon and Mo, *Economic Crisis and Structural Reforms in South Korea,* 26–27; and Kim, *Two Years after the IMF Bailout,* 84–91.

43. Kim, Ibid., 78–82.

44. Eui-dal Song, "Privatization Schedule for 5 State-Run Firms Confirmed," *Digital Chosun Ilbo,* January 16, 2001, www.chosunilbo.com, accessed January 16, 2001; *Public Sector Reform in Korea,* ROK Ministry of Planning and Budget, May 27, 2000, www.reform.go.kr, accessed January 16, 2001; and Kim, Ibid., 78–82.

45. Kim, Ibid., 56; Kim Kyeong-won, ed., *Three Years after the IMF Bailout: A Review of the Korean Economy's Transformation since 1998* (Seoul: Samsung Economic Research Institute, April 2001), 102, www.korea economy.org, accessed July 20, 2001.

46. John Larkin, "Lessons Unlearned," *Far Eastern Economic Review,* September 21, 2000, p. 64.

47. Ibid.

48. Kwong-hoi Lee, "Hyundai Mt. Kumkang Tour Project at a Cross-roads," *Digital Chosun Ilbo,* January 18, 2001, www.chosunilbo.com, accessed January 18, 2001.

49. The preceding discussion of *chaebol* reform draws on Moon and Mo, *Economic Crisis and Structural Reforms in South Korea,* 28–31, 54–57; Kim, *Two Years after the IMF Bailout,* 54–68; Noland, *Avoiding the Apocalypse,* 226–237; and "Reform the External Director System," *Digital Chosun Ilbo,* September 29, 2000 (in Korean), www.chosunilbo.com, accessed September 28, 2000 (in Washington, D.C.), editorial section.

50. Sung-jin Chung, "The Dismiss Ceremony of Joint Citizen Groups for the 16th General Election—Enlarging of People's Political Right," *Digital Chosun Ilbo,* April 20, 2000, www.chosunilbo.com, accessed October 4, 2000; Sung-Jin Chung, "CAGE Holds Final Meeting," *Digital Chosun Ilbo,* April 20, 2000, www.chosunilbo.com, accessed February 28, 2001.

3 ■
Trend Three: A Human
Resources Economy

THE STUNNING ADVANCES of the twentieth century are changing the character of economic activity, even the very nature of what we know as an economy. Today's trend is toward an economy based on intellectual activity rather than on agriculture, manufacturing, or non-information-based service activities. "Economic progress," noted former Citibank president Walter Wriston, "is now largely a process of increasing the relative contribution of knowledge in the creation of wealth."[1] Most of the new economy's workers deal in knowledge—discovering, creating, applying, and distributing it in such fields as computers, telecommunications, science, education, entertainment, publishing, health, finance, social services, and law as well as in such traditional industrial activities as manufacturing. Because knowledge ultimately derives from people, this new economy is rooted in the rich soil of human resources.

Not all countries are marching in this direction at the same pace. Developing nations that hope to prosper from their integration into the world economy will need to meet its standards and play by its rules. Korea's task during 2001–2010 is to build on its impressive industrialization and accomplish essential reforms (outlined in chapter 2) to make the transition to a competitive knowledge-era economy and society.

Two well-understood implications of a human resources economy are its declining use of raw materials (on a per capita basis or per dollar of GDP) and its bias toward the service sector. In the United States, for example, the U.S. Bureau of Labor Statistics expects 23 million of the 24.6 million new jobs created between 1990 and

2005 will be in the service sector. Korea expects to require at least 50,000 workers with IT skills by 2002.[2] But, beyond raw numbers, the knowledge era is producing comprehensive, networked entities that might be termed elaborated services—companies that service a whole spectrum of integrated needs. For example, today's auto companies are involved in financing, travel, repair, fuel, and other activities related to car ownership.

An international economy based on knowledge more than on goods has witnessed rapid growth in the relative importance of service trade and foreign investment (figure 13).[3] Software programming, back-office services, product design, research and development, and customer service are increasingly traded globally. Outsourcing, a growing trend for businesses, is taking on an international character.

Korea's knowledge-based service sector was among the least developed in the OECD in 2000 although its total service sector—including knowledge-based services—is expected to expand about 45 percent between 1996, when it comprised W 204.3 trillion, and 2005, when it is expected to be W 296 trillion.[4]

Elements of the Human Resources Economy

A more fundamental implication of the human resources economy is a transformation of the nature of work. This is a change that will affect every aspect of business and labor, from the organization of corporations to the character of the workplace.

Virtual organizations that exist only on paper and that comprise employees who work independently and communicate by e-mail, phone, and fax but do not always (or ever) share the same work space are important institutions in the knowledge era. Fewer organizations today are defined by their physical work space; most are composed of groups of people performing functions for which contiguous offices may be irrelevant. The key factor driving this process is the way the various elements of the knowledge economy work together. IT encourages companies to automate, accomplish business online, and, in the interest of efficiency, reduce the number of core offices and personnel groups.

Figure 13
World Trade in Services, 1980–1999

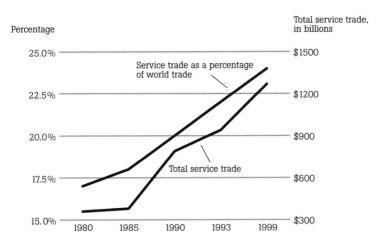

Sources: 1980–1993: Mazarr, *Mexico 2005*, fig. 13; 1999: "World Development Report 2000-2001: Attacking Poverty" (Washington, D.C.: World Bank, 2001), www.worldbank.org/poverty/wdrpoverty/report/index.htm, accessed July 14, 2001.

Virtual corporations may also shatter the traditional distinction between big and small companies. Several smaller corporations can marshal their forces and work together as if they were one institution. Yet, even as they create new opportunities, virtual organizations also have important—and vexing—implications for the concepts of trust and responsibility: How will businesses trust employees they rarely see? Not all cultures, particularly those accustomed to hierarchical social structures, can adapt equally well to a virtual world.

The nature of business competition will also change in the new era. When corporations are fragmented among dozens of smaller subentities, bits and pieces of different and competing virtual companies can cooperate on specific projects. A world of virtual or networked corporations is a world of alliance projects, and the behavior and strategies of the businesses involved will differ dramatically from the more individualistic modes of competition in the industrial era. Cooperation will become second nature; interdependence will demand cooperative alliances that vie for shares in competitive markets. Cooperative, often disruptive, new alliances—from partnerships between hotel and restaurant chains to ventures between traditional competitors such as Apple and Microsoft—already exist in all industries.

The principles of the knowledge era—speed, flexibility, decentralization, and empowerment—will change the nature of the workplace in fundamental ways.

The rapidly changing nature of employment has already produced frequent turnover and career shifts that demand great flexibility on the part of workers. Multiple career paths, serial careers, and less loyalty on both sides of the employer–employee relationship are now the norm. Employees' affiliations with their employers is more tenuous, and the forms that work takes—until recently, a relatively well-defined 40-hour, five-day week in the United States and a 44-hour, five-and-one-half-day week in Korea—have become less stable and uniform. In 1993 more than 34 million Americans, more than 25 percent of the workforce, were working part-time or as contractors.[5] These new and more flexible forms of work require a new kind of worker: better educated, more accustomed to rapid change, more willing and able to take responsibility for running important elements of the company. In Korea, the 1997 financial crisis and ensuing reform programs accelerated changes in the nature of employment.

A Networked Economy

Another development in the knowledge era is the growing dominance of networked organizational forms. No longer can an economy be thought of as a fragmented collection of individual companies and people pursuing independent project objectives. As virtual companies seek partners for cooperative ventures, as information highways and superhighways bind together various forms of economic activity, as finance becomes global, an appropriate metaphor for the new economic arrangement is "the network."

James F. Moore, in *The Death of Competition,* assembles these themes in a compelling vision of the future. He suggests we are witnessing the "end of industry," or the end of a time in which independent businesspeople in the midst of intensifying competition can think of their industries as unique, separate things. The trick in the new economy is to break out of industry boundaries and "hasten the coming together of disparate business elements into new economic wholes."[6]

Finance and Capital

Money is essentially an information product or a form of information, and it should come as no surprise that finance and capital markets have attained unprecedented importance in the human resources economy. Even the stark numbers—perhaps in excess of $2 trillion (up from $10 or $20 billion in the early 1980s) in foreign exchange is traded every day in the world currency markets while another $250 billion is traded daily in bond and equity transactions—do not do justice to the critical role of finance in the new economy.

Finance serves as an enforcer and ratifier of socioeconomic convergence. Only countries that reform and liberalize attract the investment they need to remain prosperous and maintain growth. *New York Times* columnist Thomas Friedman calls this coercive pressure "the paradigm," an international model of social and economic organization demanded by capital markets. While the long-term effects of democracy and economic liberalization are generally positive, heavy short-term costs are paid by nations dragged into such transitions more quickly and more deeply than they expect.

The 1997 financial crisis provided such a shock to Korea. However, the crisis powerfully motivated Koreans to implement long overdue reforms in several sectors, including the finance sector, prompting significant increases in foreign direct investment (FDI) of more than $15 billion in 1999 and again in 2000. Such reforms, if faithfully brought to fruition, will establish a foundation for sustainable economic growth.

Perhaps the most important financial trend is the elimination of middlemen (such as stockbrokers) who are being replaced by educated laypersons who have the ability to manage their own financial affairs online and who understand and can manipulate electronic cash (e-cash, which Koreans are increasingly using). Within a decade, money for some may no longer be a tangible object; it may exist only as e-cash in cyberspace, shuffled instantaneously among bank accounts, mutual funds, insurance funds, loans, and dozens of other applications. Modern cultures are entering a world of virtual economics, in which the strength of an economy will be judged by perceptions as much as by reality. Virtual economies may well be more prone to sudden peaks and valleys and more susceptible to boom-and-bust cycles than industrial-era economies.

Worsening Income Distribution

A globalized human resources economy threatens to widen the gap between the haves and the have-nots in both industrial and developing countries:

- new distinctions in income between high-paying, high-tech jobs and low-paying service jobs;
- social divisions fostered by the demand for highly educated workers in many new positions;
- the stratifying effects of a global economy that imposes global wage standards on industrial economies; and
- the stark divisions created by the rise of alternatives to full-time employment, including temporary and part-time jobs.

Evidence for a growing income gap is widespread. In the United States during the 1980s, an astounding 62 percent of new national wealth went to the top 1 percent of the population, while 37 percent went to the next 19 percent, and a paltry 1 percent to the remaining 80 percent of Americans. The worldwide story is much the same: between 1960 and 1990, the incomes of the richest 20 percent grew three times faster than those of the poorest 20 percent. In 1960 the richest one-fifth held three-quarters of the world's income and the poorest one-fifth just 2.3 percent. By 1990 the richest one-fifth held 85 percent of global income and the poorest one-fifth an astonishingly meager 1.4 percent.[7]

An especially disturbing pattern is the immense disparity in college degrees acquired by children of wealthy and middle-class families in the United States. Families with incomes of $67,000 or greater see 80 percent of their children attend and graduate from college.

The corresponding figure for families with incomes between $20,000 and $67,000 is only 20 percent, and for poorer families, less than 10 percent,[8] a preparation gap that cannot persist if the United States is to retain an egalitarian nature in the knowledge era.

Korea, on the other hand, does quite well in promoting egalitarian education. In 1996, for example, more than 80 percent of all high school graduates nationwide entered college, and most who entered graduated. Some students came from wealthy families and some earned scholarships or qualified for financial assistance. Others, however, could attend because their parents sometimes worked excruciating second or third jobs or assumed onerous debt to gain the funds required.

In an age that emphasizes specialized knowledge, education, and high-technology skills, a social and economic wedge can be driven between the knowledge proficient and the knowledge deprived. And with the ascent of market-based solutions and the accompanying decline in governmental authority, policymakers in the knowledge era may find it more difficult to effectively lessen the problem of socioeconomic inequity. In Korea, since 1998, the rise of high-tech, knowledge-based venture companies indicates that the new economy in Korea has great potential for worsening income disparities that are already a problem exacerbated by the 1997 financial crisis.

Shift to the Developing World

The broad knowledge-era trends considered here will promote a relative shift of power, especially economic power, toward the developing world, with the new locus in the emerging markets in Asia. Industrial countries are already growing less than 3 percent per year compared with approximately 5 percent on the average in developing countries (figure 14). East Asia's Crisis-5 countries—South Korea, Thailand, Indonesia, Malaysia, Philippines—are generally expected to grow in excess of 5 percent annually through 2008.

This tectonic redistribution of power from industrial nations to developing ones is making the world community more multipolar. This will not happen overnight; many developing nations will maintain low per capita incomes. In 2005, for example, China's will likely be around $1,250.[9] Even according to traditional measures,

Figure 14
Annual Change in World GDP Growth, 1981–2008

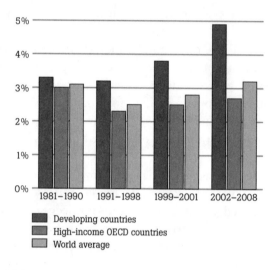

Developing countries
High-income OECD countries
World average

Source: Global Economic Prospects and the Developing Countries (Washington, D.C.: World Bank, 2000), www.worldbank.org/prospects/gep2000/chapt1.pdf, accessed February 23, 2001.

however—instead of the purchasing-power-parity measures that inflate economic importance—the clout of developing nations is growing. By 2010, developing nations are expected to account for 30 percent of world imports and 22 percent of exports (up from an estimated 22.5 and 19 percent in 2000). The World Bank concluded in 1995 that "by 2010 more than one billion consumers in developing countries could have per capita incomes exceeding those of Greece or Spain today,"[10] an estimate that an informed World Bank official said in April 2001 was still thought to be accurate. By 2010, U.S. exports to emerging-market countries will outpace exports to Europe and Japan combined. Successful knowledge-era companies will find ways to reach this immense new market with goods and services.

The Human Resources Economy and Korea

By 2010, Koreans will very possibly have made good progress in the transition to the knowledge era although significant hurdles must be overcome. One factor that inspires confidence in Korea's ability to make progress is Korea's demonstrated ability to move its poor agrarian society rapidly—roughly within one 30-year generation—into the industrialized ranks of the OECD. Another is the demand for better democratic government that prompted many Koreans to go online to influence the April 2000 National Assembly election (see the final section of chapter 2). A third factor is the exceptionally positive acceptance of electronic business despite a relatively weak financial service sector. Finally, there is the development of high-technology venture companies since 1998 despite some setbacks in late 2000.

Korea's road to the knowledge era is unfortunately cluttered with obstacles that weaken Korea's international competitiveness and engendered a poor 22nd position among the 29 OECD countries in 2000.[11] The need to complete the array of political and economic reforms outlined in chapter 2 will persist until the structural weaknesses that impede progress toward the knowledge era are eliminated. Transforming the government's role in the economy and the corporate work cultures is likely to be among the more difficult challenges.

An important step toward building a knowledge-based society and economy—that prizes human abilities to discover, create, apply, and distribute knowledge—is the establishment of an environment in which every person is not only technically competent but is also regarded as a vital asset capable of contributing intellectually to the common good. The Internet with its range of technologies and knowledge-based services provides fertile ground on which to develop the requisite modern skills and attitudes. A number of Korean citizens—enthusiastic "netizens"—were embracing the efficiencies and enabling opportunities inherent in the Internet at the beginning of the twenty-first century.

Figure 15

Percentage of Households with Internet Connections, South Korea, by monthly income, 1997–1999

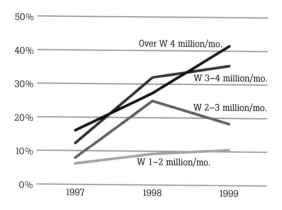

Source: "Internet Distribution Rate among Households" (Seoul: Samsung Economic Research Institute, January 29, 2000), www.koreaeconomy.org/, accessed October 28, 2000.

A Networking Economy

The Korean government has led by example since the early 1990s and has promoted the Internet as a tool to improve transparency and efficiency. Not only did the government invest heavily in building the infrastructure, but government bureaucracies and associated organizations quickly went online. Public access to government records and positions on a broad range of issues was much improved, which facilitated public sector–private sector communications. A number of Korean knowledge-based organizations, including research institutes, nongovernmental organizations (NGOs), newspapers, and private companies followed suit.

ROK government efforts to develop the Korean IT industry and promote transition toward the knowledge era began to bear fruit during the final years of the twentieth century. These high-tech developments were the bow wave of Korea's movement deeper into the knowledge era. By the end of 2000, the business of mobile

Figure 16
Percentage of Households with Internet Connections, South Korea, by education level, 1997–1999

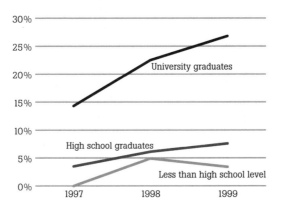

Source: "Internet Distribution Rate among Households" (Seoul: Samsung Economic Research Institute, January 29, 2000), www.koreaeconomy.org/, accessed October 28, 2000.

telephones, personal computers, and other information and communications technology products constituted an increasingly greater share of GDP and exports while the knowledge-based service sector also was growing, albeit more slowly.

Korean Netizens

Personal computers abounded in South Korean government offices, NGOs, private companies, and private homes at the turn of the century. Over 64 percent of all Korean homes were estimated to possess a personal computer by the end of 2000; 45 percent of all homes had Internet accounts, and 4 million households subscribed to broadband services, making Korea a world leader in using this technology.[12] Millions of additional Koreans regularly use computers installed in public gathering places—Internet plazas—to go online. Figures 15 and 16 show Internet distribution by household income and level of education through 1999.

Figure 17
Exports, South Korea, 1995 and 2000

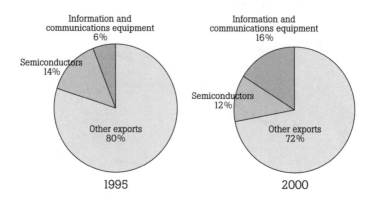

Information and
communications equipment
6%

Semiconductors
14%

Other exports
80%

1995

Information and
communications equipment
16%

Semiconductors
12%

Other exports
72%

2000

Source: Monthly Statistical Bulletin (Seoul: Bank of Korea, September 2001), 108.

Almost 20 million Koreans aged 7–59 accessed the Internet at least once during July 2000, according to a survey by the e-Trend Internet Research and Consulting Institute.[13] These Internet users represented more than 40 percent of Korea's 47.5 million population. The survey also stated that

- 69 percent of Korean Internet users were aged 10–29;
- 43.6 percent of Korean Internet users accessed the Internet daily;
- average log-on time was 90 minutes;
- the male-to-female user ratio was 6:4; and
- the top three access venues were the home (51 percent), an Internet plaza (22 percent), and the workplace (13 percent).

Mobile telephones were ubiquitous, and Korea was the world's largest market for CDMA wireless technology.[14] More than 27 million Koreans used mobile phones by mid-2000, representing approximately 56 percent of the population.[15] Using these and other information technologies, individual Koreans increasingly embraced e-cash, e-commerce (both wholesale and retail electronic commerce), online banking and investing, and credit cards.

Figure 18
Information Technology Exports, South Korea, 1994–1999

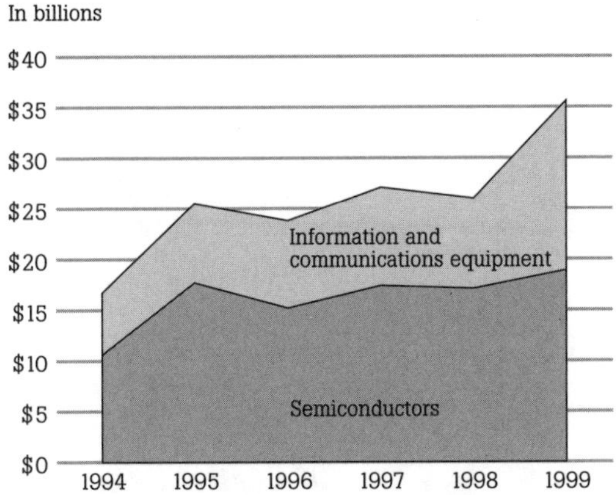

In billions

Source: Monthly Statistical Bulletin (Seoul: Bank of Korea, September 2000), 108.

Export-Driven Economy

Korea's export-based economy drives its domestic economy. Korea grasped the importance of exports in the early 1960s, and its economic development miracle rested on an export strategy with strong government support, as described in chapter 2. From 1962 through 1996, Korea's exports expanded from less than 5 percent of nominal GDP to approximately 30 percent,[16] with steady improvements in technological sophistication (figure 17). For example, primary exports in the 1960s comprised such basic products as textiles and human-hair wigs. By the end of the twentieth century, however, Korea had become a major global supplier of advanced technology items such as ships, automobiles, semiconductors, personal computers, and other information and communications equipment.

The importance of the electronics sector increased significantly during the 1990s. In 1994, for example, semiconductors and information and communications equipment exports earned about $16.7 billion, approximately 17 percent of all Korean exports. By 1999 this share had grown to $36.8 billion, which was 25 percent of total exports (figure 18).[17]

Figure 19
Growth of Electronic Commerce, South Korea, 1996–2001

Note: Data for 2000 are estimates based on data for the first half of 2000; data for 2001 are estimates.

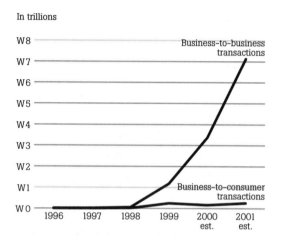

Source: Korea Information Society Development Institute (KISDI), August 2001.

Electronic Business

Domestic demand for personal computers and other information age products has been strong in Korea. Following a brief 2 percent dip in demand in 1998 caused by the recession, demand saw a strong 6.5 percent growth in 1999,[18] resulting in more empowered citizens communicating and conducting business electronically.

Electronic commerce. E-commerce in Korea increased dramatically during 1998–2000, especially with respect to business-to-business transactions although consumers warmed to business-to-consumer transactions as well. Prospects for e-commerce in Korea are promising (figure 19).

Online banking. Korea's 20 private banks all offered some online banking services by mid-2000 (figure 20). Eleven banks also provided a limited range of services to mobile telephone users, and the other nine banks expected to provide mobile banking services by

Figure 20
Registered Online Banking Customers, South Korea, 2000

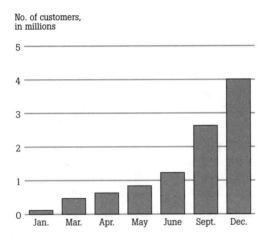

No. of customers,
in millions

Source: Bank of Korea official, communication with author, 2000.

the end of the year. The number of Koreans registered to conduct online banking soared during the first three quarters of 2000. By the end of September 2000, 2.63 million Koreans had signed up for online banking services with domestic banks, a 114 percent increase over June 2000 and a 2,067 percent increase over 1999. The most popular services were account balance inquiries, money transfers, and loan applications, which as a group increased 55 percent over online services reported in June. For example, customers submitted up to 97,000 loan applications for W 30.08 trillion, of which 20 percent were approved.[19]

Online investing. Korean investors also embraced online securities trading: over 90 percent of Korean investors used the Internet in September 2000. Total online securities trading expanded from W 548 million in January 1998 to W 136 trillion in September 2000 (figure 21). Total online securities trading between September 1999 and September 2000 increased 89 percent. Online stock trading made up 60.6 percent of total stock trading, according to

Figure 21
Online Securities Trading, South Korea, Jan. 1998–Sept. 2000

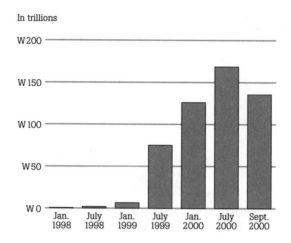

Source: Korea Securities Dealers Association, http://ksda.or.kr.

the Korea Securities Dealers Association (KSDA).[20] By comparison, online stock trading in the United States was in the 40–45 percent range in late spring 2000.[21] Figure 22 shows trends in online securities trading as reported by the top five securities firms (Daishin Securities, Daewoo Securities, Hyundai Securities, LG Securities, and Samsung Securities).

Credit card use. Another telling indicator of Korean attraction to electronic business is the increasing use of credit cards since 1997. Koreans used credit cards for less than 30 percent of total private consumption in 1997–1998; however, credit card use increased to approximately 35 percent of consumption in 1999 and was expected to account for more than 70 percent of private consumption by 2002.[22] The Kim Dae-jung government has built on previous government programs and has strongly promoted the use of credit cards.

To increase corporate tax revenue by catching businesses that underreport income, the National Tax Service (NTS) began encouraging credit card use in 1999. The NTS decided to promote credit

Figure 22
Online Trading by the Top Five Securities Firms, South Korea,
Aug. 1999–Sept. 2000

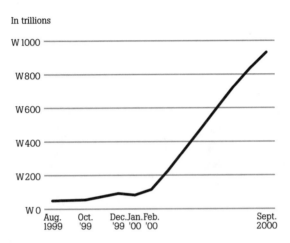

Sources: "Trend in Cyber Trading by the Five Largest Securities Firms," (March 11) and "Top Five Domestic Securities Companies, E-Trade Trends," (January 22) (Seoul: Samsung Economic Research Institute, 2000), www.koreaeconomy.org/, accessed October 28, 2000; Michael Kim, "Korean Online Trading Hits 63 percent of Total," Asia Internet.com, October 11, 2000, http://asia.internet.com/, accessed November 2, 2000.

card transactions, confident that audit trails would enable tax auditors to assess real company income more accurately than in a cash environment. The NTS monitored credit card transactions through information supplied by the credit card companies, compared consumer purchases with the vendor or service provider's business income declaration, and then requested the company provide a second declaration when there were discrepancies. NTS incentives to encourage credit card use included tax deductions for consumers making large credit card purchases and tax benefits for companies that submitted credit card receipts for entertainment expenses exceeding W 50,000 (about $40 in late 2000). In addition, in September 2000 the government advised over 50,000 small businesses to begin accepting credit cards or face potential audits—a powerful incentive.

Figure 23
Sales of Seven Leading Credit Card Companies, South Korea, 1998–Sept. 2000

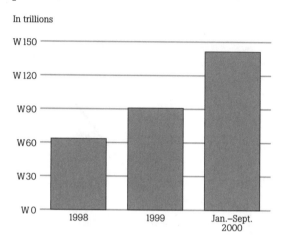

Source: "Healthy Hike in Credit Card Usage," *Korea Economic Weekly,* October 23, 2000.

Consequently, credit card use surged after 1999. The seven leading Korean credit card companies[23] reported steady growth from 1998 through September 2000, when sales exceeded W 141 trillion (figure 23).[24]

Service Sector

Korea's knowledge-based industries expanded 12.5 percent from 1985 to 1996, the highest rate among OECD countries. Despite such explosive growth, however, Korea's knowledge-based activities in 1996 accounted for only 40 percent of business added value attributable to knowledge-based industries and services, notably below the OECD average of 50 percent. Korea was held back by its relatively low share of knowledge-based business services, which—at 19.5 percent—compared unfavorably with the OECD average of 38.3 percent. As a result, Korea's knowledge-based business service

Figure 24
Trade in Information Technology Goods and Services,
South Korea, 2000

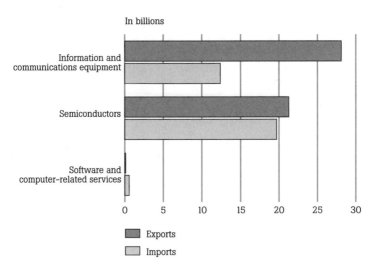

Sources: Monthly Statistical Bulletin (Seoul: Bank of Korea, April 2001), 108–109; *Information Technology Overview of Korea (Statistical Profiles)* (Seoul: ROK Ministry of Information and Communications, April 2001), 11.

sector ranked 21 among 22 assessed OECD countries; only Mexico ranked lower.[25]

In 2001, predictions were that Korea's service sector would likely expand from W 238 trillion in 2000 to W 296 trillion in 2005. Such growth would represent a 45 percent expansion since 1996, when the sector was valued at W 204.3 trillion. Korea's expanding service sector is expected to make up an increasingly larger share of knowledge-based business service providers.[26]

Strong demand and a number of economic reforms helped Korea improve its knowledge-based services. Although the increase in knowledge-based service providers was difficult to quantify, the ratio of Korea's total service sector to nominal GDP increased significantly after 1997, slightly exceeding 60 percent in 1999. By comparison, the ratios in the United States, Singapore, and Japan were 73.1 percent, 69.4 percent, and 61.5 percent, respectively.[27]

Figure 25
Balance of Trade for Technology, South Korea, 1996–1999

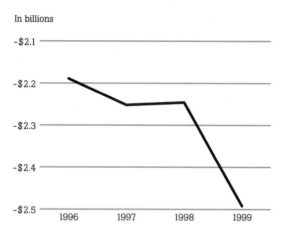

In billions

Source: "Technology Imports Surpass Exports by a Large Margin," *Korea Economic Weekly*, October 30, 2000, p. 2.

In 1998, the government began to promote small and medium-sized, high-technology, knowledge-based companies called venture companies. By May 2000, there were 7,110 venture companies, of which roughly one-third were service providers, a percentage extrapolated from the fact that 67 percent (4,733 companies) were manufacturing enterprises.[28] Although venture companies made up less than 1 percent of Korea's companies in late 2000, they had great potential to drive development of the knowledge-based business service sector.

Knowledge Creation

To succeed in the knowledge era, an economy must be able to create knowledge. Korea, however, has remained highly dependent on imported technology (figures 24 and 25). In 1999, Korea's technology exports earned only $193 million while its technology balance of trade was a negative $2.5 billion, which included payments for foreign technology licenses, consulting commissions, and personnel who accompanied imported capital goods. Electric and electronic technology imports made up 55 percent of all technology imports, followed by machinery sector imports. "The sharp increase in technology-related overseas payments is because [Korea's] high-tech industries . . . are highly dependent on technologies of advanced nations in . . . mobile telecom, software, and other critical parts and components," reported the *Korea Economic Weekly* in October 2000.[29]

The Samsung Economic Research Institute (SERI) noted the poor competitiveness of six important Korean industries—semiconductors, IT, automotive, steel, textiles, and finance—in an October 2000 report regarding Korea's industrial competitiveness. SERI concluded that Korea's IT sector suffered from "weak competitiveness in its core technology," with the "major component and upstream industries" being highly dependent on foreign technology "due to inferior domestic technology in areas such as the design of nonmemory core technology, key components of CDMA, materials for semiconductors, and production equipment."[30]

Korea's high dependence on foreign knowledge was consistent with the OECD's low assessment of Korea's "technological strength," which the Paris group's secretariat calculated by multiplying the number of Korean patents with a standard OECD index of their impact. Korea ranks 16th among 19 OECD-assessed countries.[31]

Korea has not skimped on spending for R&D; it ranked sixth among OECD countries in terms of its absolute level of R&D spending, estimated at W 13 trillion in 1999. Part of the problem may derive from the fact that private sector firms with more than 300 employees funded and performed most of Korea's R&D, spending an estimated W 10 trillion in 1999. The private sector emphasis has focused Korea's R&D on short-term projects, especially in the automotive, information, and communications sectors. More than three-quarters (78 percent) of R&D spending in 1997 was directed at these sectors. Spending on basic research was low, which may explain Korea's low technological strength.[32]

Shortcomings in the area of knowledge creation imply that Korea's problems might be greater than funding priorities. They might reflect shortcomings in workplace conditions and cultural factors that powerfully affect the ability of an organization's human resources to discover, create, apply, and disseminate knowledge.

Transforming the Work Culture

Korea's market-economy reforms since 1998 have explicitly changed the rules on corporate governance, capital acquisition, and workforce layoffs. Reforms have required companies to focus on transparency and profitability. Many firms could not meet the new standards and, consequently, an average of over 200 firms per month declared bankruptcy in Korea's seven major cities throughout 1999 and in January 2000.[33] One of the more notable cases involved the giant Daewoo *chaebol*, whose collapse in 1999 particularly alarmed workers throughout the economy because Daewoo had been thought to be too big to fail. In 2001, scores of additional companies were expected to be sold off under bankruptcy laws in the second phase of financial-sector restructuring that began in the third quarter of 2000. On November 3, 2000, 21 Korean creditor banks jointly named 52 companies to be put under court receivership, immediately liquidated, or sold off.[34]

Such reforms and results coupled with the emergence of venture companies had significant implications for Korea's traditional work culture, which typically comprised highly structured and vertical labor–management relationships consistent with Korea's industrial age economy and neo-Confucian value-based culture. The cultures in the new venture companies, however, more closely resemble those of the new knowledge-era economy based on the ability of human resources to generate knowledge. Venture companies represent a sharp departure from traditional Korean company cultures.

Emergence of Knowledge-Based Venture Companies

Korea's National Assembly approved legislation in October 1997 to establish a venture business sector to create a high-technology economy through small, dynamic companies that would also create more knowledge-based jobs in high-technology fields including telecommunications, IT, and biotechnology. To be legally recognized as a venture company, the candidate firm had to meet one of four conditions: have a high level of R&D, sell products that incorporate patent rights, have substantial investment by a venture capital company, or use advanced technology.

The law facilitated the development of venture companies by improving the availability of financing, technology, manpower, and work facilities while also providing tax incentives. The Kim Dae-jung government encouraged banks to provide candidate venture companies with credit guarantees or loans based on the value of their technology instead of on tangible collateral.

The government also provided funds to venture capital companies because other sources of capital were not yet well established and venture capital firms were relatively new to Korea. The venture capital companies were authorized to provide promising venture companies with up to 20 percent of their capital. For the balance of their capital, the venture companies had to turn to family members, friends, and other financial sources such as the angel market—other businessmen and investors—and the Korean Securities Dealers Automated Quotation (KOSDAQ) market.[35]

The venture company sector almost doubled between October 1997 and May 2000. There were 3,600 venture companies when the 1997 legislation was approved, but the financial crisis caused the number to decline by May 1998. The Kim Dae-jung government, inaugurated in February 1998, strongly promoted the venture sector, and it expanded to more than 7,000 venture companies by May 2000. Approximately two-fifths of them were in the computer or telecommunications industries. The sector was on track to reach 11,000 companies by the end of 2000 and meet the government's vision of 20,000 companies by 2003.[36] Korea will require at least 50,000 IT professionals by 2002.[37]

This new breed of Korean company requires a knowledge-era business climate of reasonable access to capital, intellectual property protection, an open and competitive market, a skilled and flexible workforce, and a corporate culture that inspires and highly rewards each worker's contributions. These new venture businesses greatly appeal to Koreans who are embracing information age technologies, recognizing that skills are more important than personal relationships in the knowledge-era economy, and craving both genuine recognition and company appreciation.

Many relatively young employees have left traditional jobs in *chaebol*, state-owned enterprises, and government to join or start venture companies.[38] This surge into the knowledge era supports trend predictions in this chapter:

- Employees like the new venture companies, which meet their professional objectives and needs for recognition, and provide satisfactory, performance-based compensation;
- Distinctions between the workplace and home have begun to blur;
- Firms hire more temporary, daily, and part-time workers than full-time workers, and opportunities for female workers have expanded;
- Outsourcing has become more common;
- Venture companies can pay their employees very well; this might create income disparities between their typically young employees and older employees in other types of employment.

Although venture companies represent fewer than 1 percent of all Korean companies, they set a new standard for corporate work cultures, with a potential ripple effect that could change Korea's work culture writ large, assuming Korea stays the course on economic reform.[39]

A W 220 billion scandal in the second half of 2000 indicated that venture companies are not immune to traditional issues regarding inappropriate personal relationships, however. In October 2000, the Korea Digital Line Company, a venture company listed on the KOSDAQ, failed to meet its debt payments, which prompted KOSDAQ officials to ask the Financial Supervisory Service (FSS) to investigate. The FSS asked the Seoul district prosecutor's office to take the case. The government's investigation revealed inappropriate relationships and illegal activities involving the Korea Digital Line Company chairman, the vice-chairwoman of a mutual savings and finance company, and FSS officials. One of the FSS officials apparently committed suicide during the investigation although homicide was not ruled out. On November 13, 2000, the government indicted the vice-chairwoman of Dongbang Mutual Savings and Finance Company for illegally borrowing W 19.5 billion, embezzling W 92 billion, and perpetrating a W 48 billion fraud through investment funds she had established. The Korea Digital chairman was indicted for illegally raising W 52.7 billion and for bribing an

FSS official. The surviving FSS official under investigation was indicted for accepting W 49.5 million in kickbacks.[40]

While the long-term implications of the scandal remained to be seen, it had near-term potential to damage public confidence in the government and in the venture sector. The news media, opposition politicians, and others expressed concern that the Seoul district prosecutor's office had not thoroughly investigated all government officials suspected of wrongdoing. The scandal also had potential to further damage investor confidence in the venture sector, which had been in recession since March 2000. From March to November 2000, the KOSDAQ's Venture Index dropped 80.4 percent.[41]

The good news in the scandal was that institutional checks and balances now built into the Korean financial and business sectors through the Kim Dae-jung administration's four-sector reforms identified wrongdoing and started a corrective process. The scandal took nothing away from the positive aspects of the work cultures promoted by the venture companies. It did, however, provide a reminder that Korea's road to becoming an open, knowledge-based economy remains encumbered with past practices and expectations.

Evolving Workforce Flexibility

The work environment in Korean firms obviously has been adequate for manufacturing advanced technology products, including products in the information and telecommunications sectors. But the environment has been generally inadequate for developing new technology and providing the knowledge-based services that are so important to knowledge era economies.

Korean labor flexibility improved significantly by the late 1990s. The Korean workforce in 1999 comprised permanent/regular workers who expected lifelong employment and nonregular workers[42] who did not. The average tenure of nonregular workers in 1997 was 6 years for men and 4 years for women, which was substantially below the OECD average of 10.4 and 8.3 years for men and women. The percentage of nonregular workers increased from 42 percent in 1995 to 52 percent in 1999, the highest in the OECD. The proportion of regular workers correspondingly declined over the same five-year period from 58 percent to 48 percent. Factoring the self-employed, unpaid family members, and nonregular workers into the total workforce, the number of regular workers declined to 30 percent of the workforce by 1999, giving Korea the smallest percentage of regular workers in the OECD.[43] Although the government has discouraged layoffs,[44] job security has become a worry for both regular and nonregular workers, particularly in light of the knowledge era's demands for significantly new skills.

Compensation in traditional Korean firms comprises a salary, usually negotiated within the company on an annual basis, supplemented by overtime and bonuses, a policy that provides a high degree of wage responsiveness to business and labor conditions. Workers are highly motivated to work as much as possible because overtime pay and bonuses could provide up to one-third of overall annual compensation.[45]

Bonuses in principle provide a sound method of rewarding performance, and knowledge-era managers could use bonuses to reward success in discovering, creating, applying, and/or disseminating knowledge or other quantifiable productivity factors. In traditional industries, however, anecdotal evidence indicated that some managers based bonuses on an employee's efforts to strengthen personal relationships with management more than on quantifiable performance. While such awards would be consistent with the importance of personal relationships within the general culture, they can frustrate a company's efforts to improve competitiveness.

Contentious labor–management relations have been a factor limiting workforce flexibility. Despite new policies authorizing layoffs, labor union leaders often mistrust company managers and have been unwilling to work with managers of financially troubled, noncompetitive, nonproductive companies to find solutions to turn the company around.

The bankruptcy of Daewoo Motors in November 2000 is a case in point. In the face of debt exceeding $10 billion, insufficient cash flow, and a loss of confidence by foreign investors, Daewoo management prepared a restructuring plan in October 2000 that would have laid off approximately 3,500 workers, about 18 percent of Daewoo's 19,000 member workforce. Daewoo's labor union refused to cooperate, prompting creditor banks to reject the plan and put Daewoo into court receivership. In December 2000, the court approved a restructuring plan that would lay off at least 5,000 workers, and massive layoff rumors worried workers. Their concerns were affirmed by late February 2001, as Daewoo laid off more than 6,800 workers and announced intentions to lay off another 1,700 to accelerate its planned sale to General Motors (GM). Taking note of deteriorating labor–management relations and a decrease in sales and production from 1999 to 2001, Korea Development Bank governor Uhm Rak-yong warned that the Daewoo Motors sale to GM could be in jeopardy if union leaders and management did not agree on reform measures to help improve cash flow.[46] Whether Daewoo Motors could have survived with a more cooperative workforce is debatable, but labor's recalcitrant attitude during this episode was not unique. At the beginning of 2001, it remained to be seen if managers and labor would be able to replace their traditional mutually critical views with the mutually respectful views commonly associated with an empowered human resources economy.

Worker Empowerment

A full-fledged knowledge-era worker feels empowered in the workplace. A successful knowledge-era organization encourages, inspires, and empowers technically competent workers with a variety of job skills to discover, create, apply, and distribute knowledge for the purpose of improving organizational effectiveness across the spectrum of economic activity, from agriculture to mining to manufacturing to the most sophisticated services. Empowerment inevitably will affect more than the workers; it will affect the nation.

Empowering Korea's workforce is likely to be difficult, however, because it clashes with Korea's neo-Confucian cultural norms. Senior management telling employees they are "empowered" is not enough. Private, public, and government organizations throughout the economy must create a work culture in which each worker— regardless of position—believes management places high value on every worker's ability to contribute intellectually to improving the organization's effectiveness. Corporate culture in the knowledge era must permit a great deal of decentralization because the need for close supervision declines as empowerment increases.

All workers must believe that their contributions will be appreciated and appropriately rewarded through increased recognition, promotion, pay, or other meaningful ways. Relationships required to establish such a work culture are more likely to resemble the collaborative, horizontal, mutually respectful organizational relationships typically found in advanced Western organizations, not in Korea's vertical and often contentious traditional labor–management relationships. It will not be easy for Korea's organizations—corporate, governmental, and social—to change, but Korea's proverbial "if you try, you can do" attitude may help smooth the way.

Worsening Income Disparity

Korea's rich were getting richer and the poor were getting poorer between the financial crisis in fourth quarter 1997 and the end of 2000. Real average income for urban households, adjusted for inflation since 1995, in the second quarter of 1997 was W 2.03 million. By the second quarter of 2000, it had fallen to W 1.93 million. When the top and bottom income quintiles for 1999 and 2000 are compared, the top 20 percent earned 5.28 times more than the bottom 20 percent in the second quarter of 2000 compared with 5.24 times more in the same quarter in 1999.[47] In first quarter 2001, the top quintile earned an even greater share: 5.76 times the bottom quintile.[48] The Gini coefficient, a mathematical expression of the degree of concentration of wealth or income, increased for Korea after 1997, indicating increasing income disparities within the population (figure 26).[49]

At least two factors contributed to this widening income gap. One was the high unemployment in Korea after the 1997 financial crisis. Unemployment peaked at 8.6 percent in 1998 and then decreased to 3.6 percent by summer 2000. But the second round of financial restructuring in the fourth quarter of 2000 was expected to add 100,000 more workers to the ranks of the unemployed, increasing the unemployment rate to 4.1 percent.[50]

The gap widened also because of differences in the sources of income for the haves and the have-nots in Korea. The wealthy regularly gain supplemental income from their property, investments, and interest earned on their savings accounts while the poorer citi-

Figure 26
Gini Income Distribution Index, South Korea, 1990–2000

Note: A score of 1 indicates all income is pooled in one group; 0 indicates equal income distribution throughout a society.

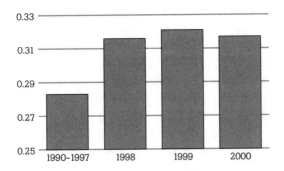

Source: Florence Lowe-Lee, "Where is Korea's Middle Class?" *Korea Insight* 2, no. 11 (November 2000): 1, www.keia.com/Insight-November2000lpdf, accessed June 3, 2001.

zens usually rely exclusively on their wages and bonuses. The wealthier group benefited immensely after 1998 because interest rates on savings accounts approached 30 percent, the stock market was expanding, and costs for rental housing increased. As a result, the gross income of the wealthiest 10 percent of the population was more than 21 times greater than the gross income of the poorest 10 percent although the salaries of the wealthy were only nine times greater.[51]

To help reduce future income disparities and to equip all members of the society—especially the poor—with the requisite skills and intellectual tools to survive in the knowledge economy, Korea will need to do a better job of providing educational and training opportunities. Formal education in primary and secondary institutions needs to be modernized, and continuing education opportunities for adults currently in the workforce or unemployed especially need to be expanded. Improved education and training should address both technical and problem-solving skills.

Summary of Challenges

Korea's future is taking shape as a knowledge-era society that will combine an increasingly responsive democratic government with a well-regulated market economy to create unprecedented economic freedom. The evolving business climate created by ongoing political and economic reforms will enable individuals and business enterprises with good ideas and management expertise to obtain capital to pursue those ideas. Merit, mettle, and market factors will matter much more than the personal relationships that previously dominated Korea's business culture. Korea, by implementing a number of long-overdue financial, labor, public sector, and corporate reforms, has made a good start in building the road toward this vision. Discipline in seeing these reforms to completion is essential for expanding an economy that is built upon people's ability to discover, create, apply, and disseminate knowledge.

The technologically savvy middle and junior managers, entry-level workers, and college and high school students of 2000 will make up a significant part of the workforce in 2010. Accustomed to the empowering efficiencies of the online world, they will demand reasonable approximations in their work settings.

Painful, socially wrenching changes are coming, however, as Korea works to reform its political–economic system and implement a market economy. The second round of financial restructuring provides a reminder that many companies need to change their operating practices to become profitable. More bankruptcies and more unemployment are to be expected.

Challenges

Korea faces four important challenges in building a competitive, human resources economy:

Implementing stipulated reforms. The first challenge is to implement fully both the specified and the implied financial, public sector, labor, and corporate reforms outlined in chapter 2. Domestic political opposition and popular demands for government action reminiscent of the outmoded but entrenched Korea Inc. model will make reform difficult.

Developing a national vision of the new economy. The second challenge is to establish a nationally accepted vision of the new human resources economy and the appropriate role of Korea's democratic government in the economy. Continuing confrontations over the 1998 structural reforms indicate consensus is still needed. The government should set policies to promote fair competition while it strongly supports a market economy and eschews direct intervention in that economy. Long the engineer of Korea's economy, the government in the new economy should be the referee instead: it should provide fiscal policy, broad guidance, and oversight. Individuals and companies need to chart their own courses and be responsible for their successes and failures. The envisioned new political–economic system would reward merit and mettle over personal relationships.

Improving labor–management relations. The third challenge is to replace quickly with mutually respectful relationships the poisoned relationships between labor unions and company management. This requires constructive leadership from the top down, an expanded social safety welfare net, and continuing education to provide workers with new skills.

Promoting a human resources economy. The fourth challenge is to develop an environment conducive to discovering, creating, applying, and distributing knowledge in organizations across the spectrum of economic activity. Korea needs to provide better formal and continuing adult education and training to meet knowledge-era requirements, establish appropriate public and private R&D organizations, set funding priorities, and protect intellectual property to empower and equip all Koreans—especially the poor—with the requisite knowledge, problem-solving skills, and intellectual tools to survive in the knowledge economy. Not only will success improve each worker's employability, it will ultimately help reduce income disparities.

As important as these measures are, however, they pale in comparison with the requirements and benefits of empowering the workforce. Organizations that limit their workers through the use of narrow job descriptions, micromanagement, and work cultures that inhibit individual initiative cannot compete with organizations that fully use all their human resources. Despite implications for supervisors and less-gifted workers, Korean private and public organizations will increasingly benefit as they implement measures that inspire workers to reach deep into their pools of knowledge, experience, and energy and empower themselves to move bravely forward to claim uncharted territory for the organization.

Prospects

In building its human resources economy, Korea faces a stark choice:

- Establish competitive, profitable firms by increasing productivity at the risk of eliminating jobs, or
- Maintain jobs at the risk of sacrificing productivity and competitiveness.

To avoid bankruptcy, some companies have been forced by their creditors to accept the first option. Additional Korean firms will also choose productivity. As time passes they will do so with less fear of labor strife because their workers will be either sufficiently skilled to be attractive to other firms or eligible for social welfare.

Because the government recognizes that for Korea to thrive in the global economy Korean firms must improve their competitiveness, it likely will continue to expand Korea's social safety net and implement job training and other measures to facilitate workers' transition into the new economy.

Notes

1. Walter B. Wriston, *The Twilight of Sovereignty: How the Information Revolution Is Transforming Our World* (New York: Scribner, 1992), 5.

2. Nayan Chanda, "The Tug of War for Asia's Best Brains," *Far Eastern Economic Review*, November 9, 2000, p. 39.

3. Current methods of gathering statistics often underestimate the scope of the service trade.

4. "Country Forecast South Korea: Data Summary," Economist Intelligence Unit, 2001.

5. Jeremy Rifkin, *The End of Work: The Decline of the Global Labor Force and the Dawn of the Post-Market Era* (New York: G. P. Putnam's Sons, 1995), 190–191.

6. James F. Moore, *The Death of Competition: Leadership and Strategy in the Age of Business Ecosystems* (New York: HarperBusiness, 1996), 3, 11–12, 15.

7. Sheldon Danziger and Peter Gottschaulk, *America Unequal* (Cambridge, Mass.: Harvard University Press, 1995); Rifkin, *End of Work*, 169-177; and Kevin Phillips, *Boiling Point: Democrats, Republicans, and the Decline of Middle-Class Prosperity* (New York: Random House, 1993).

8. *Washington Post,* February 3, 1997, p. A6.

9. "Country Forecast China: Data Summary," Economist Intelligence Unit, 2001.

10. *Global Economic Prospects and the Developing Countries* (Washington, D.C.: World Bank, 1995), 63, and discussions with informed World Bank officials in April 2001.

11. "The World Competitiveness Scoreboard—2000 Results," *World Competitiveness Yearbook,* International Institute for Management Development, www.imd.ch/wcy/, accessed October 26, 2000.

12. "Analysis of Factors Leading to Sharp Increase in Internet Users in Korea," Korea Network Information Center, http://stat.nic.or.kr, accessed October 10, 2000; *Information Technology Overview of Korea (Statistical Profiles),* Seoul: ROK Ministry of Information and Communications, April 2001), 16.

13. *1ˢᵗ Survey about Korea Internet Users,* e-Trend Internet Research & Consulting, www.e-trend.co.kr, accessed November 3, 2000; *Information Technology Overview of Korea,* Ibid., 15.

14. CDMA—code division multiple access—technology was one of the leading-edge wireless technologies in 2000.

15. "Korea's Online Population", *Cyberatlas,* July 25, 2000, http://cyberatlas.internet.com/big_picture/geographics/article/0,,5911_300981,00.html, accessed November 2, 2000.

16. Noland, *Avoiding the Apocalypse,* 26.

17. *Monthly Statistical Bulletin* (Seoul: Bank of Korea, September 2000), 108.

18. Kim, *Two Years after the IMF Bailout,* 30.

19. "Internet Banking Growing at Explosive Rate," *Korea Economic Weekly,* October 23, 2000, 17; and "Korea Net Banking Users Up 2000 Percent," *Asia CyberAtlas,* October 17, 2000, http://asia.Internet.com/cyberatlas/001017Korea.html, accessed November 2, 2000.

20. "Online Securities Trading for November 1999" and "Online Securities Trading for September 2000," Korea Securities Dealers Association,

www.ksda.or.kr/Portfoliokorea/publications/publications.htm, accessed November 3, 2000.

21. Yu Yong-Ju, *Digital Finance*, Samsung Economic Research Institute, June 6, 2000, http://seriecon.seri.org/, accessed October 28, 2000.

22. John Larkin, "Pushing Plastic," *Far Eastern Economic Review*, October 12, 2000, p. 68–70.

23. The seven leading credit card companies were BC Card, Dynasty Card, Korea Exchange Bank (KEB) Card, Kookmin Card, LG Card, Samsung Card, and Tong Yang Card.

24. "Healthy Hike in Credit Card Usage," *Korea Economic Weekly*, October 23, 2000.

25. *OECD Economic Surveys, 1999–2000: Korea*, 250, 251 (table A-4).

26. "Country Forecast South Korea: Data Summary," Economist Intelligence Unit, 2001.

27. Kim, *Two Years after the IMF Bailout*, 30–31.

28. *Change in the Number of Venture Companies* (Seoul: Samsung Economic Research Institute, August 5, 2000), and *Change in the Number of Manufacturing Companies among Total Venture Companies* (Seoul: Samsung Economic Research Institute, August 6, 2000), http://seriecon.seri.org/, accessed October 28, 2000.

29. "Technology Imports Surpass Exports by a Large Margin," *Korea Economic Weekly*, October 30, 2000, p. 2.

30. Kim Hak-sang, "The Current State of Korea's Industrial Competitiveness and Related Tasks," *Korea Economic Trends* 4, no. 41 (Seoul: Samsung Economic Research Institute, October 28, 2000), 13–17.

31. *OECD Economic Surveys, 1999–2000: Korea*, 252 (table A-5).

32. Ibid., 250–252; and "R&D Investment is Expected to Increase Greatly in 2000," Samsung Economic Research Institute, January 22, 2000, http://seriecon.seri.org/, accessed October 28, 2000.

33. *OECD Economic Surveys, 1999–2000: Korea*, 149 (table 35).

34. "The List of Ailing Companies to Be Forced Out of Business...," *Korea Economic Trends* 4, no. 43 (Seoul: Samsung Economic Research Institute, November 11, 2000), 4.

35. *OECD Economic Surveys, 1999–2000: Korea*, 152; and "SMBA Assistance for Venture Businesses," ROK Small and Medium Business Administration, www.smba.go.kr.

36. *Change in the Number of Venture Companies; Change in the Number of Manufacturing Companies among Total Venture Companies; OECD Economic Surveys, 1999–2000: Korea*, 150; and "Importance of Venture Companies," *Business Korea*, June 1998, http://www.fba.nus.edu.sg, accessed November 11, 2000.

37. Nayan Chanda, "The Tug of War for Asia's Best Brains," *Far Eastern Economic Review*, November 9, 2000, p. 39.

38. *OECD Economic Surveys, 1999–2000: Korea,* 150–153.

39. Lee Jeong-il, *The Digital Revolution and Changes in Korean Companies' Human Resources Strategies,* Issue Report, Samsung Economic Research Institute, February 26, 2000, http://seriecon.seri.org/, accessed October 28, 2000.

40. "14 People Indicted over Loan Scandal," *Korea Times,* November 14, 2000; and "Probe of Loan Scandal Virtually Ends," *Korea Times,* November 13, 2000, www.koreatimes.co.kr, accessed November 18, 2000.

41. "The Recession of the Venture Industry Is Expected to Continue for the Time Being," *Korea Economic Trends* 4, no. 42 (Seoul: Samsung Economic Research Institute, November 4, 2000), 6.

42. Nonregular workers include temporary and daily workers.

43. *OECD Economic Surveys, 1999–2000: Korea,* 188–189; and Lee Jeong-il, *The Digital Revolution.*

44. Moon and Mo, *Economic Crisis and Structural Reforms in South Korea,* 44.

45. *OECD Economic Surveys, 1999–2000: Korea,* 188.

46. "Daewoo Motors Face Suspension of Court Receivership," Korea Times, February 19, 2001, www.hankooki.com/kt_plaza/200102/t200102191439104A20158.htm, accessed July 18, 2001; "Strikes loom after Daewoo layoffs," CNN.com, February 16, 2001, http://asia.cnn.com/2001/WORLD/asiapcf/east/02/16/korea.daewoo/, accessed July 18, 2001; "Daewoo Motors Lays Off 1,750 as Talks Fail: Workers to Strike," *Dow Jones,* 2001, www.dowjones.com, accessed February 16, 2001; and Jong Ho Kim, "Daewoo Accelerating Layoffs," *Digital Chosun Ilbo,* January 10, 2001, www.chosunilbo.com, accessed March 1, 2001.

47. Jun Lee, "Income Gap Widens as Real Income Average Shrinks," *Digital Chosun Ilbo,* September 7, 2000, www.chosunilbo.com, accessed September 7, 2000.

48. Florence Lowe-Lee, "Income Gap Worse Last Year," *Korea Insight* 3, no. 6 (June 2001): 2.

49. The Gini coefficient, developed by an Italian statistician, is used by social scientists to describe inequality or compare inequality among nations. Scores range from 0 to 1; a score of 1 indicates all income is pooled in one group, and 0 indicates equal income distribution in a society. Scores normally fall in the 0.200–0.450 range; a Gini coefficient of approximately 0.400 is normal for most developed economies.

50. During the second round of financial restructuring, 21 creditor banks decided on November 3, 2000, to close scores of nonviable debtor companies.

51. This discussion borrows heavily from Florence Lowe-Lee, "Where is Korea's Middle Class?" *Korea Insight* 2, no. 11 (November 2000): 1, www.keia.com/Insight-November2000.pdf, accessed July 12, 2001.

4 ■

Trend Four: An Era of Global Tribes

THE KNOWLEDGE ERA is a time of paradox and contradiction, a time when theses and antitheses meld to produce unexpectedly powerful engines of social change. Conflicting trends gain speed at the same time, pulling societies in two or more directions. Nowhere is this more evident than in one of the greatest puzzles of our time: the simultaneous acceleration of globalism and pluralism, which is producing what might be called "global tribes." Somehow the world is at once becoming both more cosmopolitan and more insular; expanding global trade, communication, and travel arouse a deeper interest in local, national, ethnic, and religious identities. And all too often, the forces of globalism have an uneasy relation to the local, tribal, national, and individual reactions they inspire.

The Process of Globalization

To say that "globalization" is one of the most overused words of our time does not deny the reality of the process it describes: the increasing convergence of the world's economies and societies. But globalization is not a uniform phenomenon; it is more pronounced in some areas and less in others.

The world economy is increasingly globalized: not only can investors rapidly assess investment risks and opportunities and shift capital, but trade in merchandise and services is growing faster than worldwide economic growth. The world economy is growing more dependent on trade, and is thus more globalized, with each passing

Figure 27
Growth of Merchandise Trade, 1991–2007

Note: World output is measured as percentage change in real GDP; the trade growth rates of the world and of the high-income countries, OECD countries, and developing countries are measured as the sum of the relevant import and export volumes.

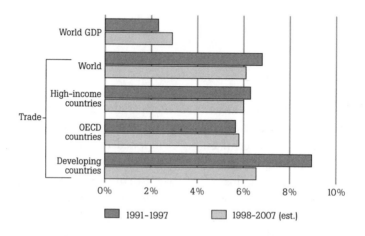

Source: Global Economic Prospects and the Developing Countries (Washington, D.C.: World Bank, 1999), table 1-5, www.worldbank.org/prospects/gep98-99/02-chap1.pdf, accessed February 23, 2001.

year. The World Bank forecasts that this current trend is likely to persist into the long term. Global trade levels by 2004, for example, are estimated to be equivalent to just under half of the world's estimated GNP (figure 27).

Trade at the turn of the century retains a highly regional focus. The vast majority of world trade—a majority that continues to grow—takes place within each of the three major trading blocs—the Americas, Europe, and East Asia—rather than between them. Between 1990 and 1999, U.S. exports to and imports from other countries in North America increased, showing a regional increase in merchandise trade share of 2.5 percent for exports and 0.9 percent for imports. Trade among the countries of the European Union appeared to decline slightly over this period, with regional exports down 1.4 percent and imports down 0.8 percent. Part of this decline can be attributed to slow growth in Europe following German unification. Within Western Europe, the EU still holds almost 70 percent of total trade accounts. Intra-Asia trade greatly increased between 1990 and 1999 owing to Japan's 5.5 percent increase in exports and 9.5 percent increase in imports from other Asian nations.[1] Most of Korea's trade is within the Asia-Pacific region.

With growing trade—even regional trade—comes increasing global awareness and an emerging tendency toward global homogenization—a willingness to accept tenets of democracy, market economics, and other global values described in chapter 2. A global mentality has become evident in increasingly specialized professions; some professionals have more in common with colleagues halfway around the world than with their own neighbors.

The pace of globalization will accelerate during 2001–2010 as a result of advances in communications. *The Economist* summarized the direction of global communication technologies:

> Over the next few years, the price of making a long-distance call in and between some countries will fall to the point where it costs little more to telephone from Hollywood to Glasgow than to nearby Beverly Hills. At the same time, telephone companies will begin to switch the basis of charging their customers from the length of time for which they talk to a flat subscription. Within a decade or two, most ordinary telephone conversations will cost nothing extra, whatever their duration or distance.[2]

This process will revolutionize service activities, recalibrate cost calculations, and "may well prove the most significant economic force shaping the next half century."[3]

A globalized world is characterized by global production and multinational corporations. By the early 1990s, 37,000 parent multinationals controlled 206,000 foreign affiliate corporations.[4] As long ago as 1992, foreign affiliates operated by multinational corporations showed total sales of $5.5 trillion, more than five times the value of world exports that year. Multinational corporations may already be a much more powerful engine of globalization than traditional trade in manufactured goods and services.

Meanwhile, knowledge-era technologies are working to transcend the distinction between global companies and local companies. In a world of virtual companies and alliances networked around the globe—doing business with intense local and niche focus but coordinating and trading globally—the emerging model is a paradoxical one.

Tribalism, Fragmentation, and Pluralism

If the knowledge era is a time of globalism, it is also, paradoxically, an era of pluralism—of fragmentation in social organization; diversity in careers, politics, and religion; a renewed search for identity in local, tribal, and national contexts. The knowledge era is pluralistic for a number of reasons. It draws on and expands the natural pluralism of modern industrial society, with its hundreds of careers and millions of products. The difference is that we now have access, through information and global marketing, to this dizzying array of options. Examples of tribalism are everywhere.

The business world is fragmenting as well. In a fast-moving, pluralistic era, it hardly seems surprising that smaller and more decentralized corporations have an edge in flexibility and innovation. But the story is not that simple: in important sectors of the economy, massive size and scope rather than fragmentation are the rule. That a trend toward bigness should emerge alongside the growing importance of small business is another symptom of a paradoxical time. The central message for businesses, then, is not so much big versus small as the effort to be both at once. Today's corporate challenge, says IBM's Louis Gerstner, is "how to incorporate small-company attributes—nimbleness, speed, and customer responsiveness—with the advantages of size."[5] Successful businesses will combine, either within their own organization or through alliances and networks, small- and big-company attributes, along with characteristics of both local and global operations.

Tribalism within Globalism

The above review might seem to imply that pluralism and universalism, tribalism and globalism, are independently important. And so they are. But even more decisive is their interaction, the complex and profound dynamic of a world that is not merely global, but plurally global; not merely plural, but globally plural. In short, major implications for the coming decade are to be found at the intersection of these two trends.

The writer Patrick Glynn predicts a coming clash between "ethnic (and other types of) particularism" and "what might be called democratic universalism." This impending conflict "seems to be replacing the old Left–Right and class polarities that have governed political life for nearly a century." The contest between pluralism and globalism, which "has every appearance of becoming the new bipolarity of global politics, the new dialectic of a new age,"[6] has a number of ramifications. One is social instability, tension, or outright conflict in many areas of the world. This process, after all, is the engine of the clash of cultures as described by Samuel Huntington. "The forces of integration in the world are real," he writes, "and are precisely what are generating counterforces of cultural assertion."[7] But at the same time, globalism in all its guises enhances interdependence among and within nations.

Korea and the Global–Tribal Intersection

Korea benefited immensely from its export-based approach to globalization that began in the 1960s, but at the end of the twentieth century it was embroiled in an internal struggle over its future. The modern descendants of the "hermit kingdom" are choosing between two fundamentally different systems: one a free-enterprise market economy based on Western economic and business practices of decentralization, pluralism, transparency, accountability, and global competitiveness; the other a continuation of Park Chung-hee's managed economy based on Korea's outmoded statist model rooted in traditional neo-Confucian culture that propelled Korea into the ranks of the industrialized economies. Some Koreans believe the market-economy model threatens Korea's national identity.

This struggle has given rise to the typical paradoxes associated with the transition to the knowledge era. The Korean economy had become so dependent on foreign markets and capital by the late 1990s that further movement into the new global economy required Korea to improve its competitiveness by adopting internationally accepted economic and business principles. This step called for nothing less than a complete revision of long-established practices associated with the Korea Inc. model.

To stay ahead of creditors and competitors, Korea had to act quickly and comprehensively, prompting protests particularly from *chaebol* and labor union leaders. The *chaebol* resisted government efforts to impose internationally accepted rules and protocols of corporate governance. Labor protested government efforts to force financial and corporate restructuring that led to unemployment. Most Koreans, however, supported the major structural reforms—and democracy.

A nationwide survey in November 1999 determined that 92 percent of respondents believed Korea's political–economic system required fundamental change; most supported measures to break up the *chaebol*, reduce the size of government, and privatize state-owned enterprises, while one in two respondents agreed with laying off unnecessary workers in private corporations. More than four of every five wanted their government to become a more open democracy. Almost three-fourths (72 percent) of respondents believed the best way to prevent a recurrence of the economic crisis would be to make the government "more democratic so that the process of policy formulation and implementation can be more transparent and accountable to the public." The percentage of respondents endorsing a more democratic government was greatest among the technologically savvy, 18- to 29-year-old netizens: 80 percent. Among older respondents, 69 percent of those aged 30–59 and 65 percent of those over age 60 also believed that a more democratic government was the best insurance against another major economic crisis. Advocates for a more authoritarian government were in a clear minority, comprising only 20 percent of respondents who were mostly over age 30.[8] Popular support for reform continued throughout 2000, although frustration arose over its slow pace caused, in part, by labor protests that delayed financial restructuring.

At the end of 2000, Koreans wanted the government to complete the restructuring reform process, the sooner the better. Most Koreans supported democracy, the devolution of government power, and reduction of government intervention in the economy.

This pervasive support for democracy coupled with widespread acceptance of the four-sector reforms to establish a free-enterprise market economy display global homogenization in Korea. By embracing these foreign values that require informed, active, empowered citizens and workers, Koreans are showing how far they are moving from the authoritarian roots implicit in their culture. However, some labor leaders and others, rooted in the past and denying the reform effort under way, are still looking to the government to intervene and fix the nation's economic problems.

Engines of Globalization

Trade. One of the dozen or so top trading countries since the late 1980s, Korea was firmly tied to the world through trade at the end of 2000. It had a commercial presence in nearby China and Japan and in distant Australia, Zimbabwe, Canada, Qatar, Poland, Thailand, the United Kingdom, the United States, and Uzbekistan. Korean exports earned more than $143 billion in 1999, with manufactured goods accounting for roughly 95 percent.[9] Korean imports that year exceeded $119 billion, with raw materials and capital goods making up about 89 percent of the total.[10]

Korea traded mostly with Asia, followed by North America and Europe, including the European Union and Eastern Europe. Asia's importance surged after Seoul and Beijing normalized relations in 1992 (see figures 28 and 29). Despite the surge in Asia, the United States has consistently been Korea's largest single trading partner. In 1999, the United States imported about 21 percent of Korea's exports and supplied about 20 percent of Korea's imports, producing an $8.3 billion trade surplus for Korea with the United States. Korea's other top export destinations in 1999 (in descending order) were the European Union, Japan, China, Hong Kong, and Taiwan. On a regional basis, Asia was the primary source of Korea's imports, followed by North America, Europe, the Middle East, Oceania, Africa, and Latin America.[11]

Although Asia has been Korea's largest regional trading partner, in early 2001 Seoul had not yet joined a regional trading bloc along the lines of the European Union, South America's Mercosur, or the

Figure 28
South Korea's Export Markets, 1990–Nov. 1999

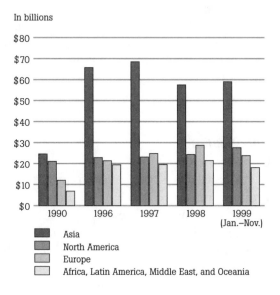

Source: Jun-sok Yang, "Korea's Economy: Korea's Foreign Trade," *Korea's Economy 2000* (Washington, D.C.: Korea Economic Institute of America, 2000), table 3, www.keia.com/2korea's%20Economy-full.pdf, accessed March 15, 2001.

North America Free Trade Agreement (NAFTA). But South Korea was working to lay the foundation for an East Asian trade zone that would include China, Japan, and the ROK in Northeast Asia and the members of the Association of Southeast Asian Nations (ASEAN). By the end of 2000, ASEAN's leaders had agreed to expand trade with their Northeast Asian neighbors while they also supported ROK president Kim Dae-jung's proposal to form an East Asia study group regarding closer cooperation among the East Asian countries.[12] Seoul also was considering free trade agreements with Mexico, Chile, and New Zealand. By diversifying its trading relationships, Seoul slightly reduced Korea's dependence on the United States and positioned the country to join a regional trading bloc.

Figure 29
South Korea's Import Suppliers, 1990–Nov. 1999

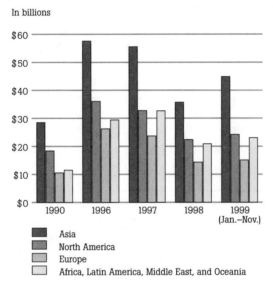

In billions

Asia
North America
Europe
Africa, Latin America, Middle East, and Oceania

Source: Jun-sok Yang, "Korea's Economy: Korea's Foreign Trade," *Korea's Economy 2000* (Washington, D.C.: Korea Economic Institute of America, 2000), table 3, www.keia.com/2korea's%20Economy-full.pdf, accessed March 15, 2001.

Foreign investment. Foreign investment also closely tied Korea's economy to the world's economy, both before and after the economic crisis of 1997. In 1992, for example, the Korean government first approved foreign investment in the Korean stock market but limited it to no more than 10 percent equity in a given issue. FDI in 1992 amounted to only $895 million, a slim 0.3 percent of GDP.[13] However, after 1997, Korea changed long-standing policies that severely restricted foreign investment, actively sought FDI, and lifted all restrictions on foreign portfolio investment. Nevertheless, the noticeable impact of capital flight out of Korea during the financial crisis—before the policy changes—suggests that even under the old, restrictive rules Korea was linked tightly to the world economy.

Foreign portfolio investors responded quickly to the full opening of the stock market in December 1997. During the months follow-

Figure 30
Foreign Direct Investment (FDI) in South Korea, 1997–2000

Characteristics	1997	1998	1999	2000
FDI (in billions)	$6.97	$8.85	$15.54	$15.69
Increase (year-on-year)	117.0%	27.0%	75.6%	1.0%
Percent of GDP	1.4%	2.8%	4.0%	3.4%

Source: ROK Ministry of Commerce, Industry, and Energy.

ing the opening, they helped send the Korea Stock Price Index (KOSPI) from 351 points to 574 (March 1998) and then to over 1,000 points (July 1999). Foreigners invested $4.78 billion in Korean stocks and bonds in 1998 and an additional $5.19 billion in 1999, a year-on-year increase of 8.6 percent.[14] FDI also expanded greatly after 1997 (figure 30).[15]

Korea's multinational corporations. The proliferation of multinational corporations is another indicator of globalism. Between 1997 and 2000, a number of foreign firms increased their presence in Korea's manufacturing and service sectors, including Germany's BASF in petrochemicals; Sweden's Volvo in the heavy-equipment industry; Mexico's Seminis in the plant-seed industry; and the U.S. companies Loral, Motorola, and Coca-Cola in the IT, telecommunications, and food industries. Foreign multinationals gained over 50 percent of market share in 13 industries, including plant seeds, film, and beer.[16]

Korea's multinational corporations—its *chaebol*—by contrast were contending with the reform process. Much of the difficulty in implementing *chaebol* reform lay in the historically close government–*chaebol* relationship inherent in the Korea Inc. development model. The *chaebol* depended on the government for resources and the government depended on the *chaebol* to provide jobs and spur economic growth. As a result, many Koreans believed the major *chaebol* were too big to fail despite the fact that the top *chaebol* accounted for more than half of Korea's corporate debt in 1998.[17] Koreans noted the government's willingness to let the relatively small Hanbo and Kia *chaebol* fail in 1997 but believed the government would never let any of the major *chaebol* collapse—until 1999 when Daewoo, shocking the nation, declared bankruptcy.

By the end of 2000, creditors, shareholders, and the ROK government were forcing the *chaebol* to become profitable, but profitability demanded numerous new and painful strategies to improve productivity and competitiveness. All *chaebol* struggled; some failed. Following Daewoo's collapse, among the remaining top *chaebol,* Hyundai's future was in question, and legendary Samsung's profitability appeared fragile as the price for semiconductors softened in 2000.[18] Many *chaebol* affiliates were under financial workout programs,[19] court receivership, court mediation, or additional but temporary payment extensions by their creditors.[20] Some firms—Hyundai Motors, for example—that particularly depended on global markets remained focused on expanding their presence internationally.

Korean global awareness greatly increased after the 1997 economic crisis, especially among Koreans not normally engaged in international commerce. They were stunned by the rapidity with which international financial institutions and investors brought their country to its knees, necessitating a humiliating appeal to the IMF. Average Koreans gained a much keener appreciation of how greatly interdependent their economy had become with the world economy, how Korean companies compared with competitors, and how quickly Korea's economic situation could deteriorate should foreign investors and creditors lose confidence. For many it was a sobering experience and provided a needed base of support for Kim Dae-jung's reforms.

Tribalism—Nationalism and Regionalism

In the late twentieth century, in spite of strong nationalist sentiments and regional rivalries, there were signs that South Korea was becoming a much more sophisticated country as the knowledge era took root. Kim Dae-jung's administration was making a deliberate effort to reduce the role of the government in the economy by replacing the Korea Inc. model with market-economy principles. The public, using knowledge-era tools including the Internet, was increasing its awareness of the country's problems. Historic nationalistic tendencies were being reduced but not completely eliminated. Regional differences within the ROK persisted; and, despite prospects for improved relationships following an unprecedented summit meeting between the national leaders of South Korea and North Korea in June 2000, public opinion was in flux regarding how much economic assistance North Korea warranted.

In the face of foreign pressure, Koreans "rally around the flag," which is how their grudging acceptance of so-called IMF reforms is sometimes described. At the end of 2000, however, a growing number of Koreans perceived some value in foreign solutions and appeared to be less influenced by highly nationalistic appeals of various interest groups.

Nationalism. Koreans have possessed a strong sense of nationalism since the seventh century, when the Silla dynasty conquered the kingdoms of Koguryo and Paekche to unify the Korean people into a single nation-state.[21] Korea's strategically important location at the crossroads of Northeast Asia gave its powerful neighbors a strong incentive to control it. But foreign powers could not eliminate Koreans' sense of identity and national culture, which sustained their culture, customs, and language during such difficult periods as domination by the Mongols in the thirteenth and fourteenth centuries and by Japan in the first half of the twentieth century.

Korea's ability to resist foreign efforts to assimilate the country and eliminate all traces of Korea's culture bears powerful testimony to the people's national pride and strong character. Such experiences taught Koreans to mistrust foreigners. In the second half of the twentieth century, Korea's so-called military governments built on Koreans' xenophobic tendencies and exploited Korean nationalism to legitimize their regimes and Korea Inc. industrial policies that inadvertently led to the 1997 economic crisis.

Nationalism remained a powerful force after the onset of the 1997 financial crisis. At the height of the crisis, in January 1998, more than 3 million Koreans donated their gold jewelry and other gold holdings through 106 NGOs to augment the national treasury, producing $2.2 billion.[22]

But nationalism has also complicated reforms to increase foreign participation in the economy. Labor unions have used nationalistic arguments successfully to protest plans to sell such companies as Daewoo Motors to foreign bidders. Bank workers have struck to protest foreign acquisition of their banks. *Chaebol* leaders have been reluctant to engage foreign directors to improve the quality of business planning and management.

Even as some Koreans despair at growing foreign participation in their economy, many also recognize that foreign stakeholders will promote sounder business practices than Korean managers had used in the past. Koreans' growing consensus to support—if not urge—reforms coupled with their lack of consensus for major strikes against layoff plans and foreign ownership have suggested that ordinary Koreans are becoming inattentive to highly nationalistic arguments that focus on selfish interests more than on the common good.

Nationalism lost some of its grip as the twentieth century came to an end. The public demonstrated broad support for the IMF-mandated reforms,[23] for example, even though the reforms led to the closure of a number of financial institutions, increased bankruptcies, greater unemployment, and reductions in the standard of living. Critics assailed the so-called IMF reforms (which underpin Kim Dae-jung's four-sector reforms) as being unnecessarily stringent, and many Koreans remained concerned about selling Korean firms—including banks and state-owned enterprises—to foreigners. Nevertheless, in a November 1999 nationwide survey, 71 percent of Koreans gave credit to the IMF for helping Korea overcome its economic crisis; 14 percent responded that the IMF had helped Korea "a lot," and 57 percent responded that the IMF had helped "somewhat." Only 7 percent felt the IMF had hindered recovery.[24] When asked about privatizing state-owned enterprises, 57 percent of respondents to another national survey in early December 2000 felt this measure was inevitable; however, almost 40 percent viewed privatization negatively as an outflow of national wealth.[25]

By 1999, most Koreans finally understood that their country faced significant endemic problems that required informed, thoughtful, and deliberate solutions followed by disciplined implementation over the 2001–2010 decade.[26] Nationalistic appeals still continued to stir some Koreans in 2000, but many believed that purely nationalistic solutions could not solve the nation's problems and were not necessarily synonymous with patriotism. By the beginning of 2001, Koreans increasingly accepted the values associated with globalism, hoping they would promote economic growth. Koreans were showing less confidence in nationalistic solutions for long-term problems.

Regionalism. Koreans have often disagreed over domestic issues while presenting a unified front against foreign pressure. Internal disagreements have frequently been expressed along regional lines, presenting difficulties in establishing national consensus. Each of Korea's regions has its own personality, often reflected in traditional proverbs extolling various virtues. For example, people from Kangwon province are renowned for their sincerity and the two Chungchong provinces are famous for their gentlemen. Not all the stereotypes are flattering, particularly those for the Honam region—today's North and South Cholla provinces that were part of the former Paekche kingdom in southwest Korea.

An unfortunate result of the regional outlook has been a nation divided on key domestic issues. People from Honam, especially, believe the ROK government has helped North and South Kyongsang provinces in southeast Korea (the Yongnam region) industrialize at Honam's expense, thus denying Honam the capabilities to participate in the global economy and its enriching potential.

Regional rivalries and the three Kims. The people of Honam believe the national government has discriminated against them for most of the ROK's modern history through 1997. They note that all four of South Korea's presidents between 1961 and 1997 were from North or South Kyongsang provinces (the Yongnam region)[27] and argue that these four presidents, deliberately ignoring Honam, approved significant infrastructure projects in their home provinces.

The presidents used national revenue to build the first express highway connecting Seoul and Pusan and massive industrial complexes in Changwon (west of Pusan) and Taegu, but they neglected to make similar investments in Honam. The Honam people also assert that the four presidents disproportionately appointed Yongnam people to important positions in the national government, military, and police, while they also provided employment for people from their home regions. The people from the two Cholla provinces felt left out of the mainstream of Korea's economic development.

The view from Honam seems valid, especially regarding the initial years of industrialization. Central government planners recognized Honam's high value as Korea's breadbasket and chose not to pay the relatively higher costs (compared with the Southeast region) of developing industrial infrastructure, including world-class ports, in the Southwest, with its famously difficult tides. Seoul's cost–benefit analyses led planners to concentrate Korea's limited financial resources in the areas most likely to yield the quickest and highest return on investment. From a political perspective, however, it would have been better if Honam people had been represented in the decisionmaking process.

Acutely aware of regional rivalries, President Kim Dae-jung pledged to reduce them. But after the opposition Grand National Party won a working majority in the National Assembly in April 2000, it assailed the Kim Dae-jung administration for trying to use reverse discrimination to correct regional imbalances, a policy that actually exacerbated rivalries. This issue promised to linger until all the involved parties agree that perceived wrongs have been rectified.

This sense of discrimination has intensified regional politics at the national level. The Honam people have their champion in Kim Dae-jung, who had represented them for most of the ROK's history and who won the presidency in 1997 on a platform that included a commitment to reduce regionalism. Kim Young-sam had similarly represented the people of South Kyongsang province and was elected president in December 1992. Kim Jong-pil, an influential official under President Park Chung-hee, was from Kongju in South Chungchong province and was supported largely by the people of North and South Chungchong provinces.[28] These were the famous "three Kims" who dominated Korean politics for the second half of the twentieth century and who could remain politically active in the twenty-first century.

Local autonomy. In addition to the Honam–Yongnam rivalry, local autonomy remained an issue. The Kim Young-sam administration in 1995 reinstated local autonomy elections, previously held in the 1950s. Although the reestablishment of local governments headed by popularly elected officials suggested significant devolution of government authority, this has not proved to be the clear outcome.

Seoul, with its large national budget, continues to maintain control over local governments because localities have little authority to impose local taxes. Regional and local governments thus remain highly dependent on the central government. By the summer of 2000, Korea's 248 local governments had sufficient funds to meet only about 60 percent of their budget obligations. Some counties were almost bankrupt and unable to pay their civil servants or satisfactorily stimulate their local economies through public works programs. People were fleeing the provinces for Seoul, with its relatively numerous job opportunities.[29] The respected *Chosun Ilbo* newspaper summarized the problem in August 2000:

> Local government is massively in debt, economies are failing, finance is paralyzed, pollution is rampant, and unemployment is rising as graduates from regional universities fail to find work."[30]

The local governments' great dependence on Seoul limits their ability to serve their constituents and suggests a dismal future for the practice of local autonomy without significant improvements in local government funding and the devolution of central government power.

Provincial access to credit also became more difficult by the end of 2000. More than 140 financial institutions with a nationwide presence were closed or merged between November 1997 and August 2000, with the survivors remaining largely in Seoul. The demise of these financial institutions led to closures of 3,600 branch offices outside Seoul, which limited credit access for regional businesses. Koreans believe the financial sector's growing reluctance to extend risky loans has hurt local economies.[31]

Even new venture companies have preferred to establish their businesses in Seoul because of difficulties acquiring capital in the provinces. As of August 2000, only 17 of 155 venture capital firms had invested in companies outside Seoul. Venture company entrepreneurs understood that they needed to be in Seoul if they wanted venture capital.[32]

North Korea

In 2000, roughly one-third of Koreans lived in the northern half of the Korean peninsula,[33] ruled by a totalitarian government hostile to the ROK since 1945.[34] By the end of 2000, it had become inconceivable that the Korean nation would remain permanently divided although predicting the date and conditions of unification remained problematic. The continuing existence of North Korea powerfully affects South Korea politically, economically, and socially.

The tragic national division—reinforced by war—has greatly complicated South Korean nation building and development in at least three ways. First, it destroyed a national economy that was the most industrialized in continental Asia in 1945. Most of the country's heavy industry was located in North Korea. Second, it divided many families and created enduring anguish among Koreans, for whom the family is central.[35] Finally, it led to a national security environment that has required significant ROK resources and investments. National security concerns require the ROK to maintain a large standing military force. Security concerns also have enabled successive authoritarian governments to justify the Korea Inc. development model and to defer progress toward full democratization. The ROK has invested incalculable sums to fund

- economic development programs to build a modern industrial state essentially from scratch;
- military capabilities (in coordination with U.S. forces) to defeat another North Korean invasion should deterrence fail;
- domestic security programs to reduce the effectiveness of North Korean subversive activity against South Korea;
- humanitarian relief for starving North Koreans; and
- diplomatic programs to promote business investment in the North.

The ROK could have used the vast sums instead to stimulate ROK economic development, support social programs, and perhaps accelerate the democratization process that South Koreans by 2000 considered essential.

Berlin and Seoul are on opposite sides of the globe, but when Germans tore down the Berlin Wall in 1989 and began unification,

South Koreans paid close attention. They concluded that Korean unification in the near term would likely be too expensive and devastating to their personal standard of living because of the significant disparities between the economies of the two Koreas. In 1996, the South Korean economy was roughly 40 times that of North Korea, with per capita annual income amounting to roughly $10,000 in the ROK and $500 in North Korea.[36] The ROK government began to take a somewhat more calculated approach toward unification than it had in the past.

The Kim Dae-jung administration's North Korea sunshine policy began in 1998 and supported diplomatic, economic, and commercial initiatives to improve the North Korean economy as quickly as possible while it took a long view on political unification. President Kim's near-term objective was to end the legacy of the Cold War on the Korean peninsula and over time lay a foundation for inter-Korean rapprochement—not achieve rapid unification per se. The policy achieved a significant objective in June 2000 when Chairman Kim Jong-il of the DPRK hosted a summit meeting with President Kim Dae-jung in Pyongyang. In October 2000, Kim Dae-jung was awarded the Nobel Peace Prize for promoting reconciliation with North Korea.

By November 2000, however, South Koreans had become increasingly concerned that Kim Dae-jung was too focused on North Korea, with no tangible return on investment, while *chaebol* and labor challenged key structural reforms in South Korea, threatening to prevent the timely implementation of the reforms and discouraging foreign investors. South Koreans, represented by the National Assembly and news media editorials, for example, demanded Kim Dae-jung pay more attention to implementing fully the four-sector reforms. This popular demand reflected South Koreans' willingness to restructure their system and their unwillingness to provide additional economic assistance to North Korea in the absence of reciprocity on even symbolic issues such as a security hot line between the two countries.

Pluralism

For a number of reasons, including its neo-Confucian culture that emphasizes the preeminence of authority, South Korea has never been a highly pluralistic society. However, the widespread popularity of knowledge-era tools (including the Internet) plus progress in achieving Kim Dae-jung's objectives to reduce the government's role in the economy and establish a more decentralized political–economic system have created fertile ground for the growth of a more pluralistic society in the future:

- The financial sector has become more responsible for allocating capital and holding debtors accountable for their financial obligations although the government has retained significant—some say undue—influence; many companies have collapsed, releasing capital for more productive use;
- Shareholders are more empowered to influence corporate decisionmaking;
- Growing foreign investment has induced more accountability and transparency on the part of company managers;
- A growing number of companies realize they must focus on profitability with the attendant requirements to become globally competitive;
- Corporate governance has become more transparent and managers more accountable to both shareholders and their boards of directors, which increasingly include foreigners;
- The government has lessened its participation in the economy by privatizing some state-owned enterprises despite significant opposition by labor unions and the National Assembly; but the National Assembly passed legislation in November 2000 to privatize the largest state-owned enterprise, KEPCO, clearing the way for movement with this important structural reform;
- Interest groups (labor unions, for example) have retained influence but are finding they need to use persuasive facts to argue their case to the public, which has become less responsive to emotional arguments;

- Private citizens increasingly endorse reforms that are in the national interest and reject nationalistic appeals by interest groups that conflict with the common good;
- The government has assumed a greater regulatory and enforcement role than it had in the past;
- Knowledge-era tools are much more available to ordinary citizens, who readily embrace them and their empowering potential; and
- NGOs seem to be gaining an increased ability to influence their issues of concern. The 16th general election is one case in point (see the final section of chapter 2).

At the turn of the century, some of the above developments were in an embryonic stage, and South Korea is not yet a highly pluralistic society. The changes in progress suggest, however, that the four-sector structural reforms are forming the foundation for a more global and pluralistic society. Cautious optimism—but not certainty—that the reforms can empower individual Koreans and make the economy globally competitive is warranted.

Summary

The venerable Korean society is clearly in transition. Koreans approve of some aspects of globalism and pluralism and are struggling for balance as the pace of change accelerates with each new generation of computer microprocessor chips and structural reform. They recognize that Korean companies need to make significant changes to survive vis-à-vis global competitors and that the government cannot continue to protect nonviable companies despite the pleas of some laid-off workers. Although they recognize the government's limitations in managing the economy, they also want the government to step in and restore social and economic harmony—elusive goals as Korea rushes headlong into the increasingly fast-paced knowledge era. Koreans want to improve relations with North Korea without sacrificing their standard of living, which forces the Kim Dae-jung government to focus on South Korea more than on North Korea. Koreans, especially the younger generations, seem to question the wisdom of working for the *chaebol* as the light of reform has revealed vast management problems. At the same time, establishing or working for a small or medium enterprise is problematic due to their difficulties in acquiring capital. Under such conditions, Koreans traditionally rely on their families for comfort; they now also look to the Internet and other modern authorities for guidance in setting a course toward becoming a more pluralistic society in an increasingly competitive globalized economy.

At the turn of the century, critics often found fault with the pace of change, calling it too fast or too slow. They were also properly disturbed by indications of continuing corruption among government officials and the government's dominant role in transforming the economy. However, because the ROK government engineered the Korea Inc. model, the government was the best candidate to dismantle the corrupt, discredited system and lay the foundation for a new market economy to be refereed by a more hands-off government. The ROK government still needs to demonstrate it has the discipline to reduce its role in the economy, privatize banks, and let market factors prevail after the reforms are fully implemented.

Korea Inc. will not dissolve immediately. Too many Koreans cannot clearly envision a workable replacement, their role in the new model, or new authorities worthy of their confidence. However, young Korean netizens—especially in their 20s and younger—promise to be critical change agents in the first decade of the twenty-first century.

Korea's great hope for the future depends on full implementation of the 1998 four-sector reforms, and the generations born after 1970 must have the energy and enthusiasm to sustain the reforms. Among Koreans, these younger members of society demonstrate the most confidence in transparent and accountable democracy and the most intolerance for authoritarianism. They also are most attuned to knowledge-era tools, benefits, and opportunities—the Internet and venture companies, for example. While no one imagines that young Koreans will begin decorating their personal cars with bumper stickers such as "Question Authority" and "Don't Trust Anyone over 30," such attitudes are becoming more evident in the society.

Notes

1. *International Trade Statistics 2000,* Chapter 3, Trade by Region (Geneva: World Trade Organization, 2000), tables III.15, III.37, III.71, www.wto.org/english/res_e/statis_e/chp_3_e.pdf, accessed April 13, 2001.

2. "The Revolution Begins, At Last," *Economist,* September 30, 1995, p. 5; and "The Death of Distance," *Economist,* September 30, 1995, p. 15.

3. Ibid.

4. *World Investment Report: Transnational Corporations, Employment and the Workforce* (New York: United Nations, 1994), 3–5.

5. John Naisbitt, *Global Paradox: The Bigger the World Economy, the More Powerful Its Smallest Players* (New York: W. Morrow, 1994), 15.

6. Patrick Glynn, "The Age of Balkanization," *Commentary,* July 1993, p. 21.

7. Samuel Huntington, *The Clash of Civilizations and the Remaking of World Order* (New York: Simon and Schuster, 1996), 129.

8. Doh C. Shin and Richard Rose, "1999 New Korea Barometer Survey," Studies in Public Policy, no. 327 (Glasgow: University of Strathclyde, Centre for the Study of Public Policy, 2000), questions 17, 18, pp. 12–13; questions 25, 26, p. 16; questions 33, 34, pp. 18–19.

9. Korea exports a broad range of finished products including computers, telephones, and other information and communications equipment; microwave ovens, televisions, and other consumer electronics; semiconductors; steel; ships; automobiles; and textiles.

10. "Exports and Imports," Korea Development Institute, http://kdiux.kdi.re.kr/, accessed December 4, 2000; Jun-Sok Yang, "Korea's External Economic Relations," in *Korea's Economy 2000,* vol. 16 (Washington, D.C.: Korea Economic Institute of America, 2000), 53–59; and Caroline G. Cooper, "Korea's Trade Continued to Rebound Throughout 1999," in *Korea Trade Insight* (Washington, D.C.: Korea Economic Institute of America, March 2000).

11. Yang, Ibid.; and Joseph A. B. Winder, "U.S.-Korea Trade Hits a Record Level in 1999," in *Korea Insight* 2, no. 2 (Washington, D.C.: Korea Economic Institute of America, February 2000), www.keia.org/Insight-February2000.pdf.

12. "ASEAN Leaders Pledge to Study Possibility of East Asian Trade Zone," *International Trade Reporter* (Washington, D.C.: Bureau of National Affairs, November 30, 2000), 1819.

13. The value 0.3 percent is based on dividing $895 million of FDI by $314.7 billion GDP; see Lister, "Leading Economic Indicators."

14. Kim, *Two Years After the IMF Bailout,* 18–20, 26.

15. Lister, "Leading Economic Indicators."

16. Kim, *Two Years After the IMF Bailout,* 31–32.

17. "Dollars & Sense," Muriel Siebert & Co., Inc., 1998, www.msiebert. com, accessed February 26, 2001.

18. Ibid.

19. Under financial workout programs, debtor companies collaborated with creditors to develop and implement plans to transform the debtor company into a profitable enterprise capable at least of servicing its debt. Workout programs could require restructuring, managerial changes, and debt rescheduling. Debtor companies that failed to meet the terms and conditions of their workout programs risked liquidation.

20. In-cheul Choi, "Issue Report: Changes in Corporate Management during the Three Years after the IMF Bailout," in *Korea Economic Trends* 4, no. 45 (Seoul: Samsung Economic Research Institute, November 25, 2000), 15.

21. The kingdom of Koguryo was in the northern portion of the Korean peninsula; Paekche was in the southwest part. Silla was roughly in the center and the eastern part.

22. Kavaljit Singh, "Economic Crisis and People's Responses: S. Korean Case," *Asia Europe Dialogue,* 2001, www.ased.org/documents/global/countries/korea/singh1.htm, accessed March 5, 2001.

23. The IMF in December 1997 agreed to lend Korea $57 billion to recover from its financial crisis if Korea implemented major reforms (see chapter 2).

24. Shin and Rose, "1999 New Korea Barometer Survey," 15.

25. Poll conducted by the vernacular *Hankyoreh News,* reported on March 21–22, 2000, http://poll.hani.co.kr:9200/oldResult.asp?id=558&chkdate=200003&Flag=, accessed March 21, 2001.

26. Shin and Rose, "1999 New Korea Barometer Survey," 15.

27. Presidents Park Chung-hee, Chun Doo-hwan, and Roh Tae-woo came from North Kyongsang province; Kim Young-sam is from Pusan, in South Kyongsang province.

28. Kim Jong-pil was the only one of the three Kims who had failed to win the presidency by 2000.

29. "The Death of Local Communities (1)–A Dark Picture," *Digital Chosun Ilbo,* August 4, 2000, www.chosunilbo.com, accessed August 29, 2000.

30. Ibid.

31. "The Death of Local Communities (3)–Credit and Construction Collapse," *Digital Chosun Ilbo,* August 10, 2000, www.chosunilbo.com, accessed August 29, 2000.

32. "The Death of Local Communities (4)–Lack of Venture Capital," *Digital Chosun Ilbo*, August 11, 2000, www.chosunilbo.com, accessed August 29, 2000.

33. Details of the differences between South Korea and North Korea are beyond the scope of this book. This section highlights a few key points that affect South Korea's development and planning.

34. To facilitate the surrender of Japanese army units on the Korean peninsula at the end of World War II, the Soviet Union and the United States agreed in August 1945 to divide Korea along the 38th parallel. The United States envisioned this line as a temporary military boundary between Soviet and U.S. military units, but it became a national border. South Korean and North Korean governments formally declared themselves in August and September, respectively, of 1948. In June 1950, North Korea invaded South Korea to reunify the Korean nation by force. North Korea failed and signed an armistice agreement on July 27, 1953. Technically, the two countries remained at war with each other at the end of 2000 because they have not established a peaceful settlement to replace the Korean War armistice agreement.

35. There were approximately 10 million South Koreans (about 21 percent) related to family members living in North Korea as of December 2000.

36. Joseph A. B. Winder, "The Economic Dynamics of the Korean Peninsula Peace Process," in *The Two Koreas in 2000: Sustaining Recovery and Seeking Reconciliation* (Washington, D.C.: Korea Economic Institute of America, 2000), 95.

5 ■

Trend Five: The Rise of
New Authorities

THE TRENDS REVIEWED so far have dramatic implications for a key concept of political and social life: authority. In the knowledge era, the extent and nature of authority in all of its forms are undergoing a profound change. Not only are the social institutions that wield authority affected, but the very character of authority itself. This shift involves something far more complex than a mere "decline of authority," a trend examined for decades. Instead, what is happening today is a transformation of authority and the replacement of its traditional forms by knowledge-era ideas and institutions that exercise great influence over people. Sometimes the new institutions are modified versions of older forms—the partial replacement of monolithic religions, for example, by more diverse and diffuse churches, cults, and self-help gurus—and in other cases, such as the mass media, the form they take is entirely new. But old forms of authority will not give way to new ones overnight, and bridging the gap between the two structures is an immense task. This is particularly true in Korea, with its well-established Confucian-based authoritarian relationships.

Phase One: The Decline of Hierarchies

The knowledge era is characterized by a crisis of authority or a decline in the strength of major social institutions. In a fragmented and diversified world, a world of widely available information and greater personal autonomy, a world of relative moral values, ruling groups face unprecedented challenges to their authority. A main

119

reason for this is that the monopolies on information, capital, force, and ideology that were once the source of power for absolute rulers are fading away.

The sociologist Richard Sennett points out that "authority is not a thing. It is an interpretive process which seeks for itself the solidity of a thing."[1] And this interpretive process has begun to move in a new direction. By radically expanding the individual to participate in it, knowledge renders authorities incapable of preserving a solid front. The weakening of forms of social authority is a measure of the scope of this change. This weakening is not unique to the United States or the West; indeed, the whole world is undergoing a similar kind of stress. In Korea, the pace and scope of change are presenting major challenges to each of this ancient society's five major social institutions—family, religion, education, economy, and government—greatly affecting their ability to sustain social harmony and transmit cultural values to coming generations.

The well-known decline of the American family, for example, is signaled by dramatically higher rates of divorce and single-parent families. What is not appreciated is that this family decay is global: in many developing countries divorce rates doubled between the 1970s and 1990s. In Korea, an industrialized nation, the divorce rate more than doubled in the 1990s, with a daily average of 113 Korean couples filing for divorce as of July 2000.[2]

These pressures also conspire to undermine communities, both local and national, around the world. As social mobility and remote forms of interaction have emerged, the strength of civil society has waned. Weaker community institutions contribute to higher levels of crime and corruption, raising concerns that the next decade could witness a rise in global corruption of epidemic proportions.

Knowledge-era forces tend also to reduce the strength of centralized, hierarchical religions. This does not imply a decline of spirituality or faith—far from it: the next decade could be a time of intensifying religious belief, in part as a reaction to the more alienating trends of our transitional era. But it does suggest that these newer forms of faith will be more plural, decentralized, and flexible. Finally, the force of tradition declines in times of rapid change, when it no longer makes sense—or no longer appears to make sense—to imitate the behavior and values of one's elders.

The most profound effect of the decline of old authorities is social instability. Old, hierarchical forms of authority typically fall away before new ones have fully taken their place, and the result is a weakening of social bonds. An obvious result of this complex interaction is the growth of ethnic strife and conflict. Ethnic tension is growing both within societies—for example, racial tensions in the United States and Europe—and between them, in the form of ethnically and culturally defined disputes over land or values or trade practices, to include intellectual property rights protection and market access issues, for example. The decline of the old authorities and the rise of the new make people intensify their search for identity. This same process, when combined with the uncertainty of the knowledge era, can produce in the individual a dangerous level of alienation from the society and once-familiar institutions.

Phase Two: The Rise of New Authorities

The fate of authority in the knowledge era is not simply one of decline, deterioration, or the permanent victory of alienation. New authorities arise to replace those that have declined, and in many cases they are more empowering and respectful of freedom than the old (figure 31).

One form of new authority is the virtual state. Today's basic level of authority, the nation-state, will give way to a less centralized, more flexible, and more adaptable institution. Nation-states will not simply disappear or fall into obsolescence; as virtual states they will share the stage of authority with more actors, accomplishing their tasks with more efficiency and greater frugality. The virtual state's main purpose is to make itself an attractive area for investment, with highly educated populations, modern infrastructures, and moderate tax rates and regulatory schemes.

Peter Drucker suggests that this process of privatization will produce a second and related new form of authority in knowledge-era society, which he calls the social sector—or nongovernmental organizations performing services previously held to be government responsibilities. Recent numbers do indeed show the dramatic growth of the social sector. Not only does the United States alone boast almost a million and a half nonprofit groups; the economic activity

Figure 31
Characteristics of Knowledge-Era Authorities

In their organization they will be decentralized, small, and flexible—most often specialized, single-issue groups. In an age of micromarketing and diversity, few broad-based institutions will succeed.

In many cases their physical structure will be virtual instead of concrete; many will consist of far-flung, pluralistic conglomerations working together.

Their approach to power will not be coercive; they will seek influence rather than control or outright power. These new institutions will be centers of information and knowledge competing for allegiance rather than rigid authorities as we have known them.

Their method of acquiring influence will be through performance, competence, and effectiveness rather than through brute force or tradition.

of these groups, at roughly 7 percent of U.S. GNP, exceeds the GNP of all but seven nations in the world. The number of NGOs in South Korea has expanded significantly since 1987 as well, although their economic impact is yet not as clear as in the United States.[3]

A concept that functions as a sort of social authority in the knowledge era is a novel set of dominant business strategies, perhaps best reflected in Gary Hamel's notion of "strategy as revolution." The idea is that, in an era of "hypercompetition" and rapid product turnover, trying to preserve existing market share without innovation is disastrous and pursuing "incremental improvements while rivals reinvent the industry is like fiddling while Rome burns."[4] Never before "has the world been more hospitable to industry revolutionaries and more hostile to industry incumbents." The knowledge era demands an "innovation-rich economy," writes former Citibank president Walter Wriston. "Nations that wish to flourish . . . will have to foster a climate of innovation."[5]

The principles of new business strategies lead directly to a new form of business authority: new management styles. Modern management theories aim to place more and more control in the hands of workers at the expense of middle management. Knowledge-era corporate leaders have decentralized decisionmaking and have empowered their employees more than at any time in the modern era.

Direct democracy constitutes the political expression of new forms of authority in the knowledge era. The combination of television, telephone, and computer lines that is developing under the rubric of "the information superhighway" is changing the way Americans—and Koreans—participate in politics. Public opinion polling, referenda, ballot initiatives—all someday conducted perhaps via voting boxes attached to televisions—are bringing politics closer to the people.

The character of businesses will also change in the knowledge era as businesses accept new roles beyond mere profit making. "Ten years from now, I am firmly convinced," writes James Moore, "business leaders will be actively and daily addressing social and environmental issues."[6] The reasons are not altruistic: they include the corporate need for a well-trained workforce, competition to attract mobile workers, efforts to increase retention and productivity, and concerns for public image and trust. Companies that express a sense of broader social responsibility will reap the rewards, both internally and externally.

Finally, the ultimate authority in the knowledge era is the most decentralized of all: the individual human being. Our era empowers human beings with more freedom, choice, and opportunity than at any other time in human history. This new age calls for self-sufficient, self-motivated, self-navigating people—individuals who express the new degrees of social and personal responsibility that are so necessary in an era of rapid change.

Applying the Trends to Korea: Renewing the Social Order

Korea was immersed in a struggle for its future—indeed, a revolution of sorts—at the end of the twentieth century. Established authorities were being significantly challenged in each of Korea's five major social institutions: family, religion, education, economy, and government. Thus, Korea was wrestling with itself over whether to adapt or eliminate values and practices developed throughout its 4,000-year history that were incompatible with and impeding the transition into the knowledge era. Some of these practices and values—family loyalty and respect for education, for example—ennoble Koreans and are likely to be retained.

Certain practices have persisted, however, that corrupt and suppress Korean individuals and institutions or otherwise constrain the society from developing new institutions and confidence to achieve its goal of becoming a prosperous, knowledge-era society. For example, the government still used traditional Korea Inc. practices to bail out questionable business enterprises three years after initiating its modern four-sector reforms.

Nevertheless, by 2001, new institutions and values helped Koreans interact effectively with a world that was becoming smaller with the development of each new computer chip. Traditional authorities were slowly yielding under pressures caused by the wrenching industrialization process that thrust Korea from an agrarian society into the industrial age and still forward to the brink of the knowledge era. Institutions based on traditional Confucian values were strongly affected.

The Decline of Korea's Traditional Authorities

Korea's Confucian foundation and its traditional authorities—family, religion, education, business, and government—were losing credibility and beginning to lose influence at the end of the twentieth century because of the impact of the industrial age, the revelations of the 1997 financial crisis, and the transition to the knowledge era.

Family

The family is the bedrock of Korean society, but Korea's rapid economic development since 1960 placed great stress on three important Confucian relationships within the family.

Father–son relationship. The eldest son has a particularly important role in the traditional Korean family. As the father's first-born son, he bears the responsibility for implementing the father's will in the family by guiding and caring for his siblings. He is also responsible for achieving the family's security and honor in his generation and the following generation and for providing for the parents in their old age. These heavy responsibilities further enhance his stature in the family.

The father–son relationship has been in transition owing to changes in the Korean family structure. Large extended families living in rural areas were the norm in the 1950s; small nuclear families living in urban areas were the norm in the 1990s. By the 1990s most families comprised only two children, and many families had no sons. By necessity, the role of daughters also has been in transition but has not yet been institutionalized as has the role of sons.

Parents traditionally relied on their eldest son for their support as they aged. They traditionally lived with him and his wife, who bore much of the practical responsibility for their care. By the end of the twentieth century, this practice was creating a problem for families lacking sons, forcing the parents to rely on their daughters for support. Daughters in modern families without sons are torn between traditional responsibilities to parents-in-law and concerns for their own parents who lack the traditional family caregiver. In trying to care for both sets of parents, the daughter risked incurring the anger of her mother-in-law and disappointing her own needy parents. To meet the growing problem of care for the elderly, the government implemented a national pension plan and assumed some responsibilities for elder care, but both citizens and officials knew that government programs could not satisfactorily replace society's traditional mainstay—the family.

Another delicate matter pertained to the father's estate, which the eldest son traditionally handled. The son traditionally divided the inheritance among all family members, but he had room for discretion. By 2000, the government had implemented laws to dispose of estates in a relatively equitable fashion—every child regardless of gender or marital status receives an equal portion, and the surviving wife receives 150 percent of a child's share—when the deceased leaves no will.[7] As a result of such changes, the role of the eldest son as a mainstay in the family has declined.

Husband–wife relationship. The husband–wife relationship also was in transition at the end of the twentieth century. Methods for selecting a spouse changed, the marriage rate declined, and the divorce rate increased.

Traditionally, marriages were arranged by parents, but as industrialization continued, Koreans increasingly took responsibility for selecting their own spouses. In 1958, for example, 62 percent of parents selected their children's spouses while another 26 percent selected the spouse and then solicited their child's consent. Fewer than 3 percent of Koreans selected their own spouses without their parents' involvement. But by 1980, within the space of one generation, 14 percent of Koreans selected their own spouses. The percentage of parents who fully decided for their children dropped from 62 percent to 18 percent, while the percentage who selected a spouse contingent on their child's concurrence increased from 26 percent to 37 percent.[8]

Koreans' newfound preference for selecting their spouses themselves continued to grow through the 1990s and into the twenty-first century. A 1994 study of 1,554 college students revealed that 77 percent of the students intended to select their own spouses, according to the Korea Socio-Cultural Research Institute. If parents were to disapprove, 44 percent claimed they would marry the person of their choice regardless, while 17 percent believed they could persuade their parents after "living together" for awhile. Only 18 percent said they would comply with their parents' opinion, and 16 percent envisioned giving up on marriage, living "forever" as a single.[9] In early 2001, an overwhelming majority (87 percent) of almost 14,000 respondents to an Internet survey favored living out of wedlock with a potential spouse in a trial marriage. Among the respondents, 90 percent of the women and 85 percent of the men considered such an arrangement to be agreeable.[10]

The popularity of marriage declined in the late 1990s, perhaps due to concerns over job security during the economic reform process. The number of couples marrying dropped roughly 17 percent from the annual high of almost 435,000 couples in 1996 to just

Figure 32
Marriage Rate and Divorce Rate, South Korea, 1990–1999

Note: per 1,000 people

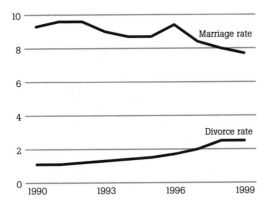

Source: ROK National Statistical Office, www.nso.go.kr/eindex.html.

under 363,000 couples who married in 1999. The marriage rate per 1,000 persons in the 1990s rose from 9.3 in 1990 to 9.6 in 1991 and then slipped during the rest of the 1990s to reach 7.7 in 1999 (figure 32). The average ages of men and women when they married were 29 and 26, respectively.[11]

Once married, couples in industrialized Korea faced pressures that were significantly different from those in traditional, pre-industrial Korea. In the last 40 years of the twentieth century, husbands typically spent more time out of the home than they had previously. Many also spent time in the evenings and on weekends with professional associates to cultivate personal relationships that were considered essential for success. Such schedules denied many fathers the requisite time to bond with their families and earn more than their children's obligatory affection and respect; this weakened the father's personal authority within the family. Consequently, mothers raised the children while fathers provided the economic necessities and sometimes became virtual strangers to their children.

Some wives worked outside of the home, which presented issues of child care and spousal relationships. To care for her children during the workday, the wife often relied on her mother or mother-

Figure 33
Marriages and Divorces, South Korea, 1990–1999

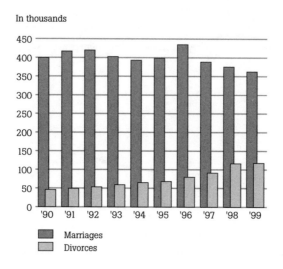

In thousands

Source: ROK National Statistical Office, www.nso.go.kr/eindex.html.

in-law. The wife's experiences outside the home as a valued, if not empowered, worker with certain rights and financial compensation could produce frustration if the husband hewed to the traditional view that the wife should be totally dependent and subservient to the husband. Husbands laid off from work could experience a devastating loss of self-esteem, which could increase anxiety and tension in the home.

Rising divorce rates in the 1990s (figure 33) suggest that an increasing number of Koreans found the evolving husband–wife relationship unsatisfactory. In 1999, 118,000 Koreans divorced—a significant 158 percent increase compared with 45,700 divorces in 1990. The divorce rate per 1,000 persons escalated from 1.1 in 1990 to 2.5 in 1999. Korea's divorce rate of 2 people per 1,000 in 1997 compared unfavorably with that of France, Japan, and Italy, which were 1.9, 1.8, and 0.6, respectively.[12]

The primary reason couples gave for divorcing was their interpersonal relationship. Only about 7 percent of couples cited economic difficulties as the reason, despite a spike in divorces during the 1998 recession. Men and women on average were 40 and 36 years old, respectively, when they divorced, and more than 71 percent of divorced couples had minor children. Twilight divorces involving Koreans over age 50 constituted 5 percent of the total.[13]

Elder brother–younger brother relationship. The eldest brother traditionally held great influence in the family and was responsible for his siblings, who owed him their obedience, support, and loyalty. Koreans at times apply this elder brother–younger brother family relationship to international relationships, which can confuse foreigners unfamiliar with its cultural implications.

The elder brother–younger brother relationship has also been in transition, however, because many smaller families have no sons or a son may have only an elder sister, not a brother. Daughters have assumed responsibilities formerly associated with elder brothers, which has made them more independent than in the past and somewhat at odds with traditional expectations of parents, siblings, and extended-family members.

The new family. The Korean family still is an important institution at the dawn of the twenty-first century, but the demands of the industrial age and Korea's transition to the knowledge era have put it in a state of flux. Fewer Koreans married and more divorced in 1999 compared with 1990. Within families, there were new demands on women to meet nontraditional expectations associated with roles formerly performed by males. Young women in Korea today are relatively more independent and able to make greater contributions to their families than in the past.

Many of today's children are online—no surprise as most Korean Internet users are young. A survey of 2,900 fourth- to sixth-grade students and their parents in November 2000 found that 95 percent of the children in Seoul households had their own computers. Nationally, more than 96 percent of children had used the Internet in the preceding month, and over 42 percent use it almost daily. Of these, 83 percent use it to do homework, 37 percent sought "necessary information," and about 10 percent used it for entertainment. Among children in Seoul, over 78 percent had Internet access, which was higher than the national access rate of 69 percent. Average use per day was about 1 hour and 15 minutes.[14]

During the hectic pace of work and school days, such access challenges parents who try to instill traditional values in their children—witness the declining marriage rate and growing divorce rate. In the late 1990s Korean teenagers aged 14–17 reported a higher degree of dissatisfaction than did their counterparts in France and the United States:[15]

- Only about one in three Korean teenagers (37 percent) were happy with themselves, compared with almost 90 percent of U.S. teenagers and 71 percent of French youth, although they were slightly happier than Japanese teenagers who reported that fewer than one in four (23 percent) was happy.
- Only one in two Korean teens (50.5 percent) was satisfied with family life compared with approximately 84 percent in the United States, 64 percent in France, and 40 percent in Japan.
- A surprisingly low number of Korean youths were eager to seek financial independence within the next 7–10 years. Approximately one-third wanted to remain financially dependent on their parents until after graduating from university, one-fifth wanted to remain dependent until becoming employed, and one-eighth did not envision becoming financially independent until after marriage. By contrast, more than 64 percent of U.S. teens envisioned becoming financially independent after graduating from high school, and almost 75 percent of French teens anticipated financial independence after graduating from university.
- Only 41 percent of Korean youths were satisfied with their schools compared with approximately 73 percent of U.S. and 58 percent of French teenagers. Koreans' dissatisfaction was partly attributable to the years of intense preparation they endure for highly competitive university entrance exams, the results of which profoundly affect their future livelihood. This pressure notwithstanding, Korean teenagers, like their Japanese counterparts, considered making friends to be the most

important aspect of school. French and U.S. students placed more importance on their studies and higher education.

■ Only 15 percent of Korean teenagers were satisfied with their general society; this compares with 72 percent of their U.S. and 53 percent of their French counterparts.

The intense pressure to excel on university exams no doubt contributes to Korean teens' dissatisfaction, but it may not be the only factor. Changes in the family probably also contribute. And, because Korean teenagers are avid computer users, their dissatisfaction could derive from the intense difference between their stimulating and empowering online experiences and their highly regimented schools that neither stimulate nor reward individual expression.

Government

Confucius patterned the ruler–subject relationship of government on that of the father's relationship with his family, making government inherently paternalistic. The result in modern Korea, especially Park Chung-hee's Korea Inc. model, has been a system in which the central government has assumed wide-ranging responsibility and authority to manage in detail the affairs of the people and the economy. Many government officials in contemporary Korea continue to refer to their responsibilities in clearly paternalistic terms, revealing a view that citizens lack the ability to survive in a free-market economy without government assistance. Such views justify government intervention to rescue mismanaged, debt-ridden companies. However, this centralized Confucian system conflicts with the decentralized nature of liberal democracy, free-market economics, modern nuclear families, and empowered individuals. Moreover, noble Confucian concepts of righteousness to assure moral government have proved to be unattainable for ordinary people in Korea's modern, fast-paced, industrial, and increasingly pluralistic knowledge-based society.

At the close of the twentieth century, Koreans' greater political activism consistent with empowering aspects of information technology and liberal democracy could be seen during elections to the National Assembly in 2000. Reduced trust in a number of political

Figure 34
Trust in Political Institutions, South Korea, 1997

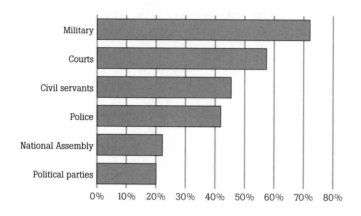

Source: Doh Chull Shin, "Monitoring the Dynamics of Democratization in Korea: The Korea Democracy Barometer Surveys," *International Journal of Korean Studies* 4, nos. 1, 2 (Fall/Winter 2000): 53.

institutions also led some Koreans to seek new institutional checks and balances to restrain government officials and organizations from abusing their powers. Roughly three of every four Koreans (77 percent) were wary of the National Assembly's ability to properly represent the people, and even more Koreans (80 percent) were skeptical of the political parties. Approximately 54 percent mistrusted civil servants and almost three in five (57 percent) mistrusted the police. By contrast, slightly more than one in two Koreans (57 percent) trusted the courts and over 70 percent trusted the military, perhaps because they considered it to be apolitically committed to the welfare of the nation (figure 34).[16]

By 2000, Koreans wanted improved democracy and devolution of power. A slim majority (53 percent) wanted to limit the powers of the president. A stronger majority (63 percent) wanted the National Assembly to be autonomous and independent, and 70 percent wanted the political process of selecting candidates for office to be opened to the public.[17]

Despite these indications of strong support for democracy, a slight majority of Koreans "were yet to be fully dissociated from the political practices of the authoritarian past," according to Doh Chull Shin of the University of Missouri, who, since 1988, has conducted eight parallel Korea Democratic Barometer Surveys of Korean attitudes toward democracy. In 2000, he noted that almost all Koreans strongly reject the idea of either military or civilian dictatorship except in the case of an economic crisis. More than 40 percent of Koreans would support a dictatorship to overcome an economic crisis.[18]

Koreans thus want higher-quality democracy but mistrust the ability of their established institutions to provide it. To achieve better democracy, Koreans have used knowledge-era tools to influence politics, with the most clear example being the grassroots movement to change the course of the 16th general election in 2000. In Korea's developing knowledge era, such activism is likely to grow.

Planned devolution of power. President Kim Dae-jung entered office in 1998 with the objectives of promoting democracy and significantly changing the Confucian-based ruler–subject relationship that previous governments depended on to operate Korea Inc. Kim's 1998 structural reforms centered on reforming the economy by weakening the power of the central government and diminishing the relationship between the government and the governed. Key objectives were to enable Korea to participate effectively in the global economy by replacing Korea Inc. with a market economy and to improve Korea's democracy. The central government could be much less dominant than in the past because the four-sector reforms are expected to

- reduce significantly the size of the government workforce; by the end of 2000, the central government had released 21,400 employees and the regional governments had released 49,500; an additional 11,100 positions were due for elimination by the end of 2001;[19]
- privatize 87 of 108 state-owned enterprises, including four parent companies—Korea Heavy Industries Co. and POSCO were two of the four—and seven subsidiaries by the end of

2000; the government began in March 2001 to privatize the giant Korea Electric Power Company;[20]

- replace Park's concept of operating a managed economy through "guided capitalism" with modern methods of regulating—or refereeing—a free-enterprise market economy;
- establish the principles, institutions, and practices for a properly functioning market economy, and add appropriate institutional checks and balances to prevent crony capitalism and other corrupt practices; and
- empower the private sector to allocate capital and other resources throughout the economy after fully privatizing all financial institutions, selling the government's shares in financial institutions, and withdrawing the government's direct involvement.

Success in implementing these reforms would be a historic accomplishment for a number of reasons. First, the government would have significantly reversed and reduced its intervention in the economy, thus improving the nation's economic freedom and potential standard of living.[21]

Second, the government would have established a new model for its role in Korea's developing market economy while greatly complicating the ability of future governments to return to the Korea Inc. managed-economy model.

Third, but no less important, the government would have improved the prospects for containing if not reducing corruption, a major problem in Korea.

The four-sector reform process was incomplete at the end of 2000. The government remained closely involved in the financial sector and, in a sense, appeared hostage to labor demands to sustain nonviable firms and protect workers in state-owned enterprises targeted for privatization. Kim Dae-jung addressed these obstacles in his speech to the nation on January 1, 2001, when he specifically apologized for the government's failure to complete restructuring, which he cited as the primary reason for the slowdown in Korea's economy at the end of 2000. Kim also pledged that his administration would

- complete the second stage of basic reform tasks in the four major sectors (financial, corporate, labor, and public) during the first half of 2001;
- then switch to a system of constant reform controlled by the market;
- let competitive enterprises survive while not hesitating to allow unhealthy companies to close down;
- carry out thorough financial reform in 2001 so that the words "insolvent financial institution" would disappear for good; and
- make efforts to make the public sector a model of reform.[22]

Although Kim in his speech reaffirmed his commitment to implement major structural reforms, subsequent government action quickly raised questions about the administration's ability to succeed, at least with respect to financial sector and *chaebol* reforms. Within a week of the January 1, 2001, speech, the government announced its intention to purchase more than $1 billion in corporate junk bonds that six companies—four Hyundai affiliates[23] and two cement companies—lacked liquidity to redeem when they were scheduled to mature in January and February 2001. Moreover, the government planned for creditor banks to assist the bailout by buying 20 percent of the bonds. The government stated that it was aiding these particular companies because they were considered to be viable firms in the long term. Opponents argued the government's move was politically inspired because the companies were not viable, a point that was affirmed when one of the Hyundai affiliates, Korea Industrial Development, declared bankruptcy on March 2, 2001.

The government's decision to bail out the six companies suggests disagreement within the Kim Dae-jung administration about letting arguably unhealthy companies collapse and ceasing the Korea Inc. practice of intervening in the economy.[24] It remains to be seen whether Kim Dae-jung has the power to complete the reform of the financial sector and change the behavior of government officials enough to create a government of the people as he envisioned it in 1997.

Perceived injustice. Public confidence in Korea's judicial system was weak in late 2000, in part due to the widespread perception that the Seoul district prosecutor's office did not thoroughly investigate government officials involved in financial scandals and thus facilitated perceived government cover-ups. A public poll of more than 20,000 mobile-telephone users in November 2000 found that 78 percent of respondents did not believe the prosecutor's office had adequately investigated and prosecuted officials.

Two cases in the public consciousness in 2000 were the W 220 billion Korea Digital Line bribery case (see page 82) and a W 100 billion illegal loan that a Hanvit Bank official made to the brother of a senior government official in 1999 but that came to light in 2000. The Seoul prosecutor's office promised a full investigation of the Hanvit scandal, but many Koreans believed the prosecutor's final report in September 2000 was inadequate and, as one respected Korean newspaper stated, ultimately raised ". . . suspicion that the investigation was [conducted] according to a well-choreographed script, just as the people have been left with suspicions about previous large-scale 'power scandals'."[25] The November 2000 survey of mobile-telephone users indicated that public skepticism of the prosecutor's office had increased since 1994 when a Gallup Korea poll concluded that 65 percent of Koreans were skeptical of the Seoul prosecutor's office,[26] whose potential ability to check abuse of power by government officials is so important.

Another poll, reported in September 2000, also provided disturbing views of the judicial system. More than two-thirds of respondents believed that judicial decisions in Korea were unfair, and about 8 percent of respondents considered the decisions to be "strongly unfair." Moreover, approximately 65 percent of respondents believed that people with a personal contact in the judicial office would be more likely to receive a favorable judgment than those without such contacts. More than 80 percent of respondents would welcome the introduction of a jury system in Korea.[27]

Political parties. Korea's political parties are another established authority suffering from low credibility at the beginning of the twenty-first century; in 1999 only about 20 percent of Koreans put trust in them. Korea's parties reflect regional concerns and are dominated by charismatic leaders to a degree that key differences among political parties are based less on ideology and issues and more on the charisma of leaders who usually establish their own parties. The custom of patronage throughout Korean society permits the party leader to play a key role in selecting subordinate leaders and candidates for public office. Most of the relatively young political parties have not yet dealt with the challenge of transferring leadership to a new generation.

At the end of the twentieth century, Koreans increasingly wanted changes in Korean democracy: one in three agreed with the concept of forming new political parties that pursue definite policies, and a strong majority (71 percent) favored opening the process by which the party selects candidates for public office.[28] In 2000, ordinary citizens used the Internet to mobilize support to defeat 59 candidates they believed were unfit for office (see the final section in chapter 2). Such newfound activism suggests Koreans in the first decade of the twenty-first century will increasingly demand greater say in determining party candidates, if not the party leader and platform issues.

Local autonomy. The future of local autonomy was in doubt at the end of 2000 primarily due to insufficient funding of local mandates and questions regarding the integrity of local officials. Local governments' financial dependence on the central government (see page 110) can promote corruption as some local officials, for example, reportedly lease public land to private corporations to raise money for political purposes. In addition, some Koreans believe some elected officials are not technically capable of guiding efficient economic development, protecting the environment, and performing other duties. Advocates for replacing elected officials with appointed officials argue that appointees would be able administrators who would not be obligated to meet campaign promises and therefore would not engage in corrupt activity or practices that could produce corruption.

In October 2000, National Assembly member Lim Inbae of the opposition Grand National Party, confident of the support of at least 41 opposition and ruling party members of the 273-seat National Assembly, submitted a bill to revise the law on local autonomy.[29] The bill, which could be formally considered during 2001, would empower the central government to replace directly elected local government heads with persons appointed by the central government.[30]

Despite some support for terminating the post-1995 practice of electing local officials, no one could predict at the end of 2000 how this issue would be resolved. Koreans' strong approval of democracy suggests many will resist proposals for the central government to appoint local officials, which was the practice under former military governments. Voters will likely insist on other solutions to the plethora of problems that exist at the local level, but passage of the bill cannot be ruled out.

It is difficult to envision how Kim Dae-jung can successfully devolve power from the central government if local governments revert to their former role as extensions of central power.

Freedom of Speech

Freedom of speech and the power of the press, like democracy, are relatively new concepts in Korea's 4,000-year-old Confucian culture. Although newspapers date back to the nineteenth century in Korea, newspapers' role as the people's watchdog guarding against a government's abuse of power clashes with Confucian values of loyalty and obedience to the government. Nevertheless, since independence in 1945, Korean newspapers have sought the watchdog role in the face of government control of the press, which persisted through the Chun Doo-hwan administration.

Press freedom grew under elected civilian governments, and some news organizations routinely report balanced stories that inform readers of developments the government would prefer not be publicized. However, it will take time—perhaps another generation—before Korean reporters, editors, and news media organizations will feel comfortable in routinely reporting stories critical of the government to the extent common in Western democracies. As democracy depends on free speech, elected Korean governments should see it in the national interest to protect and nurture the press and promote freedom of speech.

Concerns arose in 2000 and 2001 regarding a potential decline in government commitment to freedom of speech. South Korean media at times appeared reluctant to publish stories that might offend the governments of both South Korea and North Korea; also, the ROK government apparently tried to control some Internet communications, discourage political activism, and (critics charged) use tax audits to pressure news media organizations.

North Korean influence on South Korean free speech. President Kim Dae-jung of the ROK and Chairman Kim Jong-il of the DPRK conducted an unprecedented summit meeting in June 2000, laying a historic foundation to improve inter-Korean relations. Afterwards, Kim Jong-il quickly invited ROK news media organizations to visit North Korea from August 5 to 12, attracting 48 representatives from 46 of South Korea's 100 news media organizations. The highlight of the trip was Chairman Kim's relatively candid two-hour meeting with ROK media representatives on August 12.

Freedom-of-speech concepts were challenged, however, on August 11 when representatives of the media organizations of the two countries signed a five-point agreement, promising to avoid harsh criticism of the other side and seek greater cooperation. The second point of the agreement specifically limits South Korean free speech by calling on "the media organizations of the North and the South [to] avoid confrontation between compatriots and stop slanders and calumnies, which hurt national reconciliation and unity, in keeping with the prevailing situation."[31] The agreement is not legally binding because of the unofficial nature of the South Korean media delegation, which comprised representatives from fewer than half of the companies in the industry.

Pyongyang's insistence on the media agreement illustrates its desire to control freedom of speech in South Korea with respect to North Korea stories and maintain control through the illusion of harmony, if not widespread public support. The agreement also accords with a Korean neo-Confucian value—a value unchallenged in North Korea and also present to a lesser degree in some South Korean groups—that regards public criticism of the government to be inconsistent with the ruler–subject relationship wherein the subject is loyal and uncritical. This neo-Confucian value also helps explain South Korean media and government acceptance of the agreement.

Although South Korean news organizations may not feel bound by the agreement, immediately afterwards there occurred a marked decline in South Korean news stories highly critical of North Korea and Kim Dae-jung's sunshine policy. In late 2000, however, ROK press coverage of controversy surrounding the head of the South Korean National Red Cross raised questions about the South Korean press commitment to free speech.

The Red Cross president, Chang Choong-shik, granted what turned out to be a surprisingly scandalous interview with a prominent monthly news magazine following his return in August 2001 from South Korea's first family reunion in Pyongyang.[32] Chang described North Korea as a very poor country, a controlled society where there is far less freedom than in South Korea. Pyongyang took umbrage and threatened to cancel two family reunions scheduled for November and December if Chang did not apologize. When Change refused to do so, an ROK government agency reportedly sent an apology to the North Koreans in his name, smoothing over the incident. Chang resigned his post in December.[33]

The news media and the ROK government backed away from supporting Chang's right to free speech, impolitic though it was. The low level of South Korean news coverage of the incident raised questions about the media's and the government's zeal for freedom of speech, allowing North Korea to essentially force Chang out of office for speaking his mind. The government's dismay at Chang's undiplomatic comments was certainly understandable although the media usually do not share those government concerns. South Korean media inattention could have occurred because the media did not consider Chang's situation to be newsworthy; or they downplayed the story because of the August 11 media agreement; or, as conservative Koreans believe, they imposed self-censorship because they were influenced by ROK government officials concerned that negative reporting would prompt North Korea to suspend family reunions and other improvements to inter-Korean relations.

Internet anti-sites. So-called anti-sites on the Internet, which increased in the late 1990s with about 50 actively operating in August 2000, also raised questions about the ROK government's commitment to freedom of speech. Korean netizens, offending established authorities, use these sites to criticize *chaebol* and the government. In a major victory for free speech, a Korean court in June 2000 found that one anti-site's criticism of Samsung was legal and the persons operating the site, who had been arrested for their on-line statements, were within their legal rights.[34]

Undeterred, the national police in fall 2000 arrested a different anti-site operator in Pusan on charges of distributing pornography. Free speech advocates countered that the site's main purpose was to criticize the Kim Dae-jung administration and complained that the government was suppressing free speech.[35]

Supreme Court rules against private negative campaigning. ROK law forbids negative campaigning. However, in early 2000, members of grassroots citizen groups, including the Citizens' Alliance for the General Election (CAGE), campaigned against more than 80 National Assembly candidates they considered to be unfit for office. After voters did not elect 59 of these candidates during the 16th general election in April 2000, charges were brought against CAGE for waging a negative campaign. The Supreme Court on January 26, 2001, ruled that the citizen groups had violated the campaign law.[36] The ruling strictly interprets the law and presents another potential hindrance to the rights of private citizens in a democracy to voice their views. The 2002 presidential campaign will show whether the ruling discourages political activism.

News media audits. In February 2001, the Seoul regional office of the National Tax Service (NTS) and the Korea Fair Trade Commission (KFTC) announced their intention to audit the tax records and investigate the business practices of 23 Seoul-based news media organizations. These concurrent major investigations alarmed free speech advocates who were concerned that the government intended to use these powerful tools to muzzle the press, and they provided fodder for political opponents.

Government critics based their arguments in part on their presumption that the Kim Dae-jung administration sought to silence the news media's critical coverage of two particularly important topics: South Korea's declining economic performance and its sunshine policy toward North Korea. South Korea's GDP growth rate in 2000 dropped almost two percentage points to 8.8 percent compared with 1999 and was forecast to slip approximately 4 percentage points more in 2001. Unemployment had increased since the third quarter of 2000 because of the implementation of the second round of financial restructuring reforms and the increase in the liquidation of financially weak companies.

South Korean critics also were offended that the North Koreans had spurned what they believed were Seoul's generous efforts to improve North Korea–South Korea relations. For example, Pyongyang refused to install a crisis-management communications link between the two national capitals or military headquarters, a modest military confidence-building measure. Despite Pyongyang's lack of cooperation, the Kim Dae-jung administration in late 2000 and 2001 continued to exhort DPRK chairman Kim Jong-il to visit Seoul and reciprocate the South Korean president's June 2000 visit to Pyongyang, a stance that disturbed conservative South Koreans who faulted the government for being too lenient with the DPRK.

The ROK government pointed to numerous consumer complaints and allegations of wrongdoing by news media companies and announced that the time had come to assess this sector's compliance with laws that companies throughout the economy were required to obey. ROK law calls for the government to audit major companies every five years, and the most recent news media sector audit had been in 1994. In addition to the government, private organizations such as the People's Coalition for Media Reform, an NGO, had concerns about improper government–news media relations and had been calling for news media reform since 1998.[37]

In June 2001, the KFTC and NTS announced the results of their investigation and tax audit. The KFTC reported that 13 media groups had conducted illegal internal dealings in excess of W 543 billion between April 1997 and March 2001 and fined the involved companies and their subsidiaries a total of W 24.2 billion ($19 million). The NTS found evidence of tax evasion throughout the audited companies and levied the largest assessment on a single business sector in ROK history: W 505.6 billion ($389 million) in back taxes on the 23 news media companies and their subsidiaries.[38] The government also fined some individuals for irregular business transactions and planned to indict several executives for tax evasion.[39]

How has the tax audit and KFTC investigation affected news media reporting of the government? Was the press silenced? Reporting in selected English language newspapers during the time of preparing this book indicated little if any significant change in the intensity of news media criticism of the government. Prime Minister Lee Han-dong in February 2001 described the investigations as "routine government inquiries designed only to ascertain fairness and due payment of taxes," but added that the government would comply with ROK law and not release the results to the public.[40] The June findings suggested that the NTS and KFTC investigations had been conducted in accordance with the prime minister's explanation although more transparency could help ease public concern.

Free speech advocates regarded the Supreme Court's interpretation of negative campaigning and the government investigation of news media companies as constituting a de facto official backlash against free speech and a free press sometimes critical of the government. Although such actions as well as the case against the former Red Cross president can suggest that freedom of speech is not yet a firmly entrenched Korean institution respected by all members of the society, the continuing critical press coverage of the government may in fact indicate that Koreans are moving toward a more liberal knowledge era in which freedom of the press will be increasingly respected as essential for a prosperous knowledge-era democracy. The more transparently the government conducts tax audits and other investigations, the easier it will be to assure the public that the government is upholding freedom of speech while enforcing the rule of law. Changing the laws to require the prompt publication of tax audit methods and results could illuminate such investigations and build public confidence.

Education

The Korean education system also lost credibility at the end of the twentieth century. Koreans prize education—an important Confucian value. Not only do they expect a good education to improve their intellectual quality of life, but they also expect education to enable financial success. The changing nature of Korea's economy, the inability of many high school and university graduates to gain satisfactory employment, and difficulties in fostering innovation—key to success in the knowledge era—all reflected negatively on the education system.

Korean students perform very well in international examinations of selected skills. In 1995, for example, Korean fourth and eighth graders scored best in the world on international standardized tests in mathematics.[40] However, the Korean education system has not yet distinguished itself internationally by producing significant numbers of graduates at any level with the demonstrated skills and attitudes to regularly create an array of universally respected, indigenously developed, knowledge-era products. Moreover, the Korean approach to education appears to alienate students; the survey of students aged 14–17 indicated that roughly 60 percent were dissatisfied with their schools. Their dissatisfaction may derive from too much rote memorization, inflexible teaching styles, and little overlap between academic and vocational studies, which the OECD identified as problem areas in 2000.[41] The education system acknowledges its need for substantial reform, which it was attempting to accomplish.

Although South Korea ranked first in the OECD in 2000 with respect to the proportion of university graduates among young adults—double the average among OECD members[42]—fewer than 50 percent of university graduates outside of Seoul found employment when they graduated in 2000. Roughly 31 percent of all registered university students dropped out of school by November 2000 due to concerns about their ability to find work in a weak economy. Of the 527,000 dropouts, approximately 60 percent entered the military, and 37 percent went abroad to study or dropped out due to financial difficulties, according to the Ministry of Education.[43]

These statistics raise questions about the efficacy of Korea's higher education system. Korean universities in the twenty-first century will need to produce graduates with skills and attitudes quite different from those of the past. The new knowledge-era economy requires workers who can innovatively contribute to improve their organizations and who have a sufficiently broad education to make sound decisions and take informed risks once empowered to do so.

Business

The Korea Inc. business model also lost credibility in the 1990s owing to its culpability for the 1997 financial crisis and inadequacy in equipping Korean companies for the competitive challenges of the knowledge-era global economy. The financial crisis in 1997 clearly demonstrated that Korea's business model had outlived its usefulness and had become an anachronism. The *chaebol*—historically family owned and managed, impervious to outside scrutiny, and financially and politically supported by a government that provided protection from foreign competition in domestic markets and a steady cash flow to penetrate export markets—were not competitive with foreign firms except in certain limited sectors. Korea's small and medium enterprises were usually not competitive with foreign firms either. Extensive changes across the political, economic, and business spectrums were required and were in progress at the end of the twentieth century (see pages 46–52).

Religion: Buddhism

Many religions are represented in the ROK, which has no state religion. Buddhism has been the dominant religion for much of Korea's long history, and certain of its tenets have blended naturally with Confucianism over the centuries to influence Korea's culture. In past centuries, Buddhists led the nation in resisting foreign invasion and were associated with nationalistic causes. By 1995, however, it appeared that Buddhism had failed to keep pace with the spiritual needs of modern Koreans caught up in the society's tumultuous transition to an industrialized economy en route to the knowledge era.

By 1995, the percentage of South Korean believers[44] adhering to Buddhism had slipped to 46 percent while Christians comprised 52 percent of the total faith population, according to the Korean Information Service.[45] Christianity, the nontraditional religion, is no bar to high government position. A Buddhist newspaper reported in March 2000 that 62 percent of 100 senior government officials were Christian: 20 were Roman Catholic (including Kim Dae-jung) and 42 were Protestants.[46] However, other sources indicate the Korean faith population was divided more evenly, with 47–48 percent accepting Buddhism and 48–49 percent accepting Christianity. In any case, it appeared that in the 1990s the long-standing

Figure 35
Corruption in Asian Nations, 2001

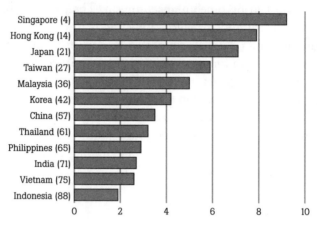

0 indicates highly corrupt; 10 indicates highly clean

Source: Transparency International, www.transparency.org/documents/cpi/2001/
cpi2001.html#cpi, accessed July 15, 2001.

spiritual authority of Buddhism had lost its historic role as Korea's
major religion.

Transitional Risks:
Symptoms of Social Instability

"Power tends to corrupt and absolute power corrupts absolutely."
—Lord Acton

Corruption

Koreans acknowledge that the economic model of their recent past—
Korea Inc.—and, in fact, the whole of Korean society are perme-
ated by the dangers inherent in the concept of moral hazard. To
illustrate: If both the lender and the borrower in a private sector
transaction expect that a third party (in Korea, the government) will

bail out the lender if the borrower is unable to repay its debts,[47] lenders will be willing to provide financially unjustifiable loans if benefits are satisfactory, in other words, if a bad loan leads to an improved relationship with the borrower or other interested party. A Korean lender's expectation of third-party (government) intervention also reduces the requirement to assess thoroughly the envisioned project from a profit-and-loss perspective. Government intervention in favor of unjustifiable loans forgives incompetence and encourages various vices; it is the proverbial free lunch for borrower and lender alike.

Financial institutions and *chaebol* in the Korea Inc. era learned they could usually rely on the ROK government to bail out lenders that made bad loans to *chaebol,* a fact that established the factors that led to the 1997 financial crisis and has promoted corruption and crony capitalism.

The 1997 financial crisis, subsequent difficulties with implementing structural reforms, and numerous corruption scandals weakened the moral authority of the central government by the end of 2000. More than 70 percent of Koreans in late 1999 believed the level of political corruption remained the "same as in the past" or had increased since 1998.[48] In September 2000, another survey of 11,000 Koreans indicated that 62 percent of the respondents were not happy about living in Korea; they cited five reasons that included corrupt politicians and government officials as well as government–business cronyism prevalent throughout the society.[49]

Transparency International (TI), an international NGO dedicated to increasing government accountability and curbing international and national corruption, corroborated Koreans' assessment that internal corruption remained a significant problem despite progress in implementing structural reforms (figure 35). The TI 2001 Corruption Perception Index ranked South Korea 42 among 91 nations, an improvement over its ranking of 48 in 2000. Compared with its Asian neighbors, Korea was cleaner than China, Thailand, Philippines, India, Vietnam, and Indonesia. However, it was more corrupt than Singapore, Hong Kong, Japan, Taiwan, and Malaysia. In 2001, TI's 2001 index rated Korea 25 of the 30 members of the OECD; it was followed by Poland, Czech Republic, Mexico, Slovak Republic, and Turkey.[50]

Figure 36
Number of Crimes, South Korea, 1994–1998

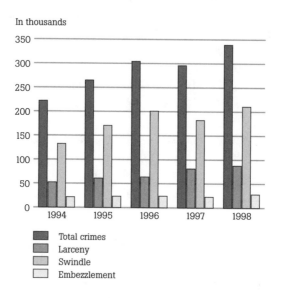

In thousands

Legend:
- Total crimes
- Larceny
- Swindle
- Embezzlement

Source: ROK National Statistical Office, www.nso.go.kr/eindex.html.

In 1999, TI also rated 19 leading exporting countries to assess the propensity of their exporting companies to bribe senior public officials. TI's Bribe Payers Index for 1999 ranked Chinese and South Korean exporters as the most corrupt of the 19 countries, with South Korean exporters slightly cleaner than the Chinese. In this index, Korea was ranked most corrupt of the 15 OECD countries rated by TI.[51]

The *Chosun Ilbo* newspaper in January 2001 reported on its survey of the views of 127 resident expatriate heads of U.S., European, and Japanese firms on corruption in Korea. Of the expatriate managers, 40 percent reported that Korean business representatives and government officials had demanded bribes or solicited donations or entertainment, which added to the foreign firms' costs of doing business in Korea. Korean business associations were the most demanding, followed by tax and customs officials and "media outlets and provincial governments."[52]

Figure 37
Rates of Robbery and Murder, Japan, South Korea,
United States, 2000

Note: per 100,000 people

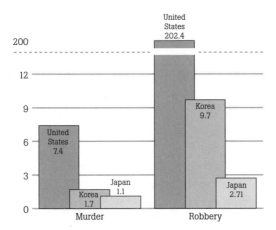

Source: ROK National Statistical Office, www.nso.go.kr/eindex.html.

Although by 2000 many Koreans believed the four-sector reforms would help improve Korea by illuminating areas previously darkened by corruption, many also had become discouraged and had emigrated or were strongly considering leaving. Discouragement was especially prevalent among middle class, white-collar workers. The *Monthly Chosun* noted in October 2000 that an increasing number of professionals including doctors, computer specialists, and *chaebol* executives decided the quality of life in Korea had deteriorated sufficiently for them to leave their homeland. Such professionals reportedly preferred "selling pizza" or "operating grocery stores" in Canada over their professional lives in Korea.[53] Approximately, 15,300 Koreans emigrated in 2000, a 20 percent increase compared with 1999 when 12,655 Koreans left, according to the Ministry of Foreign Affairs and Trade. Most Koreans emigrated to Canada, followed by the United States, Australia, and New Zealand. Emigration among professionals increased by almost 60 percent in 2000 compared with 1999. Emigration in January–February 2001 showed a 25 percent increase over the same period in 2000.[54]

Stay-at-home Koreans were bothered by the escalating trend of emigration. They feared that if Korea does not address key economic, political, and social concerns, increasing numbers of Koreans—especially white-collar professionals—will emigrate, depriving Korea of talent and hindering recovery.

If Korea is to achieve its potential as a knowledge-era society, practices that corrupt Korean individuals and institutions need to be significantly reduced if not eliminated—ideally through transparent legal mechanisms. Many corrupt practices were inherent in the Korea Inc. political–economic scheme that President Kim Daejung is addressing through the four-sector reforms. Other corruption is inherent in Korea's increasingly anachronistic neo-Confucianism, which emphasizes personal relationships over the law but lacks objective institutions to enforce moral behavior or, at least, mitigate corruption in the fast-paced industrial-cum-knowledge age. More work will be needed to reduce corruption in Korea, which not only damages the human spirit but also spawns an environment of increasing crime.

Crime

Koreans were increasingly concerned about rising crime during the 1990s (figure 36), and often compare Korean crime rates with Japanese crime rates (figure 37). The incidence of homicide, burglary, rape, theft, and violence increased 11.8 percent between 1998 and 1999. Roughly 245,000 incidents of these five major crimes occurred during the first nine months of 1998 and more than 273,000 incidents during the same period in 1999.[55]

Crimes involving narcotics also increased in the latter half of the 1990s. The number of criminals associated with drug trafficking increased approximately 28 percent in 2000 compared with 1999, when just over 4,700 persons were arrested. The number of cases dealing with mind-bending psychotropic drugs increased 33 percent to 3,015. Organized crime had not yet established a firm presence in Korea, but authorities were concerned that organized crime leaders were seeking a foothold.

Crimes committed in cyberspace—pornography distribution, swindles, and hacking—increased more than 400 percent, from 397 cases in 1999 to almost 1,700 in 2000. Compared with 1997, cybercrimes by 2000 increased almost 1,400 percent. To deal with cybercrime, the national police planned to increase its capabilities, which raised civilian concerns that the government would seek to censor political expression over the Internet.[56] Although Internet anti-sites increased in the late 1990s—with about 50 operating in August 2000 and 200 in December—and the Korean judicial system ruled that at least one anti-site operator was within his rights to criticize *chaebol* activity, Korean authorities in late 2000 were seeking ways to curtail criticism of the government on some anti-sites.

The Rise of New Authorities

> We hold these truths to be self-evident, that all men are created equal; that they are endowed by their Creator with certain unalienable Rights; . . . . That to secure these rights, governments are instituted among men, deriving their just powers from the consent of the governed; . . . .
>
> Declaration of Independence, July 4, 1776

Inspired by President Woodrow Wilson's 14 points to guide the post–World War I international order, Koreans peacefully demonstrated against colonial rule on March 1, 1919. Colonial authorities suppressed the so-called Samil Movement and the pursuit of freedom until 1945 when Korea gained its independence. Since 1945, South Koreans have increasingly demonstrated their acceptance of the fundamental and universal truths in the American Declaration of Independence. The UN Charter and the UN Universal Declaration of Human Rights also incorporate the concept of human rights, and history validates the fact that governments ultimately depend on the consent of the governed.

Koreans are likely to develop by 2010 an increasingly pluralistic set of institutions that rest on the concepts, principles, and values inherent in liberal democracy, a market economy, and an increasingly self-reliant, active citizenry. Progress in Korea will be commensurate with the pace of reform. Korea will likely make relatively rapid progress if the four-sector reforms are fully implemented by 2003 and sustained by successor governments. If reforms stall or are not sustained, however, Koreans will continue to move toward the goals, albeit more slowly, unless they abandon hopes of becoming a prosperous, knowledge-based democracy. In early 2001, it appeared likely the Korean people would stay the course.

The new Korean institutions pursuing their self-interests can be expected to employ increasingly competent, empowered workers who strive to meet clear standards and are accountable to supervisors who themselves are subject to objective scrutiny based on their measurable, transparent, institutional performance. Improved checks and balances to assure effective governance and economic activity and impede corruption should be the result.

The new institutions had not fully matured by the beginning of 2001, in part because of the tenacity of Confucian values and political concerns about unemployment as a result of permitting financially unhealthy companies to fall into bankruptcy. The government remained the locus of change, and thousands of government officials would have to recognize that power should be transferred to the new institutions. After the April 2000 National Assembly elections when the opposition Grand National Party—the ruling party from 1961 through 1997—won a working majority of the parliament, the Kim Dae-jung administration became something of a lame duck. However, Kim's Millennium Democratic Party in early 2001 formed a new coalition with the United Liberal Democratic Party that promised to improve its influence. Nevertheless, President Kim Dae-jung—a man of strong character who is highly motivated to improve Korea's political–economic climate—remained committed to implementing all of the structural reforms and making Korea a more democratic nation.

Democracy

Koreans broadly support democracy. At the end of the twentieth century, over 90 percent of Koreans agreed with the concept of democratic government while a slight majority (53 percent) believed "democracy is always preferable to any other kind of government." Almost nine of every ten Koreans (87 percent) believed the Korean democratic system "should be made more democratic," and that it would be more democratic by 2004 than it was in 1999.[57]

President Kim Dae-jung pledged in 1998 to reduce the size and influence of the central government. If he can achieve substantive and enduring changes before he leaves office in February 2003, it will be an accomplishment that bodes well for decreasing the historically pervasive role of Korea's central government. Kim reaffirmed his commitment to democracy on January 1, 2001, when, in addition to outlining the four-sector reforms, he pledged further efforts to make Korea a nation characterized by democracy and human rights.[58]

Ordinary Korean citizens are likely to become increasingly active in calling for change in their political institutions. They can be expected to insist that party officials open the process of nominating and selecting candidates for political office—including the presidency—and thus become more responsive to constituents. Citizens will also urge the formation of an independent, autonomous National Assembly and further reductions in the president's power. Voters are also likely to demand more say in the party platform-cum-legislative agenda and may also help promote national platforms that reduce regionalism. Skeptics need look no farther than the grassroots Internet campaign that influenced the April 2000 National Assembly elections. These efforts offer eloquent testimony to the determination of ordinary citizens to become part of the political process.

Two challenges confront those who are working toward achieving greater democracy in Korea. One is based on the association some Koreans make between democracy and prosperity. When they compare the importance of these two objectives, roughly 50 percent of Koreans believe economic development is more important while only about 14 percent regard democratization as being more important. About one-third (35 percent) of Koreans considered the two as being equally important.[59] These data imply that a sizable number of Koreans could embrace another form of government if economic reforms fail, prompting a turbulent reaction from democracy advocates. The other challenge derives from the lingering influence of Confucian teachings on a culture that for so long accepted the dominant role of centralized government, an authoritarian hierarchy, and a patronage system.

Freedom of Speech

Freedom of speech is an absolute prerequisite for both democracy and a knowledge-era society. The ROK government bears heavy responsibility to protect free speech and discipline officials who seek to silence the news media or quell citizens' comments. The press as a government watchdog is a relatively new concept in Korea, where Confucian values can at times confuse patriotic critical commentary with subversion. Although some news organizations may have succumbed in recent years to real or perceived pressure by government officials, others demonstrated that they were committed to reporting events as they saw them and did so in a manner reasonably consistent with international standards of competence and ethics. Such organizations inevitably improve their credibility with members of the society and become a new authority for citizens seeking to cope with increasingly difficult issues. The Internet has also emerged as an alternative source of information for many citizens whose free speech in cyberspace also merited protection.

Korea as a Virtual State

ROK governments under Presidents Kim Young-sam and Kim Dae-jung took on some of the attributes of the virtual state described on page 121. They both worked to attract foreign investors—a significant departure from their predecessors and a key function of the virtual state although in the case of Korea thus far this has been done with central government authority and means. Throughout the 1990s, the ROK government implemented and sustained programs to establish a modern infrastructure, especially for telecommunications but also for air transport (the massive, new Inchon International Airport opened in March 2001). The government also significantly liberalized trade (compared with its predecessors) and other sectors to facilitate FDI. Success in implementing the four-sector reforms should help move Korea closer to becoming a decentralized virtual state and significantly increase its attractiveness to foreign investors.

Free-Enterprise Business Strategies

Progress in implementing the four-sector reforms in the late 1990s established a basis for business enterprises to focus on productivity and profits in both domestic markets and the increasingly competitive global economy. These reforms appear likely to endure, provided the government does not relapse to the Korea Inc. model or some variant of it. Korean *chaebol* and small and medium enterprises were slowly changing at the dawn of the twenty-first century because of concerted government reform efforts to transform Korea's managed economy into a free-enterprise market economy and to conform with the realities of an international marketplace that rewards only competitive firms.

The most significant business reforms were caused by the rapid increase of foreign investment, foreign members on corporate boards of directors, foreign owners and managers, and new management styles:

- By February 2001, total foreign portfolio investment and FDI amounted to $62 billion, of which $40 billion was FDI;
- The total market value of domestic stocks held by foreigners at the end of 2000 constituted 30.1 percent of total market capitalization, or W 56 trillion (foreigners eschewed the bond market; they owned less than 1 percent of the total value of outstanding bonds);
- Foreigners held controlling equity in the financial sector and were the principal owners of such banks as Korea First, KorAm, Korea Exchange, Hana, and Kookmin; foreigners also gained influence throughout the financial sector by increasing their equity holdings in a number of other financial institutions; and
- Foreigners acquired controlling ownership in a number of manufacturing companies, including 30 auto parts manufacturers (the U.S. company, Delphi Corporation, for example, acquired Daewoo Precision Industries; France's Renault bought Samsung Motors, while DaimlerChrysler acquired 15 percent equity of Hyundai Motors; Daewoo Motors was up for sale; Volvo, Philips, Asahi Glass also gained controlling interests in heavy industry and electronics manufacturing companies).

As a result, foreigners gained unprecedented influence in Korean corporate decisionmaking, which yielded a number of benefits. Foreign influence promoted financial sector and corporate sector restructuring; management transparency; and new personnel management methods, including performance-based compensation. Moreover, foreign influence helped reduce debt–equity ratios and lay the foundation for a significantly new business environment.[60]

Korean companies are increasingly likely to cooperate innovatively with one another over the coming decade. The V Society—V stands for both value and venture—was formed in September 2000 by top executives of venture company start-ups and affiliates within such *chaebol* as Hyundai, SK, Lotte, and Kolon. They concluded they could thrive in Korea's new economy if they cooperated with each other in ways previously unthinkable; the very notion of competitor cooperation was a major break from the past. During weekly meetings, members brief the group on the business strategies of their companies. While presenters might not reveal their firm's deepest secrets, the chairman of Kolon, Lee Woong-Yeul, commented, ". . . we're up-front most of the time. We're not afraid to criticize during the presentations, and we swap advice. This is important. Sooner or later the younger generation will take over the economy." Not only did the V Society emerge as an intellectual clearinghouse for an admittedly elite group; it also offered opportunities for members to form new business teams and to invest in promising venture company start-ups.[61]

Companies are now more likely to change their internal corporate cultures to empower workers and break down barriers to cooperation. For example, the Cheil Jedang corporation, one of Korea's top companies, in 2000 required employees at every level of authority to address each other by full name and the honorific suffix *Nim* in lieu of position titles. This was a momentous change given the South Korean custom developed over centuries of calling one other by position title within the family, workplace, and general society.[62] A worker previously would have addressed his company president, for example, President Sohn Kyung-shik, as Sohn Kyung-shik Sajang Nim (*sajang* means company president), under the new protocol the worker would call the president by his full name with the honorific: Sohn Kyung-shik Nim. One would no longer refer to Miss (or Mrs.) Kim Young-cha as Miss Kim but as Kim Young-cha Nim. Managers and supervisors also began to address their subordinates in this new respectful way.

Many Korean companies recognized the new Cheil Jedang protocol was worth emulating and planned to change their own procedures when they judge the time to be right.[63] That time is likely to come sooner than they expect. After they adjust internal communications patterns, companies could further empower their employees.

Thus, at the end of the twentieth century, Korean companies were beginning to reengineer themselves to compete in an open market economy. By 2010, assuming the reforms endure, companies can be expected to be more flexible and less hierarchical than they were in the past. Nonviable companies will likely have been liquidated or face increasing difficulty in staying afloat absent productive restructuring. Companies will survive on the strength of their products, productivity, and management. Industrial relations are also likely to be quite different because managers and workers will have to pool their respective talents and capitalize on all of their human resources to compete in the global economy and domestic market. Businesspeople with sound ideas are likely to find it easier to acquire credit on the merit of their ideas and demonstrated business expertise.

NGOs

A growing number of NGOs were organized in Korea in the late part of the twentieth century, especially after President Roh Tae-woo's declaration on June 29, 1987. By 2000, an estimated 12,000 to 20,000 NGOs existed in Korea, and since 1987, they have increasingly influenced decisionmaking in both the Kim Young-sam and Kim Dae-jung administrations. NGOs had become sufficiently important for the Kim Dae-jung administration to establish an office in the presidential Blue House for NGO matters.

Korean NGOs addressed a broad range of topics that included faith-based organizations (which can be both politically active organizations and caregivers) and association communities focused on member interests, human rights, consumer concerns, education, environmental protection, and political issues. Environmental protection groups in summer 2000 successfully influenced the government to redress an issue regarding the improper disposal of formaldehyde, which they argued endangered Seoul's drinking water. Four particularly well-known, politically oriented NGOs were the Citizen Coalition for Economic Justice, Korean Federation for Environmental Movement, People's Solidarity for Participatory Democracy, and Korean Women's Association Union.

A number of Korean NGOs reportedly rely on government funding for 60–70 percent of their budgets. While this might not be a significant issue for care-giving organizations, it could constrain politically active NGOs from challenging government policies and becoming a wholly independent new authority. Nevertheless, the emergence of NGOs is another indicator of Korea's transition to the knowledge era, as they provide a means to represent the concerns of their individual members to the established authorities.[64]

Religion: Christianity

Christianity emerged as one of the two major religions in Korea at the end of the twentieth century. Approximately half of all Koreans espoused faith in some religion. Roughly 48 percent of Korean believers subscribed to Buddhism while another 48 percent accepted Christianity, according to some sources. Other sources indicate Christianity actually supplanted Buddhism as the most accepted faith in Korea at the end of the twentieth century.[65] The acceptance of Christianity in Korea is a remarkable change considering Buddhism's centuries-long influence in Korea.

The rise of Christianity in Korea may seem to be a paradox because one of the features of the knowledge era is the decline of centralized religion, but about 75 percent of Korean Christians are Protestants and not particularly susceptible to the dictates of a centralized church. They have joined independent churches that for the most part establish their policies and practices consistent with their interpretation of the gospel and Christian doctrine.

Koreans became increasingly attracted to Christianity in the twentieth century because they were impressed by the bravery of Christians in resisting tyranny in Korea, dating from the late nineteenth century. In more recent times, Christians played an important role in antigovernment demonstrations to improve labor conditions and human rights before Roh Tae-woo's June 29 declaration that set a course for democratization in 1987. Although most Korean Christians are Protestants, the Roman Catholic cathedral in central Seoul's Myong-Dong district was an important rallying site for antigovernment demonstrators in the 1970s and 1980s. The government was reluctant to violate the cathedral grounds and offend the Vatican. Christianity gained greater legitimacy with Koreans after Roh's declaration.

Some observers suggest Koreans may associate Christianity with advanced industrial nations and believe that if Korea is to be such a nation, it must be a Christian nation as well. However, there appear to be several more substantive reasons why a rising number of Koreans converted to Christianity in the late twentieth century, a time of apparently increasing corruption and economic hardship, especially in the latter years. By accepting Jesus Christ as the perfect, incorruptible, and compassionate savior, Koreans may believe they can find refuge from what they consider to be an increasingly corrupt secular environment. They may hope to find spiritual salvation; the promise of a healthy, happy, prosperous, abundant life (*kibok*);[66] and empowerment.

Another reason for gregarious Koreans—the Irish of the Orient—to convert may have been to associate with like-minded people. There are approximately 40,000 Christian churches in Korea, usually identifiable at night by a red cross.[67] One is the single largest Christian church in the world—the Yeoido Full Gospel Church that Pastor Cho Yonggi founded in Seoul in the late 1950s. In 1958, he began holding services in a surplus small military tent with a congregation of about 50 believers. He subsequently empowered the women of the church to build it up, and by 1992 the congregation had swelled to 700,000 members, making it the largest in the world. The church is capable of accommodating 25,000 worshippers at each of the many services it conducts throughout the week.

The Christian churches in Korea are more than religious and social organization. They also serve as NGOs, which might attract more converts. For example, like many Korean Christians, the Reverend Lee Sang-min and his Suh-Moon Presbyterian Church in Taegu as late as 2000 continued to assist people who had been greatly affected by the 1997 financial crisis, including the old, those with physical disabilities, the unemployed, and the homeless. They provided free meals five days a week, attracting an average of 800 people daily for lunch. They also used their cars to transport people with disabilities and conducted medical missionary work to provide free medical care to their neighbors.[68]

Despite such good works, some Koreans are critical of Christianity, especially the Protestants who make up roughly three-fourths of Korean Christians. Some critics feel individual churches should do more to alleviate suffering. Others believe some church leaders take advantage of members through highly authoritarian or self-serving practices. Some also feel the Protestant churches generally are too exclusive or narrow-minded with respect to other religions or such customs as ancestor veneration (*jeasa*).

In sum, Christianity met the spiritual needs of many, if not most, Korean believers as their society experienced tumultuous change in the 1980s and 1990s.

Individual Authority

With each click of the computer mouse to make a commercial transaction, access some source of information, or transmit a message, Koreans increasingly realize their future is in their hands. Their demands for qualified political candidates; responsive government; responsible, transparent corporate management; and greater economic freedom reflect this growing realization. Koreans also increasingly acknowledge that every person can influence events with knowledge-era tools and concepts. Equally important, Korea's leaders are beginning to realize it as well.

In light of the April 2000 National Assembly election, political parties understood they should solicit and respect popular views in nominating candidates for public office. Government officials also increasingly recognized their accountability to voters in a country where citizens had rapidly improving access to information and the ability to influence the course of events through the Internet. Corporate leaders understood that their success depended on the willingness of their employees to contribute to the company, a fact that inspired some to adapt corporate cultures to break down communication barriers and empower workers.

Individual Koreans by 2010 are likely to accept that, as empowered workers, citizens, and family members who are responsible for their future and that of their families, they are the ultimate authority in Korea's knowledge era. This is especially likely for Korea's netizens in their 40s and younger.

Summary

Korea's rapid transition from an agrarian society through the industrial age to the brink of the knowledge era in the space of roughly one 30-year generation has placed unbearable demands on ancient traditions and authorities. The pace of change greatly accelerated in the 1990s with the coming of age of postwar Koreans, the advent of the knowledge era, increasing competitiveness of the global economy, and comprehensive failure of the Korea Inc. political–economic model in 1997. Faced with a declining economy; a rapidly changing family structure; and rising unemployment, crime, and corruption, some Koreans sadly concluded in 2000 that their country was collapsing. In a sense they were correct. Korea's traditional institutions and authorities could not equip Koreans to cope with their rapidly changing environment, and replacement authorities were not fully in place.

The above social changes combined with the 1997 financial crisis presented Koreans with what psychologists call a "significant emotional event" that proved sufficiently traumatic to prompt almost unimaginable changes. Koreans elected a new president who advocated free-market economics and democratic principles anchored in new social authorities.

Most Koreans approved, unaware of the implications for their daily lives and livelihood but desperately hoping that the four-sector reforms would provide a sound foundation for Korea to move toward its goal of becoming a prosperous, knowledge-era democracy. But the pain of restructuring became more evident in 2000. Reform lagged as the society struggled with traditional attitudes and authorities that refused to yield to the new. On January 1, 2001, President Kim Dae-jung reaffirmed his commitment to implement his basic four-sector reforms in 2001 and to let the invisible hand of a free-enterprise market guide continuing reform, but significant new progress seemed problematic in the near term.

At the end of the twentieth century, Koreans seemed to be generally united in the view that the costs of moving away from such discredited authorities as Korea Inc. would be great, but not as great as the failure to become a free-market democracy. Nevertheless, some Koreans were reluctant to yield power derived from traditional institutions. Koreans have often proved the truth of their *Ha myun dwen da!* proverb (If you try, you can do!). However, it will be difficult for them to adapt their social, political, and economic institutions to reach their potential quickly as a knowledge-era society. Korea's ability to quickly make the minimum changes necessary to remain competitive in the increasingly fast-paced global economy remained a question in early 2001.

The catalysts for change during the 2001–2010 decade are likely to come from two key groups, both of which want a prosperous democracy. One group will be the current younger generation—age 30 and under—who are most accustomed to knowledge-era tools, concepts, and opportunities. They will be the natural allies of the second group: progressive older Koreans with attitudes and values similar to those of the V Society who seek to create greater wealth in the new global economy and who also acknowledge the crucial need for free enterprise and a liberal, democratic, hands-off government.

Adherents to discredited traditions—those who seek a dominant role for the central government in managing the economy; suppress initiative, innovation, and empowerment; and promote government–business cronyism—will be squeezed from both ends, depending in part on developments in North Korea–South Korea relations. The presidential elections scheduled for 2002 and 2007 are likely to be referenda for continuing reforms to blend Korea's traditions with the new ways of democratic, free-market, knowledge-era societies.

Korea's movement toward a prosperous, knowledge-era democracy during the coming decade depends on a clear national vision that captures individual hopes, fears, and aspirations amidst the incessant pounding of the engines of change. At the beginning of 2001, Koreans wanted their country to be a respected, prosperous, knowledge-era democracy. Most were willing to accept new concepts and hardships to achieve this objective, but they needed to see progress to sustain hope. Korea's major challenge in achieving a truly national vision is to press on with the four-sector reforms. Success depends on adapting new authorities inherent in the reform concepts, neutralizing the impact of Koreans holding on to attitudes derived from discredited institutions, and educating individuals to assume their roles in facilitating the transition.

Moving toward 2010 will produce some alienation, as Koreans blend old and new authorities and refine their self-image. But Koreans can do what they set their minds to do.

Notes

1. Richard Sennett, *Authority* (New York: Knopf, 1980), 19.

2. "Rejection of Twilight Divorce," *Korea Times*, December 13, 1999, www.search.hankooki.com/search_kt.htm, accessed July 16, 2001; "Divorces in Korea," ROK National Statistical Office, October 2000, www.nso.go.kr, accessed December 17, 2000; and "Daily Divorce Rate," *Digital Chosun Ilbo*, November 29, 2000, www.chosunilbo.com, accessed February 5, 2001.

3. In South Korea such NGOs include charities that provide food and shelter for the unemployed and homeless who are affected by the economic situation.

4. Gary Hamel, "Strategy as Revolution," *Harvard Business Review* 74, no. 4 (1996): 69-71.

5. Wriston, *The Twilight of Sovereignty,* 127.

6. Moore, *The Death of Competition,* 272-273.

7. *Republic of Korea Civil Code,* Article 1009, revised January 13, 1990.

8. "Changes in Spouse Selection," Indiana University, East Asian Studies Center, Bloomington, Indiana, www.easc.indiana.edu/pages/easc/curriculum/korea/1995/general/hand14_6.htm, accessed July 14, 2001.

9. Hansoo Kim, "The Conscience and Living Behaviors of New Generation College Students," *Digital Chosun Ilbo*, May 15, 1994, www.chosunilbo.com, accessed February 20, 2001.

10. "Korean Women Favor Trial Marriages," *Korea Herald*, April 19, 2001, www.koreaherald.co.kr/, accessed April 20, 2001.

11. "Korean Birth Rate Plummets," *Digital Chosun Ilbo*, September 27, 2000, www.chosunilbo.com, accessed September 27, 2000; and "Divorces in Korea," ROK National Statistical Office.

12. "Rejection of Twilight Divorce," *Korea Times;* and "Divorces in Korea," Ibid.

13. Ibid.

14. "95 percent of Seoul Children Own Computers," *Digital Chosun Ilbo*, November 29, 2000, www.chosunilbo.com, accessed December 6, 2000; and "97 percent of Elementary Schoolers Have Experienced the Internet," *Digital Chosun Ilbo*, citing a survey by the Korea Network Information Center, January 10, 2001, www.chosunilbo.com, accessed January 17, 2001.

15. Joo-Hee Lee, "Survey Shows Teens Dissatisfied with Society," *Korea Herald*, October 11, 2000, www.koreaherald.co.kr/, accessed October 25, 2000.

16. Doh Chull Shin, "Monitoring the Dynamics of Democratization in Korea: The Korea Democracy Barometer Surveys," *International Journal of Korean Studies* 4, no. 1 (Fall/Winter 2000): 50–53.

17. Ibid.

18. Ibid., 56.

19. Jang-Hae Lee, "Paying Dividends," *Korea Trade and Investment*, January/February 2001, p. 14; Kim, *Three Years after the IMF Bailout*, 129–130.

20. Lee, Ibid.; Kim, Ibid., pp. 131–132.

21. Gerald P. O'Driscoll Jr., Kim R. Holmes, and Melanie Kirkpatrick, *2001 Index of Economic Freedom* (Washington, D.C.: Heritage Foundation, and *Wall Street Journal*, pp. 18, 22, 43–44, 231–232). The Heritage Foundation and the *Wall Street Journal* publish this annual index of economic freedom, which they define as "the absence of government coercion or constraint on the production, distribution, or consumption of goods and services beyond the extent necessary for citizens to protect and maintain liberty itself." In other words, economic freedom is the extent to which the government does not intervene in the economy and consume GDP. Authors of the index contend that economically free countries are more likely to have relatively high growth rates and standards of living than countries categorized as "mostly free," "mostly unfree," or "repressed." The 2001 index ranked Korea in the mostly free category for the sixth year in a row, placing it 29 among 155 economies worldwide and 9 among 32 Asia-Pacific economies, behind Hong Kong, Singapore, New Zealand, United States, Australia, Japan, Taiwan, and Thailand. North Korea placed last.

22. Kim Dae-jung, "A New Year Message from President Kim Dae-jung to the Nation," ref. no. 409 (Seoul: Korean Executive Mansion [Chong Wha Dae], January 1, 2001), www.cwd.go.kr/cgi-bin/php/englib/view.php3?f_offset=0&f_item_num=1002&f_row_num=1, accessed July 14, 2001.

23. Hyundai Electronics, Hyundai Engineering and Construction, Hyundai Merchant Marine, and Korea Industrial Development.

24. Young-shin Yoon, "FSS Selects Companies for Bond Support," *Digital Chosun Ilbo*, January 4, 2001, www.chosunilbo.com, accessed January 18,

2001; Jun Lee, "Major Companies to Get Major Rollover Through KDB," *Digital Chosun Ilbo*, January 7, 2001, www.chosunilbo.com, accessed February 20, 2001; In-sang Kim, "Creditor Banks Protest Bond Refinancing Levels," *Digital Chosun Ilbo,* January 17, 2001, www.chosunilbo.com, accessed January 18, 2001; Ihlwan Moon, "So Long, Corporate Reform—Ssangyong's bailout shows how Seoul has lost its nerve," *Business Week*, January 22, 2001, 52–53; Jun Lee, "MOFE Introducing Measures to Ensure Soft Landing," *Digital Chosun Ilbo*, February 16, 2001, www.chosunilbo.com, accessed February 20, 2001.

25. "Another Cover Up," *Digital Chosun Ilbo* (editorial), September 7, 2000, www.chosunilbo.com, accessed September 14, 2000.

26. Yeong-lim Hong, "People Lack Faith in Prosecution," *Digital Chosun Ilbo*, November 19, 2000, www.chosunilbo.com, accessed November 20, 2000.

27. "Judgements are Unfair" (survey), *Hankyoreh 21,* no. 326, September 20, 2000, www.hani.co.kr, accessed December 23, 2000.

28. Shin and Rose, "1999 New Korea Barometer Survey," question 46/ 4-5, pp. 24–25.

29. The National Assembly has 273 seats; 227 are directly elected and 46 (proportional) are appointed according to party size; www.assembly.go.kr/ english/introduction/organization/index.html.

30. "Local Autonomy," *Digital Chosun Ilbo*, December 10 and December 15, 2000, www.chosunilbo.com, accessed December 29, 2000; and Kyosik Choi, *Digital Chosun Ilbo*, December 15, 2000, www.chosunilbo.com, accessed December 16, 2000.

31. "Joint agreement of media organizations of north and south issued," August 11, 2000; Korean Central News Agency of DPRK, August 12, 2000, www.kcna.co.jp/calendar/frame.htm, accessed August 28, 2000.

32. Family visits between northerners and southerners were a symbol of the new contacts between the North and the South.

33. "Bad Precedent," *Korea Times*, December 24, 2000, www.koreatimes. co.kr, accessed December 27, 2000; "A New Controversy on Red Cross Aide," *JoongAng Ilbo*, November 30, 2000, http://english.joins.com, accessed December 26, 2000; Jeong-ho Yoon, "Red Cross Chair Resigns Over Controversial Statements," *Digital Chosun Ilbo*, December 24, 2000, www. chosunilbo.com, accessed December 27, 2000; In-goo Kim "Red Cross Head Under Fire Again for Remarks on NK," *Digital Chosun Ilbo*, November 12, 2000, www.chosunilbo.com, accessed December 26, 2000; Shim Jae Hoon, "The Moral Cost of Engagement," *Far Eastern Economic Review*, December 28, 2000–January 4, 2001, p. 28; Ji-ho Kim, "North Protests Red Cross Chief's Remarks," *Korea Herald*, November 4, 2000, www.koreaherald.co.kr, accessed

December 27, 2000; and "A New Controversy On Red Cross Aide," *JoongAng Ilbo*, November 30, 2000, english.joins.com, accessed December 26, 2000.

34. "Anti-Sites in Internet Are on Increase," *HanKook Ilbo*, August 12, 2000, www.hankooki.com, accessed December 14, 2000 (in Korean).

35. Minkoo Kim, "Anti-DJ Site, Investigation Due to Lewdness or Insolence," *Weekly Chosun*, no. 1634, December 28, 2000, http://weekly.chosun.com, accessed December 29, 2000.

36. Won Kyu Choi, "The Supreme Court's Decision," *Digital Chosun Ilbo*, January 26, 2001, www.chosun.co.kr, accessed January 26, 2001.

37. For additional information, see the People's Coalition for Media Reform, www.pcmr.or.kr, accessed July 24, 2001.

38. "FTC Hits Media Companies with W 4.42 billion in Fines," *Digital Chosun*, www.chosun.com/w21data/html/news/200106200106210066.html, accessed June 26, 2001

39. David I. Steinberg, "The Korean Press and Orthodoxy," *Digital Chosun*, July 17, 2001, http://www.chosun.com/w21data/html/news/200107/200107170170.html, accessed July 23, 2001.

40. *OECD Economic Surveys, 1999–2000: Korea,* 255.

41. Ibid.

42. Ibid.

43. Hong-jun Kang, "One in 3 Students a Dropout, Fearful about Finding a Job," *JoongAng Ilbo*, December 4, 2000, http://english.joins.com, accessed December 6, 2000.

44. In 1995, approximately 50 percent of all South Koreans accepted some sort of religion (Buddhism, Ch'ondogyo, Islam, Christianity, or others). In this book this group is called "believers."

45. *Facts about Korea* (Seoul: Korea Information Service, 2000), 156.

46. Kiryun Kim, "Survey on Religious Inclinations of 100 People," Buddhist Newspaper no. 1759, March 21, 2000, www.buddhistnews.net, accessed January 22, 2001

47. Noland, *Avoiding the Apocalypse,* 205.

48. Shin and Rose, "1999 New Korea Barometer Survey," question 38b, p. 20.

49. Sunja Kim, "Internet Survey—Are You Happy Living as a Korean?" *Monthly Chosun*, November 2000, http:// monthly.chosun.com/, accessed November 15, 2000. The question asked, "Are you happy to live as a Korean in Korea, which is the 12th largest exporting nation, 8th largest automotive producer, 2nd largest shipbuilder, and ranked 2nd for death by automotive accident, fever for entering college, and 1st for death rate from liver cancer?"

50. "2001 Corruption Perceptions Index," Transparency International, www.transparency.org/documents/cpi/2001/cpi2001.html, accessed June 28,

2001. Transparency International publishes an annual Corruption Perception Index after it surveys the perceptions of businesspeople, risk analysts, and the general public.

51. "Bribe Payers Index," Transparency International, 1999, www.transparency.de/documents/cpi/bps.html, accessed December 16, 2000.

52. Eu-dal Song, "Expat Firms Complain of Solicitation from Officials," *Digital Chosun Ilbo*, January 15, 2001, www.chosunilbo.com, accessed January 15, 2001.

53. "Increasing Flow of Immigration of the Professionals in Korea," *Weekly Chosun*, October 31, 2000, http://weekly.chosun.com, accessed November 20, 2000.

54. "Emigration," *Digital Chosun Ilbo*, January 8, 2001, www.chosunilbo.com, accessed January 10, 2001; "South Korea: Leaving Home," *The Economist*, March 31, 2001, p. 40.

55. Seok-bae An, "Statistics Show Increase in Crime Rate," *Digital Chosun Ilbo*, November 26, 2000, www.chosunilbo.com/, accessed December 1, 2000; Chul Ok, "Five Major Crimes such as Murder and Robbery Have Increased 11.8 Percent this Year," *Digital Chosun Ilbo*, November 19, 1999, www.chosunilbo.com/w21data/htm/html/news/199911/199911190072.html, accessed December 19, 2000.

56. Soobyum Lee and Sangwon Choi, "Netizens' Backlash on the Strengthening of Control over Harmful Sites," *Hankyoreh*, February 8, 2001; Kim, "Anti-DJ Site, Investigation Due to Lewdness or Insolence."

57. Shin and Rose, "1999 New Korea Barometer Survey," 23–28.

58. Kim Dae-jung, "A New Year Message."

59. Shin, "Monitoring the Dynamics of Democratization in Korea."

60. Sang-il Park, "Impact of Foreign Capital Advancement on Domestic Corporate Management," *Korea Economic Trends* 5, no. 4 (Seoul: Samsung Economic Research Institute, February 3, 2001), 13–20.

61. John Larkin, "Turning Over a New Leaf," *Far Eastern Economic Review*, December 21, 2000, pp. 66–67.

62. "Destroying the Name That Calls Each Other," *Hankyoreh 21,* April 31, 2000, www.hani.co.kr, accessed December 26, 2000.

63. Ibid.

64. This discussion is based on Ji-young Kim, "Non-Government Organizations in Korea," *The Weekly Hankook*, October 31, 2000, www.hankooki.com/whan/200010/w200010311225800615/284.htm, accessed December 5, 2000; and Wontae Sul "NGO's Criticized by Civilians," *Newsmaker*, no. 407, January 18, 2001, http://newsmaker.khan.co.kr/society/n407c06.htm, accessed January 18, 2001.

65. *Facts About Korea*, 2nd ed. (Seoul: Korean Information Service, 1999), 156; Frank M. Tedesco, "Questions for Buddhist and Christian Cooperation in Korea," International Association for Religious Freedom, May 5, 1999, www.geocities.com/~iarf/tedesco1.html, accessed February 16, 2001.

66. "Kibok Belief of Protestant Churches," trans. Jung Kyunghwan, *Hankyoreh 21,* no. 342, January 9, 2001, www.hani.co.kr, accessed March 19, 2001.

67. The red cross on Korean Christian churches commemorates two legendary events. One is the bravery of a Canadian missionary named MacKenzie in the late nineteenth century. Rebels bent on destroying all traces of Western influence in Korea approached MacKenzie's church in Ichon near Seoul. MacKenzie courageously met them in front of his church with a disassembled pistol on a table before him while the red Cross of St. George flew over the church. The rebels were so impressed with his faith and courage that they spared him and the church, taking note of the flag. The other legend recounts the security Korean dissidents found in homes displaying a red cross after the Samil Movement in 1919. Colonial authorities reportedly would not enter homes bearing the red cross at the entrance, making them safe houses.

68. Won-soo Park, "Reverend Lee Sang-Min Says, 'The Role of Religion Is to Help our Unfortunate Neighbors'," *Digital Chosun Ilbo*, November 16, 2000, www.chosunilbo.com, accessed December 22, 2000.

6 ■
Trend Six: A Test of Human Psychology

IT IS CLEAR that the advent of the knowledge era, with its associated social and economic transformations, will put individuals under immense strain. Coping with change is never easy; coping with the compressed, comprehensive changes under way today could turn out to be one of the hardest tests ever posed for the human race. The nature of that test will determine its social and personal implications for human psychology and, in turn, the requirements for meeting it successfully.

Anxiety and the Psychological Challenge

"We have reached a moment in history," argues self-esteem guru Nathaniel Branden, "when self-esteem, which has always been a supremely important psychological need, has become an urgent economic need." The new global economy is "characterized by rapid change, accelerating scientific and technological breakthroughs, and an unprecedented level of competitiveness." While everyone in the business world understands that this fact magnifies the importance of education, Branden writes that what is not so well understood is that the new pressures "also create new demands on our psychological resources," requiring "a greater capacity for innovation, self-management, personal responsibility, and self-direction."[1] This will be a challenge for those Koreans accustomed to being directed in their daily affairs in rigid, hierarchical organizations.

As citizens of the knowledge era, we are expected to understand our own careers and life choices well enough to choose intelligently.

We are expected to master dozens of kinds of advanced technology, from computers to automobiles to videotape recorders. We have to manage a lifelong process of education in support of our careers (or interests), of the substance of this education as well as its finance. We must pay our bills, complete complicated tax forms, and manage a portfolio of insurance, retirement savings, and other investments. We must provide for our health care, wending our way through a maze of complicated insurance options and care restrictions and regulations.

The result is anxiety: our fast-moving technological society is depriving people of unifying stories and epic myths, whether religious, ideological, or other.

Our growing knowledge undermines old belief systems and authorities while our ever-expanding freedom provides us with an almost unlimited set of lifestyle, career, moral, and hobby options. Without a clear foundation of values or ideologies to guide us, this array of choices is almost paralyzing. Without a firm sense of purpose, what career can we choose that will satisfy our desire for identity and meaning? Without a firm moral compass, how can we place lifestyle alternatives, such as drug use or respect for the environment, in the proper context? How can one cope with a rising sense of anomie?

Individual human beings—cut off from the social and natural "objects" that surround them, shorn of their faith but possessing a mantle of freedom—confront a multitude of complex, fragmented roles and choices. "This," Rollo May observes, "is why anxiety is so profoundly connected with the problem of freedom. If the individual did not have some freedom, no matter how minute, to fulfill some new potentiality, he would not experience anxiety. The existentialist philosopher Søren Kierkegaard described anxiety as 'the dizziness of freedom'."[2] In the kind of world typified by trend two, where freedom of all kinds, political as well as economic, is on the rise, this dizziness seems certain to evolve into mass vertigo.

The solution to this problem is as straightforward as it is difficult: the exercise of will through self-empowerment. The knowledge era may ease such an agenda by enhancing the level of meaning and self-control available in the lives of individuals—in short, by empowering people.

A Habit of Alienation

On the road to transcendence and empowerment, a second major psychological challenge of the knowledge era emerges, a natural complement to anxiety: alienation.

Perhaps the dominant psychological reaction to the transition to a knowledge era is a growing sense of alienation in both the industrial and developing countries. Stripped of familiar moral, social, and political landmarks, caught up in the swift current of the knowledge era (or left stumbling in its wake), people in both the industrial and developing worlds are experiencing new kinds and intensities of personal and group alienation. For one thing, the death of ideologies has put an end to many of the unifying themes used to combat estrangement. Many observers have commented on the decline of the sacred, of national and religious myths, even of the socialist ideal as ideas that stand against the void. For example, today's discrediting of the Korea Inc. model and problems of strict adherence to Confucian values raise important questions among Koreans regarding the moral, social, and political values that helped them industrialize their country but are now inadequate for success in the knowledge era.

An equally powerful cause of alienation has to do with the challenge of coping with a knowledge-rich age: information overload. People can feel helpless in the midst of a bewildering array of information. A specific result is to imbue the knowledge era with an unprecedented degree of social complexity—a third route to alienation. Social issues, their characteristics as well as causes and cures, seem more complicated than ever before. This complexity is exacerbated by the frightening speed and degree of change in the knowledge era and by the pervasiveness of abstract realities. Abstraction may well be the governing principle of a knowledge era: knowledge, which represents ideas rather than things, is inherently abstract, and an era in which society and economy revolve around knowledge and information is bound to become ever more abstract—a process accelerated by rising pluralism, fragmentation, relativism, and the crisis of authority.

A global media age also alienates people from what is perhaps the most important measure of psychological stability and personal grounding: a firm sense of place, physical as well as social. Joshua Meyrowitz discussed this phenomenon in his insightful book *No Sense of Place*. "At one time," he wrote, "physical presence was a prerequisite for first-hand experience. To see and hear a president speak in his office, for example, you had to be with him in his office." This, of course, is no longer the case. "The evolution of media has decreased the significance of physical presence in the experience of people and events."[3] Our ability to locate ourselves in the world may be weakened by electronic media's constant assault on our sense of personal and social place.

The forces of alienation in our age are undoubtedly manifold, but the knowledge era is double-edged. It presents not merely the risk of alienation at least as profound as that of the industrial era, but also an unprecedented prospect for escape from alienation. The knowledge era seems likely to impel the further spread of economic and political freedom throughout the world, providing individuals with stunning educational and entertainment options. In the final analysis, through its effect on the workplace and other social institutions, the knowledge era can and should be about the empowerment of individual human beings. In the process, human alienation—from nature, from society, from self—would give way to new levels of connectedness and satisfaction.

The Pessimism Syndrome

A particular danger emerges in our age because of the naturally pessimistic bias of a prevalent and important media. It is well known that to promote sales the media have a broad tendency to report negative or pessimistic stories for their shock value. At the same time, in the knowledge era the relative balance between knowledge that we acquire through personal knowledge or contact and the knowledge that we obtain through external accounts is thrown off balance. Our personal observations seem to count for little against the vast wave of information sweeping over us each day in a dozen forms, swamping our perceptions and washing away the familiar landmarks of our experience.

Debate, the essence of democracy, can also increase a sense of pessimism among the people, especially if the economy is weak. As elections approach, it is only natural that candidates criticize the incumbent government, political party, and specific officials for various faults to build support for their campaigns. It is equally natural that in reporting these issues, the news media exaggerate their importance, if only because offsetting positive news may not be particularly newsworthy. The net result can be to discourage citizens who are attentive to political developments and make them pessimistic about their futures under current leadership. The more citizens believe they can influence domestic politics, however, the less alienated and apathetic they feel. If citizens feel they lack influence, alienation is more likely.

Together these phenomena produce the pessimism syndrome: the pervasive tendency to think things are getting precipitously worse when they are not.

People have always sought to understand the world around them. The primary source of understanding in an information age is the news media—print, broadcast, or online. The pessimistic tone of many news reports can lead people who pay attention exclusively to the press to believe that the world is going under.

"Television is now, indisputably, the primary source of news for most Americans," argues David Shaw in the *Los Angeles Times*. "[Television] may also be the primary source of the cynicism that increasingly pervades the news media and society at large." Shaw continues with a neat summary of the present hypothesis:

> Just as studies have shown that viewers who see crime-dominated local TV news shows are likely to think that crime is much more prevalent than it really is, so viewers who watch national news shows, magazine shows and the weekend political talk shows are likely to think that the world in general, and politicians in particular, are much worse than they really are.[4]

Confronted with an unrelenting tide of pessimism, it is no wonder that Americans, as well as the citizens of many other industrialized nations including Korea,[5] are depressed about both the state of their societies and their future prospects, even as they see little evidence of catastrophe around them. The message delivered to most Americans is that things are bad and the future holds enormous peril. Robert Samuelson phrases it this way: "When surveyed, about four-fifths of us say we are satisfied with our own lives. But when asked about the country—whether it's 'moving in the right direction'—Americans are routinely glum." This perceptual gap "has been true for at least two decades. Somehow, a society that satisfies most of us most of the time has also convinced many of us that it's rolling inexorably toward the edge of a cliff."[6]

Partly, then, this phenomenon involves a divergence in confidence about the present and the future, a creeping suspicion that even if things look fine for the moment, they will soon turn for the worse. But it also implies a fear that general social trends, and in particular the economic situation, are running in negative directions, even when evidence from people's own lives suggests otherwise. The prevalence of the pessimism syndrome calls into question our certainty in making the transition to a new era of human affairs and contributes to personal stress and depression.

The syndrome could have broader social effects as well. It could stifle entrepreneurship and progress and undermine faith in the ability of social institutions to address problems. It could feed anxieties about the future that could undermine future proposals for free trade. And ultimately, it could drive people of all countries, the United States and Korea included, into the arms of politicians promising solutions to problems that do not really exist—or at least not to the degree people think. Alternatively, it could prompt people, Koreans included, to support old-authority politicians who provide yesterday's invalidated solutions to current and anticipated problems.

Human Psychology in Korea:
An Ancient Culture under Stress

The psychological stresses that Korea confronts today are obvious enough. Globalization and "convergence with the world"—including the weakening of Korea's Confucian authorities and five major social institutions—seem to threaten individual needs for emotional security. The pace of change in Korea is probably faster than in many other countries: witness its rapid transition to an industrialized nation since 1961 and its urgency to become a prosperous, knowledge-era democracy. The sort of issues presented by trend five—issues that erode the foundation of Koreans' sense of identity and security—will be a particularly intense challenge over the 2001–2010 decade.

At the same time, the knowledge era is a time of opportunity as well as challenge. Over the next decade Korea can become a country enjoying notably greater prosperity, dignity and achievement, provided its people and institutions effectively manage change.

In the past, Korea adapted modern concepts—technologies, management, economics, and governance—to its traditional values as a means of meeting national psychic needs. Korea's current effort to implement the four-sector structural reforms has great potential to establish an accountable, open, free-market, democratic system, which will in turn create a more robust society and economy characterized by empowered citizens willing to assume responsibility for the country's future and better able to achieve their knowledge-era goals. But the transition remains fraught with danger: forfeiting one's illusions about traditional authorities is a traumatic prospect. If the knowledge era is an age of the empowered individual, the cultures and political systems that have traditionally suppressed individualism will confront an exceptionally difficult social and psychological transition.

Alienation: Sources and Evidence

In theory, Koreans confront the same daunting lineup of trauma and alienation as the citizens of any other nation in our transitional age. The shocks of modernization, liberalization, and other forms of change pulled by the engines of history are rocking the country as it races through the industrial era toward the knowledge era. The simultaneous process of globalization and pluralism exaggerates the impact of modernization and undermines such core elements of human identity as place and community. These changes are accelerating and becoming more far-reaching with each decade.

Perhaps most important is the assault on authority structures and value systems. The transition to the knowledge era is shaking the foundations of Korea's traditional authorities in all of its major social institutions. The decline of family stability, collapse of lifelong employment, and increase in underemployment and unemployment with their implications for self-worth are some indicators of how the transition to the knowledge era is weakening traditional authorities and increasing anxiety among Koreans. In the precarious social order that results, alienation can become commonplace.

Poor people often can be content with their circumstances if they perceive themselves to be living as well as can be expected. The same people can become dangerously dissatisfied, however, if they perceive others similar to themselves living noticeably better, or if their own quality of life drops precipitously. Their perception of relative deprivation is tied to their expectations.

The government of Park Chung-hee in the 1960s skillfully raised expectations and national pride through industrialization policies that catapulted South Korea into the ranks of the industrialized world within a 30-year generation. In this blink of history's eye, per capita income rose from less than $100 in 1962 to more than $10,000 by 1996 and was combined with Korea's typically low unemployment rate. This transformation gave rise to *Han-Tang Ju-yee,* a concept carefully nurtured if not developed by Park Chung-hee and his successors.

Han-Tang Ju-yee. Simply put, *Han-Tang Ju-yee* means becoming extraordinarily wealthy overnight, "getting a fortune through one shot without any effort,"[7] although *Han-Tang Ju-yee* also recognizes and values hard work. During Korea's industrialization, however, many people did become extraordinarily wealthy through almost no effort, validating speculative schemes as a means to get rich quick. Some of those who participated in the military coups of 1961 and 1979–1980 gained great wealth rapidly, setting a bad example for the society. Farmers and others who owned land in areas targeted for development—areas in and around Seoul, for example—also became incredibly wealthy through little effort. Another group that benefited immensely were housewives (*bok-buin*) who collaborated with friends to speculate in real estate and other hot investments and earned vast sums.

People in the business world, taking advantage of the crony capitalism spawned and nurtured by the Korea Inc. model, also appeared to achieve sudden wealth with relatively little work. In a society that rests on personal relationships, temptation to engage in corrupt behavior is especially difficult to resist. *Han-Tang Ju-yee* did not find expression only in the business world.[8] But if such expectations of businesspeople and others existed in the past, they certainly were challenged by 2001 as Korean firms and other organizations increasingly focused on employee performance rather than background.

Koreans overall experienced fantastic improvements in their quality of life from the 1960s through 1997. Many, but not all, achieved their financial goals largely as their leaders had promised. However, industrialization strongly affected key Korean institutions, especially marriage and the family. Korean workers also became disturbed in the aftermath of the 1997 financial crisis as many companies laid off workers with unprecedented government support while corporate owners and managers appeared to live quite well. This pattern violated workers' fundamental sense of fair play and weakened trust in established authorities. It also increased anxiety and alienation.

Thus, while *Han-Tang Ju-yee* raised expectations, many were unrealistic. Koreans who could not achieve their goals were at greater risk to experience the negative emotions of disappointment, stress, anger, and depression. Koreans felt that all was not well in the 1990s as cracks emerged in the foundation of their traditional authorities and mental illness in Korea became more apparent.

Stress indicators. The stresses of modernization began to take an obvious toll in the 1980s as increasing numbers of Koreans underwent psychiatric treatment. The number of beds set aside for inpatient psychiatric care, medical expenditures for psychiatric care, the incidence of depression in the society, and the suicide rate provide insight into the magnitude of these stresses.

The number of beds dedicated for psychiatric care rose significantly from 1984 through 1997 (figure 38), reflecting a significant increase in new requirements or awareness of a need for treatment. In 1984, just under 15,000 beds met the psychiatric care needs of Korea's 40.4 million people. In 1997 the number of psychiatric beds tripled to 45,000 although the total population increased less than 14 percent, to 45.9 million.[9] These data, of course, could understate Korea's mental care needs because they exclude Koreans

Figure 38
Psychiatric Beds, South Korea, 1984–1997

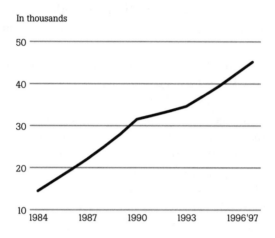

In thousands

Source: ROK Ministry of Health and Welfare, www.mohw.go.kr.

who were treated as outpatients or who did not seek professional care for their mental health problems.

Expenditures for psychiatric care increased more than 83 percent from 1992 to 1995 alone, rising from almost W 52 billion in 1992 to over W 95 billion in 1995, just three years later. The percentage of medical costs spent on psychiatric care increased from 17 percent in 1992 to 21 percent in 1995.[10]

Choi Meng-chae and Nam Chung-jah of the Korean Social Health Institute in their 1997 study of 5,417 Koreans aged 15–69 reported that 14 percent of Korean youth up to the age of 22 were depressed enough to require treatment; and within this youthful group almost one person in four (23 percent) admitted to considering suicide during the previous 12 months. By contrast, 4.5 percent of the total population, roughly 1 person in 20, had considered suicide during the same 12-month period.[11] Some of this depression may have been linked to the stress of university tests, but the impact of industrialization and institutional change were likely factors as well.

Koreans who were particularly susceptible to depression included those who were unmarried due to the death of a spouse, divorce, or separation. They were 2.9 times more likely than married people to experience depression. The rising divorce rate in the 1990s surely exacerbated this problem. Koreans with only a secondary school education were 2.5 times more likely to become depressed than better-educated Koreans. Females were 1.5 times more likely to suffer from depression than males.[12]

Note that the mental health problems outlined above occurred during a period of rising prosperity, a common occurrence in all countries. Per capita income rose from about $1,500 in 1980 to over $10,500 in 1996, when Korea was accepted into the OECD. Unemployment stayed relatively low by international standards while the government kept inflation under control. However, the increase in mental illness indicates the stresses of the industrial age were taking their toll. Available data about mental illness in South Korea possibly understate the problem owing to a shame some Koreans feel when they discuss the topic.

The financial crisis in 1997 ushered in a period of economic decline and social turmoil based in part on significant expansion in the unemployment rate and decreased income. Per capita income dropped from $10,307 in 1997 to $6,723 in 1998. It increased slightly, to $8,551, in 1999 and to $9,628 in 2000 but still remained less than 1997 and income disparity worsened (see page 86).[13] Unemployment shot up to a high of 8 percent in the spring of 1998 and averaged 6.8 percent for the year, declining to 6.3 percent in 1999. It dropped to a low of 3.4 percent in October 2000; it then increased because of the second round of financial-sector restructuring in the fourth quarter, and it averaged 4.1 percent for 2000.[14] Unemployment was projected to increase in 2001 because of reemphasized financial reforms and corporate restructuring.

Employment stresses combined with the inadequacy of such established authorities as Korea Inc., the 1997 financial crisis, and the implementation of the four-sector reforms after 1998 also contributed to the need for increased mental health care. Between 1997 and 1998 the number of beds dedicated to psychiatric care increased more than 24 percent, according to the ROK National Statistics Office.

Suicide. A person who feels valued by at least one other significantly important person generally possesses sufficient hope to endure the challenges of daily living. By 1999, however, suicide was the second leading cause of death for teenage boys and men in their 30s in Korea. It was the eighth leading cause of death for women. The suicide rate for Korean men increased 72 percent from 1990 to 1999. Between 1990 and 1997, male suicides increased almost 35 percent, from 13.2 to 17.8 deaths per 100,000 population; and they then increased 27.5 percent, to 22.7 suicides per 100,000 population, in 1999. From 1990 to 1997, Korean female suicides increased 63 percent, from 4.9 to 8 deaths per 100,000.[15] The World Health Organization estimates that in 2000, the global average mortality rate for suicide was 16 per 100,000.[16] The increase in Korea's suicide rate is worrisome when compared with several other countries whose suicide rates are decreasing (figure 39).

Korea's increased suicide rate indicates that Korea's mental health problems and feelings of alienation and isolation—leading causes of suicide—persist into the twenty-first century. This alienation has led to the growth of Korean-language Internet sites dedicated to suicide and other antisocial activities such as building bombs.

A pair of unrelated teenage suicides in early 2001 galvanized the government. Prime Minister Lee Han-dong in February directed the Ministry of Justice, the Prosecution Office, and National Police Agency to investigate Internet site operators who were providing information on how to commit suicide and murder through making bombs. He also told the Ministry of Education and the Ministry of Culture and Tourism to develop educational programs that would provide teenagers with "correct views on life and death."[17]

Political alienation. The knowledge era is one of empowerment. The government best suited to empowered people is democracy, a system in which citizens can express their views and influence the government to do their will.

Most Koreans at the end of the twentieth century wanted to improve their democracy; however, a significant majority (69 percent) believed the government paid little or no attention to their interests or opinions when it made "important decisions." Fewer than 25 percent of Koreans trusted their representatives in the Na-

Figure 39
Comparison of Suicide Rates in Selected Countries, 1990 and 1995–1998

Note: Totals are calculated by an annual standardized rate per 100,000 persons according to the world population standard of the WHO.

Country	Year	M	F	Total	Year	M	F	Total	Total Increase
South Korea	'90	13.3	4.9	7.4	'97	17.8	8.0	13.0	5.6
Japan	'90	20.4	12.4	16.3	'97	26.0	11.9	18.8	2.5
New Zealand	'90	21.7	5.4	12.4	'96	24.1	6.1	14.9	2.5
Spain	'90	11.2	4.1	7.5	'96	12.8	4.3	8.5	1.0
Italy	'90	11.4	4.1	7.6	'96	12.4	4.2	8.2	0.6
Netherlands	'90	12.3	7.2	9.7	'97	13.5	6.7	10.1	0.4
Australia	'90	20.7	5.2	12.9	'96	21.3	4.9	13.0	0.1
Greece	'90	5.5	1.5	3.6	'97	6.2	1.0	3.6	0.0
Canada	'90	20.6	5.2	12.7	'97	19.6	5.1	12.3	-0.4
France	'90	29.6	11.1	20.0	'97	28.4	10.1	19.0	-1.0
United Kingdom	'90	12.6	3.8	8.1	'97	11.0	3.2	7.1	-1.0
United States	'90	20.4	4.8	12.4	'97	18.7	4.4	11.4	-1.0
Norway	'90	23.3	8.0	15.5	'95	19.1	6.2	12.6	-2.9
Sweden	'90	24.1	10.4	17.2	'96	20.0	8.5	14.2	-3.0
Germany	'90	24.9	10.7	17.8	'98	21.5	7.3	14.2	-3.6
Finland	'90	49.3	12.4	30.3	'96	38.7	10.7	24.3	-6.0

Source: Mental Health & Brain Disorders: Suicide Rates & Absolute Numbers of Suicide by Country (Geneva: World Health Organization, 2000), www.who.int/mental_health/Topic_Suicide/suicide1.html, accessed February 22, 2001.

tional Assembly, political party leaders, and officials. Most people resented the exclusionary practices of the political parties when they select candidates for public office, and more than 70 percent wanted the parties to open up the process of nominating candidates for public office.[18] Koreans understood that democratic governments were supposed to be "of the people" and wanted to be involved.

Public sentiment to influence the 16th general election for National Assembly candidates in 2000 produced a grassroots movement to defeat candidates considered unfit for office. Members of the movement spread their message through the Internet to mobilize support. However, the Supreme Court, in a controversial decision in January 2001, stated that the public's exercise of free speech in the grassroots movement violated a South Korean law that prohibits negative campaigning. Some Koreans promptly rejected the decision on principle.

If Koreans cannot exercise free speech to influence the government to do their will, what will the outcome be? Will they increasingly insist on a responsive government—risking a government backlash—or will they feel increasingly alienated and apathetic? Global trends predict alienation and apathy. Apathy is the antithesis of empowerment; the implications are not encouraging for Korea's development into a full-fledged knowledge-era society.

Media audits. The 2001 NTS tax audits of 23 news media companies in Seoul and the accompanying KFTC antitrust investigations had the potential to polarize the body politic and contribute to political alienation. Koreans, with an impressive 98 percent literacy rate,[19] greatly depend on the news media to stay informed. In 1999, almost one-third of Koreans read a newspaper daily, and 52 percent read one five days a week. The majority paid "some" or "a lot" of attention to politics. Eight out of ten Koreans watched television seven days a week, and nine out of ten watched five days a week. Radio was not a primary source of news, as 46 percent did not listen at all and only 21 percent listened daily.[20]

In December 2000, 89 percent of Koreans polled believed the trustworthiness of newspaper reporting was "average" or "above average," with about 40 percent of the respondents believing it was "accurate" or "very accurate." Only about 15 percent were skeptical of newspaper coverage.[21] The question at hand for South Koreans was the extent to which the audits of media companies would restrict their ability to perform a vital role in a democracy: ensure freedom of information and transparency on issues concerning the public interest.

The government described the investigations of the media as essential (see page 142) and firmly rejected suggestions that the investigations were designed to suppress free speech, insisting they were designed only to "ascertain fairness and due payment of taxes."[22] President Kim Dae-jung addressed this latter point in early July after the government imposed historically high tax penalties and announced plans to indict some news media executives on criminal charges. The president commented that "justice has been fully served" and expressed hope that the investigations would serve as "a turning point for the transparent and sound development of the Korean media."[23]

However, comments by some senior officials inadvertently sparked questions regarding the government's stated motives of assuring compliance with tax and antitrust laws. A senior ruling party official reportedly asserted that freedom of speech is less important than paying taxes.[24] Also, in February 2001, as the investigations were beginning, a government minister raised eyebrows when he reportedly said:

> The time is ripe for the government to be ready for declaring war on the press . . . . When it comes to tax investigations, there should not be any sanctuary. The press is no exception. And we need a policeman who has the stomach to stand against the press . . . . Isn't the press more scary than the president? Only the press has no natural enemy until now.[25]

The minister quite possibly never intended to imply a threat against the freedom of news media organizations to report and comment on developments as they perceive them and was possibly commenting only on the suspected business practices of news media companies, as the prime minister had explained at the beginning of the audits and the president emphasized at the end. Nevertheless, such remarks, combined with the timing of the two investigations and the extent of the penalties, prompted concerns that the audits were politically inspired.

Free speech advocates and political opponents of the Kim Dae-jung administration decried the investigations as an assault on free speech and freedom of the press and claimed auditors used "different interpretations of the law" in conducting the investigations and assessing back taxes and fines.[26] Some media companies were likely to appeal the administrative decisions and file a lawsuit against the government to ask the court to decide whether the government properly conducted the audits and assessed the penalties. Political opponents, in particular, claimed the government was trying to silence media critics of its sunshine-policy efforts to encourage DPRK chairman Kim Jong-il to visit South Korea. Some critics implied the government was trying indirectly to silence the critical press by forcing certain news media companies out of business.

The government responded that it was acting with due consideration for the law, noting that part of the controversy lay in the fact that, compared with companies in other sectors, the news media had rarely been subjected to a proper tax audit or held accountable for their business practices. To assure the body politic that the audits were not intended to muzzle a free press, the government in mid-2001 was thought to be considering generous debt payment schedules that would enable the media companies to survive in the current business climate of the four-sector reforms.

Many Koreans seemed supportive of the government measures to ensure that news media companies complied with tax and antitrust laws. Yet allegations that the government intended to suppress freedom of speech had the potential to keep this issue in the public consciousness through the December 2002 presidential election. An unintended by-product of the audits as an election issue could be to increase political alienation.

Personal needs. Abraham Maslow, a famous student of human behavior, believed that humans are motivated by unmet needs, ranging from those that permit life itself to self-actualization (figure 40).[27] Maslow argued that people first seek to meet lower needs and then strive for higher levels. Some people might never reach the top tier or even get beyond levels II or III, and those people can suffer frustration, extreme stress, and mental disorders if they cannot move to the next level. People who fall from one level to another also can suffer depression or other mental illnesses.

Figure 40
Maslow's Hierarchy of Needs

V.   Self-actualization

IV.   Ego needs: respect and self-respect

III.   Social needs: belongingness and affection

II.   Security and safety needs

I.   Basic physiological needs

Sources: Abraham H. Maslow, *Toward a Psychology of Being,* 3rd ed. (New York: Wiley, 1999), 36–37; and James M. Higgins, *Human Relations: Concepts and Skills* (New York: Random House, 1982), 29–31.

People first need basics required for life, such as food, water, air, and sleep. Most Korean citizens have achieved this first level although some unemployed might not have.

Level II, security and safety, includes physical security requirements, for example, shelter, a safe neighborhood, and a strong national security system as well as the emotional security of home and family. Level III, social needs (also referred to as belongingness and affection needs), reflects a person's need to be loved and accepted by others, for example, parents, siblings, friends, and coworkers. Stress indicators in Korea suggest that some Koreans are experiencing difficulties in meeting their security and social needs as their society transitions toward the knowledge era with its emphasis on individual performance and accountability.

A global survey of 1.26 million respondents living in 251 countries or autonomous territories conducted over a three-week period in late 2000 by 3-Com, a U.S. company, found that

■ Korean respondents reported the most influential factors in their daily life in descending order were (1) family, (2) friends, (3) their companies, (4) their jobs, (5) national issues, and (6) the economy;

- in Korea, 17 percent of adults never told their spouses that they loved them; 33 percent declared their love "a few times throughout the year" (69 percent of U.S. respondents said they declared their love to their spouses on a daily basis);
- almost half of the Korean respondents (48 percent) stated they had thought about changing their nationality (only 8 percent of Americans, 10 percent of United Kingdom respondents, and 23 percent of Japanese had considered this choice);
- three in five (59 percent) of South Koreans were proud of their country; their sense of national pride placed South Korea at 149 out of the 251 countries and autonomous territories surveyed, a significant drop compared with the time before the 1997 financial crisis.[28]

It is no surprise that Koreans identify the three most influential beings in their daily lives as those who normally contribute to meeting their physiological, security, and social needs. However, the rising suicide rate and mental health care needs suggest that some Korean families may not be keeping pace with the individual needs of their members as Korea races into the knowledge era. It also suggests that Korean work and social groups also might be failing to meet some individual ego needs. The fact that Koreans ranked the economy last highlights the importance of family and friends.

Level IV in Maslow's hierarchy is the need for esteem, both self-esteem based on individual competence or mastery of various skills as well as attention and recognition bestowed by others. Underemployment and unemployment, of course, frustrate one's efforts to fulfill the need for esteem. Groups and families that reject members who express their individuality can induce alienation, which increases if one cannot receive love and acceptance from persons of significant emotional importance.

The pinnacle of needs is self-actualization: "the fully growing and self-fulfilling human being, the one in whom all . . . potentialities are coming to full development, the one whose inner nature expresses itself freely, rather than being warped, suppressed, or denied." There certainly are self-actualizing Koreans, but the importance that Koreans place on group approval (a level III need) throughout the culture raises questions about the degree to which Koreans may envision level V self-actualization over someone else's praise (a level IV need). As South Korea progresses in its transition to the knowledge era, the process—if successful—should empower growing numbers of Koreans to move toward becoming self-actualized.

Keeping Alienation in Check

One's sense of being loved and valued by others is essential for reducing alienation. The increased suicide rate and rising psychiatric care requirements suggest the transition to the knowledge era is producing a number of unmet needs.

Confucius in the fifth century B.C. recognized the importance of the family in establishing a stable society and nation. Korean families today are smaller and possibly under more stress than they were 2,500 years ago, but the more that busy Korean families can unconditionally love and accept their family members, the better. The same is true for other social groups, including those in the workplace. Two broad strategies—education and empowerment—consistent with knowledge-era trends would help Koreans reduce alienation in their society.

Education. Many Koreans do not understand what is happening to their society. In February 2001 Prime Minister Lee Han-Dong correctly identified education as one countermeasure to the growing suicide rate. Government, however, may not effectively reach parents who guide the family and employers who command workers' attention for most of the day.

To educate all Koreans—families, employers, coworkers, and friends—a broader approach would be to conduct a national bipartisan campaign to explain what the transition to the knowledge era entails: the importance of the individual and the necessity of meeting rising individual ego needs within families and groups, including in the workplace. The ideal campaign would inspire Koreans to understand and fulfill the love and belongingness needs of family members, friends, and coworkers—be they colleagues, subordinates, or superiors.

The ideal campaign should also include private corporations and other employers and highlight the great value they place on employees, which might also improve corporate cultures throughout society. The government might offer tax incentives to encourage companies to sponsor public service advertisements, for example. The objective of such a campaign would be to help Koreans understand the changes they are experiencing and develop coping strategies.

An ideal campaign would provide both a vision of a Korean knowledge-era society and a road map that would guide citizens toward the achievement of that vision. But because a clash between old and new authorities might render it impossible at first to gain consensus on a vision, any public information campaign should focus first on highlighting and commending contributions that individuals can make to society. That is the foundation for individual empowerment.

Empowerment. A public service education campaign is important, but it is not enough. The knowledge era rewards individuals—not groups—because individuals advance the knowledge era. Empowered, self-directed, prosperous, knowledgeable people—citizens of the knowledge era-society—are by definition not alienated.

Empowerment implies mutual respect, equality, opportunity, and individual accountability. The more such understanding can permeate Korea's hierarchical social groups and empower new behavior, the better. In an encouraging sign, some company managers seem increasingly willing to try modern approaches to improve productivity. Others, however, are more Confucian and traditional.

Korean social institutions—private corporations, religious groups, nonprofit organizations, the government, families—should consider ways to empower individuals for success. The society must create institutions and practices that reward, encourage, and inspire individual performance consistent with knowledge-era trends:

- Publicly address such questions as the role of the individual in the knowledge-era society, explaining the importance of each Korean becoming a change agent capable of discovering, creating, applying, and/or distributing knowledge, not simply a human machine or mere cog in a system.
- Promote a vision that enables each member of the society to understand an individual's role in various environments: at work, at home, and in a democracy.

- Encourage laid-off workers to explore ways of forming their own enterprises—business service companies, for example—and establish a business environment in which those with meritorious ideas and ability can succeed.
- Involve citizens in selecting political party candidates.
- Permit unfettered freedom of speech.
- Concentrate on creating laws that meet with public support.
- Enforce laws without regard to personal relationships and thus build respect for the rule of law.
- Focus on eliminating corruption, not just individual cases but root conditions that permit it; for example, develop executive, judicial, and legislative institutions that transparently check and balance each other.
- Break down hierarchical relationships that suppress individuals and acknowledge individual efforts to improve organizations, especially if contrary to a group ethic.
- Improve mutual respect, especially between husband and wife and among family members; and in the workplace and in the general society.
- Encourage news media organizations that report on suicides to report also on what likely created the sense of alienation that produced the suicide (reporting should increase awareness and promote constructive behavior, not sensationalize).
- Continue the four-sector reforms because with fuller implementation Korean companies can increase their competitiveness in the global economy and provide benefits throughout Korean society.
- Build a human resources economy to unleash the individual potential in every Korean.

The Role of the Media

The Korean news media are a valuable source of information to Koreans: a great majority of Koreans read a newspaper and watch television at least five days a week to stay abreast of political, economic, business, and social developments. Many also use the Internet. Since 1945, at times in the face of government opposition, the news media have sought to keep citizens informed of the news of the day, including government and economic activities. Most news organizations attempt to provide the public with a responsible, accurate understanding of events; some hew closely to a government line and others take a more independent stance. Overall, Koreans trust their news organizations.

The Korean media's tendency to emphasize abnormal developments—the bad news of declining GDP growth, rising unemployment, suicides, bankruptcies, and labor protests—is normal. Such stories are easy to write and attract readers, but the public often loses sight of positive factors:

- Korea's GDP growth rate in 2000 was 8.8 percent—slightly down from 1999's 10.7 percent but still formidable by world standards. It is forecast to be lower in 2001, perhaps 5 percent provided Korea continues its long-overdue restructuring; but 5 percent growth is not a recession and compares favorably with global growth forecasts of 4 percent.

- Unemployment statistics were much better in 2000 than in the preceding three years. Fewer than 800,000 were unemployed in 2000 compared with 1.7 million workers in 1997. The unemployment rate in 2000 was roughly 4.1 percent, which was significantly better than 1999's 6.3 percent and 1998's 6.8 percent. The government has plans to alleviate unemployment in 2001 and continue investments in the safety welfare net.

- Korea's foreign reserves in 2000 continued to grow to more than $94 billion, a healthy increase over 1997's $8.9 billion.[29]

Korea also made progress on the four-sector reforms that are designed to facilitate significant improvements in the near future. Even though the Korean media often seek to educate readers as well as inform them of developments, the steady drumbeat of daily news that highlights abnormalities can induce pessimism and discourage readers who lose sight of the broader picture. To keep from being overwhelmed by bad news, Koreans—like Americans and others—need to keep a broader perspective and access multiple sources of information such as the Internet provides. Government sources could be another alternative if they can establish credibility with citizens.

As old authorities struggle for primacy in Korea's transition to the knowledge era, society must insist on freedom of speech. To muzzle the apostles of a prosperous, knowledge-era democracy would be one of the worst things that could happen to this free people who have overcome so many obstacles to become one of the world's leading economies.

Summary

Korea's rapid industrialization and current transition into the knowledge era present Koreans with intense psychological challenges, as evidenced by growing psychological problems. It is difficult for any culture to change customs, habits, and practices developed over 4,000 years. Koreans handled the industrialization process—the first wave of modernization—relatively well. The second wave—transition to the knowledge era—is more challenging because the vertical relationships of a Confucian culture do not adapt easily to the horizontal relationships and importance of empowered individuals in the knowledge era. However, Korea's historic ability to survive stressful experiences inspires confidence it can do so again although it may take more time than expected.

In Korea, the high level of education, general respect for authority, and strength of the family provide a foundation for addressing modern psychological problems. As Koreans learn how to make the transition to the knowledge era and accept and experience personal empowerment, alienation will be reduced and a foundation will be laid for a new Korean society suitable for the third millennium.

Notes

1. Nathaniel Branden, "Self-Esteem in the Information Age," in *The Organization of the Future,* eds. Frances Hesselbein, Marshall Goldsmith, Richard Beckhard (San Francisco, Calif.: Jossey-Bass, 1997), 221.

2. Rollo May, *The Discovery of Being: Writings in Existential Psychology* (New York: W. W. Norton, 1983), 112.

3. Joshua Meyrowitz, *No Sense of Place: The Impact of Electronic Media on Social Behavior* (New York: Oxford University Press, 1985), vii, 125.

4. David Shaw, "Beyond Skepticism: Have the Media Crossed the Line into Cynicism?" *Los Angeles Times,* April 19, 1996, p. A1.

5. Koreans, like Americans, get most of their news from television.

6. Robert J. Samuelson, *The Good Life and Its Discontents: The American Dream in the Age of Entitlement, 1945–1995* (New York: Times Books, 1995), 6.

7. "The Unique Mental Structure of Modern Koreans (*Han-Tang Ju-Yee*)," attributed to neurologist Hyunsu Kim, http://newsmaker.khan.co.kr, accessed January 17, 2001.

8. Ibid.

9. "Current Situation," ROK Ministry of Health and Welfare, 1997, www.mohw.go.kr, accessed February 10, 2001.

10. Ibid.

11. "Many Koreans Suffering Depression," *Digital Chosun Ilbo*, May 8, 1997, www.chosunilbo.com, accessed January 30, 2001.

12. Ibid.

13. "Statistics: National Accounts," Center for Economic Information of the Korea Development Institute, http://epic.kdi.re.kr/home/english/, accessed July 6, 2001; "Leading Economic Indicators," *Korea's Economy 2001*, vol. 17 (Washington, D.C.: Korea Economic Institute of America and Korea Institute of International Economic Policy, March 2001).

14. "Statistics: Employment and Wages," Center for Economic Information of the Korea Development Institute, http://epic.kdi.re.kr/home/english/, accessed July 6, 2001; "Economic Indicators," *Korea Insight* 3, no. 1 (January 2001): 4, www.keia.com/insight-January2001.pdf, accessed June 3, 2001.

15. "Mental Health & Brain Disorders: Suicide Rates & Absolute Numbers of Suicide by Country," World Health Organization, 2000, www.who.int/mental_health/Topic_Suicide/suicide1.html, accessed February 22, 2001; "Male Suicide on the Rise," *Digital Chosun Ilbo*, October 15, 2000, www.chosunilbo.com, accessed February 5, 2001.

16. "Suicide Statistics," Befrienders International, http://www.befrienders.org/info/statistics.htm, accessed February 20, 2001.

17. "Investigation Launched on Anti-Social Web Sites," *Digital Chosun Ilbo,* February 7, 2001, www.chosunilbo.com, accessed February 9, 2001.

18. Shin, "Monitoring the Dynamics of Democratization in Korea," 50–53.

19. *World Factbook 2000,* U.S. Central Intelligence Agency, www.cia.gov/cia/publications/factbook/geos/ks.html#Intro, accessed July 27, 2001.

20. Shin and Rose, "1999 New Korea Barometer Survey," questions 60a, 60b, 61a, 61c, 62a, and 62c, pp. 42–45.

21. *Survey for Newspaper Reform,* survey conducted by Hangil Research Co. for the People's Coalition for Media Reform and the Journalists Association of Korea, www.pcmr.or.kr, accessed July 23, 2001 (translated by Jung Kyunghwan).

22. "Prime Minister Insists Probes Are Normal," *Digital Chosun Ilbo,* February 9, 2001, http://www.chosun.com/w21data/html/news/200102/200102090353.html, accessed February 9, 2001; "Background of KFTC Investigation into Newspaper-Magazine-Broadcasting Sectors," Office of Public Relations, Korea Fair Trade Commission, February 13, 2001, http://ftc.go.kr/ftc10/owa/wi101_3e?ctcode1=14&ymd1=2001-06-07&no1=7, accessed July 27, 2001.

23. Kim Min-bai, "President Says 'Justice Served' in Media Probe," *Digital Chosun,* July 2, 2001, www.chosun.com/w21data/html/news/200107020176.html, accessed July 9, 2001.

24. David I. Steinberg, "The Korean Press and Orthodoxy," *Digital Chosun,* July 17, 2001, http://www.chosun.com/w21data/html/news/200107/200107170170.html, accessed July 23, 2001

25. "Minister Alleges Press 'More Scary Than the President'," *Digital Chosun Ilbo,* February 7, 2001, http://english.chosun.com/w21data/html/news/200102/200102070425.html, accessed February 9, 2001.

26. "The NTS Accusation," *Digital Chosun,* June 29, 2001, www.chosun.com/w21data/html/news/200106/200106290194.html, accessed July 29, 2001.

27. Abraham H. Maslow, *Toward a Psychology of Being,* 3rd ed. (New York: Wiley, 1999), 36–37; and James M. Higgins, *Human Relations: Concepts and Skills* (New York: Random House, 1982), 29–31.

28. Young Lim Heung, "Survey Results of Various Countries Indicate Korean National Pride Ranks 149," *Digital Chosun Ilbo,* December 24, 2000, www.chosunilbo.com, accessed December 26, 2001.

29. "Employment and Wages" and "National Accounts," Center for Economic Information of the Korea Development Institute, http://epic.kdi.re.kr/home/english/, accessed July 6, 2001.

7 ■
Scenarios

W HAT WILL KOREA LOOK LIKE IN 2010? Will it be a prosperous, knowledge-era democracy, approaching the end state envisioned by the 1998 four-sector structural reforms; or will it be an also-ran, having given up on reform and bypassed by other countries that were willing to risk major change to receive the full benefits of the knowledge era?

The final endeavor of this study is to apply the trends and indicators identified as driving world politics and Korean society over the next decade to several representative scenarios for Korea. The objective is not to forecast the future, but to furnish a sense of the range of outcomes that could emerge as Korea continues its transition to a knowledge era. These scenarios are intended to help government and business planners consider the implications of alternative visions of Korea's future, not to specify the most likely outcome.

Overview

In early 2001, the Kim Dae-jung administration was focused on fully implementing the four-sector reforms before the February 2003 inauguration of the next president. It remained to be seen whether the government could accomplish all its objectives in its remaining two years. For the remainder of the 2001–2010 decade, the scope of this book, no one knows who will be the Korean presidents and hundreds of National Assembly representatives and their intentions. Will they sustain and build on the 1998 four-sector reform effort to transform Korea into a prosperous, free market, knowledge-era democracy?

Korea's survival as an independent nation-state is not in question; instead the question is: Can Koreans take full advantage of the opportunities presented by the knowledge era to achieve their goal of becoming a prosperous democracy? Subsumed in this question is the issue of the people's willingness to adapt traditional social institutions and authorities that have sustained them over centuries in favor of new authorities inherent in knowledge-era concepts. Another issue is presented by the rapidly globalizing world economy: Can Korea improve its competitiveness quickly enough to remain among the world's top economies?

Four scenarios are possible during the coming decade: full reform, partial reform, rejection of reform, and military coup d'état. These scenarios provide virtuous or vicious development cycles, continuing growth or spiraling decline.

Assumptions

History suggests several significant conditions in Korea are likely to persist over the 2001–2010 decade:

- Domestic events, concerns, and aspirations will continue to exert the strongest influence on South Korean decisionmaking, reflecting the truth that "all politics is local."[1] Accordingly, domestic politics will continue to command a great deal of attention among Koreans, especially if any but the first scenario prevails, because Korea will then continue to place relatively more importance on personal relationships. The news media will continue to strengthen their capabilities to report government activity as the public's watchdog.
- At the crossroads of northeast Asia, Koreans will be mindful of international developments, but they will process them intellectually as they consider their domestic goals. As time passes, Koreans might place even greater emphasis on international issues and less on Korean central government issues because of the possible devolution of government power and new routes to empower citizens.

- South Koreans will continue to pursue their goal of establishing a prosperous, knowledge-era democracy; however, prosperity will be their primary objective, followed by improvements to democracy.
- Social turmoil will persist at varying degrees throughout the period of transition as Koreans wrestle with new concepts (market economy and rule of law, for example) as well as new social authorities and institutions and their impact on personal roles in society vis-à-vis authorities based on traditional Confucian values. Established authorities will not easily admit their inability to meet knowledge-era challenges or yield to new authorities.
- The body politic is likely to remain divided along regional lines unless successive governments persuasively address the issues that promote regionalism. Success in resolving issues based on regional perceptions of favoritism or neglect will help reduce social turmoil.
- North and South Korea will not be a single unified nation-state by 2010. North and South Korea remained far apart economically, politically, and socially in 2001. Moreover, the pace of change in South Korea was rapidly producing increasingly empowered people striving to succeed in a globalized economy. South Koreans stood in stark contrast to their suppressed brethren living in the northern part of the peninsula who were bound by the limitations of their concepts of self-reliance (*juche*). South Koreans want unification with North Korea but not at the expense of their prosperity. Under the best conditions, the two societies could require at least a generation to bridge the gap.

Although North and South Korea will not have unified by 2010, they may trade and cooperate in various ways. North Korea will continue to exist as an independent, autocratic state that might qualify for aid from various international financial institutions and might achieve positive GDP growth, but its overall national power will be less than that of South Korea—especially in light of the ROK-U.S. relationship.

By 2010, the North Korea–South Korea relationship may evolve to peaceful coexistence, possibly including various security confidence-building measures and some reduction in military forces. However, neither country will consider the other as a wholly trustworthy and friendly power.

■ South Korea will continue to regard the United States as an important trading partner and security ally. Because Seoul and Pyongyang will not have resolved all of their differences, the threat of a resumption of war will remain a concern. Moreover, North Korea may still not have completely resolved international concerns regarding its missile delivery systems and weapons of mass destruction, a situation that will hinder rapprochement with South Korea.

The 1953 Korean War armistice agreement will remain in force. South Korean and U.S. security planners will continue to assess North Korea as a security threat. The U.S.-ROK security alliance will remain in force, and the ROK will continue to ask the United States to maintain a military force presence in South Korea although circumstances might warrant some adjustments. The mission for U.S. military forces in Korea will be unchanged: deter foreign aggression against South Korea and help defeat it should deterrence fail. This mission could help maintain peace and stability elsewhere in Asia, however, if it were expanded and restructured.

■ South Korea will continue to build and improve relations with neighboring states and many other countries around the world. The objectives will be to open markets for South Korean firms and encourage countries to normalize relations and trade with North Korea, thus reducing the South Korea–North Korea income gap and making unification economically more feasible. South Korea would then become increasingly part of the global economy, which will make new demands on Korean companies to become more competitive globally.

Scenario One: Sustaining the 1998 Reforms

This scenario assumes the Kim Dae-jung administration will implement the four-sector reforms before Kim leaves office in February 2003 and that the successor administrations will build on them.

The financial, corporate, labor, and public sectors will be significantly different in 2003 compared with 1997 when the financial crisis discredited the Korea Inc. political–economic model and highlighted the need for major restructuring. By 2003, the government will rely on the invisible hand of Korea's free market to drive business, saving, investment, and consumption decisions. The government will influence economic activity primarily through the macroeconomic tools of fiscal and monetary policy and regulations to promote fair trade, with due consideration for public safety and welfare. The government will also have strengthened its regulatory agencies—the Korea Fair Trade Commission and the Financial Supervisory Commission, for example. The government will expand the social safety net and assist the unemployed and elderly who lack satisfactory family support.

Korean democracy will be stronger in 2010 compared with 2001 due in part to increasingly active citizens using the Internet to influence government decisionmaking and political campaigns. Citizens increasingly will hold elected and appointed government officials accountable for their decisions and behavior. The news media also will be better watchdogs than they were in 2001. The central government will be smaller and more responsive to the legislative and judicial branches, which will have emerged as more effective checks and balances vis-à-vis executive power than in the past. However, neither the National Assembly nor the Supreme Court will yet be fully independent of the executive branch.

Korea's economy will also be more firmly rooted in free market principles and practices in 2010. Financial firms will carefully assess loan applications and weigh them in consideration of business prospects and the likelihood of receiving satisfactory return on investment. Koreans will not believe that government or any other third party will bail them out if a borrower defaults. *Chaebol* and small and medium enterprises will be focused on increasing profits. The manufacturing sector will remain a key component of Korea's export-based economy, but the knowledge-based service sector will have become much more important. Korean business managers will flexibly implement new strategies to increase productivity and sales domestically and abroad. *Chaebol* will be less diversified and will concentrate on profitable core specialties more than they did in the twentieth century. Automotive companies, for example, will likely no longer be *chaebol* affiliates but independent companies.

Business, government, and other organizations will increasingly prize their human resources and create new methods of retaining employees whose sense of company loyalty paradoxically will pale in comparison with developing skills to compete for more satisfying or lucrative positions in other firms. The labor market will be much more flexible in 2010 than in 2001. The unemployment rate will likely fluctuate in the 3 percent–6 percent range—high compared with Korea's industrialization period but low compared with many other OECD nations.

Socially, many Koreans will be disconcerted. The fast pace of political, economic, and business developments in the knowledge era coupled with the decline of stability within many families and a steady diet of negative news will sustain a high degree of stress. Koreans will have difficulty coping with the increasingly limited utility of the five major Confucian relationships to help them achieve their personal and professional objectives. Replacing historic Confucian relationships will likely be difficult and might make some Koreans receptive to demagogues who present simple solutions to Korea's complex problems.

Regionally, Korea's relationship with the United States will remain very important while that with North Korea will be relatively frustrating. North Korea probably will not have implemented meaningful reforms and therefore will be neither a reliable trading partner nor a significant investment destination. China and Japan will remain important trading partners for Korea, and Korea will have established free-trade agreements with several countries. Seoul's standing will have improved significantly within the OECD, the WTO, and such groups, but Koreans will continue to place the highest value on the ROK-U.S. relationship owing to the lucrative trading relationship and the security alliance. Seoul will continue to perceive the United States as a reliable ally that helps deter foreign aggression by North Korea in the near term and by other nations in the longer term. Accordingly, the ROK will continue to host U.S. forces on its soil.

Indicators of Scenario One: Sustaining the 1998 Reforms

- Korean financial institutions allocate capital through loans or investments in accordance with their own business criteria, assessments, and calculations that match international standards, not edicts from government officials. Firms focus on increasing profits by lending or investing wisely.

- Financial institutions lend with no expectations that the government or other third party will bail them out if the borrower defaults.

- Financial institutions discipline loan officers or other employees who recommend or approve unjustifiable loans if the institution suspects corrupt behavior.

- Financial institutions eagerly seek the services of outside directors and consultants to help them stay competitive.

- Government regulatory agencies and law enforcement officials investigate and prosecute politically difficult cases in a manner that earns public respect and confidence.

- Changes in the financial sector and strong government support for free-market practices encourage companies and individuals to develop good ideas, skills, and competitive products to attract capital. This combination helps to unleash the human resources potential resident in Korea's well-educated and industrious work force.

- The government is attentive to complaints by domestic and foreign firms regarding excessive regulation. The government conducts annual reviews of all regulations pertaining to the conduct of business—including those pertaining to trade and investment—and eliminates those that impede free enterprise, except as required to promote public health and safety.

- The government increasingly privatizes state-owned enterprises and sells its equity holdings in state-invested firms. The government also regularly reviews its requirements for government research institutes and reduces its reliance on them, turning instead to universities, private research organizations, and consulting firms for custom research support.

- *Chaebol* and small and medium enterprises focus on profits in domestic and foreign markets; they will have no expectation of a government bailout if they mismanage their resources. Korean and foreign members of their boards of directors, shareholders, and other stakeholders require that managers provide satisfactory return on investment and insist on lowering debt–equity ratios to manageable levels.

- Publicly traded firms provide sufficient credible information that enables investors to make informed decisions; companies that refuse to do so attract fewer investors.
- Corporate managers eagerly engage the services of outside directors and consultants as well as acquire or develop new technologies to improve profitability.
- *Chaebol* increasingly narrow their product ranges on the basis of their core competencies (compared with the diverse product ranges of the past).
- Lenders and investors are more inclined to consider advancing capital to small and medium enterprises on the basis of whether the firm's ideas, experience, and business plan inspire confidence in achieving a satisfactory return on investment.
- Throughout the society, including work places, seniors and juniors increasingly relate to each other in ways discernibly different from the past. They mutually recognize that each can add value to decisionmaking. Neither assumes the junior will unquestioningly obey the senior, which promotes mutual respect. Courtesy remains a trademark of interpersonal communications.
- Employers throughout the society—including for-profit business enterprises, private nonprofit organizations, and government organizations—strive to establish highly attractive, empowering work environments and compensation packages to attract and retain highly skilled employees. Employers increasingly replace formal hierarchical work relationships with flexible informal relationships that inspire workers to contribute intellectual capital beyond the scope of their job descriptions.
- Both employers and employees recognize the benefits of empowering workers and seek new ways to do so, which enhances productivity and morale.

- Employees tend to regard their current employment as an opportunity to work toward self-actualization as Maslow described it, at least until a better opportunity emerges.
- Managers and workers relate to each other more maturely than in the past, as each realizes that skilled workers can easily seek new employment if conditions warrant.
- The government enacts laws to expand the social safety net commensurate with the increase in labor flexibility. It also enacts legislation to provide citizens with tools to prepare for retirement, including tax-deferred individual retirement accounts, for example. Financial firms compete to provide an array of products to meet the growing investment needs of the aging Korean society.
- Annual GDP growth typically is 5–6 percent and at times is greater. Unemployment typically is in the 3–6 percent range.
- Koreans increasingly use knowledge-era tools to monitor proposed legislation, government policies, and the voting positions of their elected representative in the National Assembly. They communicate their opinions to their National Assembly representatives and hold them accountable for their votes. They also communicate to government officials to influence decisionmaking and fix personal responsibility.
- National Assembly representatives increasingly debate proposed legislation, taking into consideration the merits and demerits of the legislation, their party philosophy or platform, and voter reaction if the debate focuses too much on achieving political advantage at national expense.
- Voters also use knowledge-era tools to pressure political party leaders to open up the selection of potential candidates for public office.
- Koreans continue to seek ways to merge traditional relationships with contemporary developments, even though such efforts sometimes achieve mixed results; for example, the marriage rate may well remain relatively low and the divorce rate high, as women become less economically dependent on men and demand more equality in the marriage.

- Lingering challenges include:
  - devolution of central government power;
  - lack of budget authority at the local level;
  - government tendencies to micromanage the economy;
  - noncompetitive companies seeking government support with public funds;
  - corruption; and
  - government tendencies to suppress free speech when embarrassing scandals develop.

Scenario Two: Reform Yes, but . . .

Scenario Two also assumes the Kim Dae-jung administration will implement the four-sector reforms before Kim leaves office in February 2003, but as the decade progresses, one or both of the two successor governments will decide to adjust certain tenets or fail to enforce reforms. Advocates for only partial reform will argue, "Yes, the four-sector reforms are needed, but they are too much, too fast for Korea. Some temporary adjustments are needed now." The result will be partial reform.

Several factors could combine to prompt successors to the Kim Dae-jung administration to adjust the four-sector reforms: decreasing competitiveness of Korean companies if they lag in improving their productivity; declining GDP growth and rising unemployment if companies find it difficult to sell their products profitably; and social turmoil caused by the clash of outdated and emerging social traditions, institutions, and authorities combined with the accelerating pace of change and information overload driven by new developments in science and technology. These factors could produce a sense of crisis among voters.

To address such issues, candidates for the presidency and other public offices would likely campaign on platforms that call for minor, temporary adjustments to the four-sector reform program and a more active government role in managing the economy. Although South Koreans might at first welcome such an approach, it could promote a return to Korea Inc. practices that would probably prove ineffective in the knowledge-era global economy and thwart Korea's undertaking of becoming a prosperous democracy. It could also discourage foreign investment, reduce capital for Korean enterprises, and in some cases prompt trading partners to retaliate.

Regionally, Korea will place increased importance on its relationship with trading partners as the government emphasizes an export strategy to improve the economy. However, most of Seoul's trading partners will become dismayed at the turn of events in South Korea. They will be concerned about how new ROK government policies will affect Korea's ability to repay loans and provide a satisfactory return on investments. Trading partners may consider retaliating if Korea's trade barriers prove unacceptable; and the United States will become especially concerned because of South Korea's importance as an export destination.

The United States will also assess the implications of Korea's new stance on the ROK-U.S. security relationship, and some Americans will argue that the United States should not subsidize South Korea's defense if Seoul is unwilling to implement economic reforms that have helped countless other economies throughout history. Counterarguments will address the need to deter North Korean threats to U.S. national security objectives. While Washington officially adheres to the ROK-U.S. alliance, the bilateral relationship could become strained.

Indicators of Scenario Two: Reform Yes, but . . .

- The ROK government increasingly uses public funds on what it says is a temporary basis to subsidize certain nonviable or questionable companies. The government may also require Korean banks to fund such companies "until they recover."
- Managers of Korean financial institutions complain that the new government policy makes their firms responsible for nonperforming loans; the government responds that it will assist the financial institutions if their fears are validated.
- Managers and loan officers in Korean financial institutions conclude that the government will rescue them if they lend money irresponsibly, reestablishing the prospect of loans based

on other than free-market business principles and reenergizing behavior based in moral hazard.

■ Economists and managers of profitable companies increasingly warn that government favoritism toward nonviable and questionable companies damages the overall economy by reducing the amount of capital available for new investment.

■ Business representatives from all sectors strengthen personal relationships with government officials to gain their support in acquiring government-backed capital; in short, Koreans resurrect crony capitalism.

■ The government decides to implement some "temporary" trade barriers to protect favored but noncompetitive industries; trading partners protest such practices, raising the specter of retaliation.

■ Labor leaders again turn to government for assistance in persuading employers to increase total compensation regardless of market conditions or the employer's actual ability to provide better wage and benefit packages.

■ Korea's netizens—especially those who will be in their early 40s and younger in 2010—become discouraged by Korea's return to past Korea Inc. practices as the political–economic climate again puts more value on personal relationships and loyalty than on individual merit and initiative.

■ Social tension also builds as Korea's netizens continue to demand improvements in Korean democracy—an independent National Assembly and possibly an independent judiciary—while established authorities resist such changes.

■ Corruption, crime, and general disorder also increase, raising the prospect of strong government countermeasures to establish harmony.

Scenario Three: Reform Rejected

Scenario Three assumes the Kim Dae-jung administration implements the four-sector reforms by 2003, but at least one of the two administrations that succeed the Kim administration takes office with the express intention of halting the reform effort and returning to the "good old days" of Park Chung-hee's guided capitalism and Korea Inc.

The factors that could prompt successor governments to adjust some of the four-sector reforms under Scenario Two also apply to Scenario Three. The difference between the two scenarios is a matter of degree with respect to voter demands during, for example, the political campaigns leading up to one of the presidential elections.

Scenario Three might result from more discouragement with the economy than expected in Scenario Two: a great number of non-competitive companies, rising unemployment, or low GDP growth (especially compared with the double-digit growth rates occasionally achieved during the industrialization period). Many Koreans in 2000 nostalgically recalled social harmony and consistently strong economic growth under President Park Chung-hee and his successor. They also seemed to ignore or be unaware of the negative impact of his Korea Inc. political–economic model on democratization, the changing global economy, and other modernizing trends. Koreans also could be confused and upset with what they view as unending social turmoil as new and old authorities struggle for legitimacy while a constant barrage of negative news—which always sells well—adds to general malaise and the view that Korea is on the wrong road.

Scenario Three envisions one or more of the presidential candidates in 2002 or 2007 promising to restore Park Chung-hee's economic principles and arguing that the four-sector reforms have not solved all of Korea's economic and social problems but are instead part of the problem. Voters respond favorably to this simple message and elect the candidate who proceeds as promised.

Intent is the difference between Scenario Two and Scenario Three. In Scenario Two, Korea accepts the legitimacy of the four-sector reforms and seeks to implement them over the long term while implementing "temporary" adjustments in the near term to solve a current crisis. In Scenario Three, Korea blames the four-sector reforms for whatever the current crisis is and seeks to revert to some version of the Korea Inc. political–economic model.

Regionally, the United States and other trading partners react to Scenario Three regressive developments with greater caution than if Scenario Two had been followed. Foreign creditors lobby the ROK government to extend sovereign guarantees over private sector loans. Creditors, investors, and others negatively assess the likelihood that Korea can achieve sufficiently strong economic growth to back up the government's loan guarantees and sustain a business environment capable of providing satisfactory return on investment in the increasingly competitive, knowledge-based global economy. The ROK government may revert to former Korea Inc. practices and characterize North Korea as the ROK's major military threat that requires stronger defense capabilities, including increased domestic security controls. Some government measures degrade freedom of speech and assembly in South Korea. The United States will regard such developments with a great deal of concern.

Indicators of Scenario Three: Reform Rejected

The rejector administration will embrace some measures outlined in Scenario Two. It will also do the following.

- Gain greater control of the financial sector in order to allocate capital to firms judged able to advance economic growth and foreign policy objectives as during the Korea Inc. era.
- Develop partnership agreements with *chaebol* to encourage them to hire unemployed workers. In exchange, the government could provide low-cost capital, support low wages in lieu of no wages, and commit to suppress strikes.
- Describe North Korea as the primary threat to South Korea's security and call for significant

  - ROK defense investments,
  - strengthening of the ROK-U.S. alliance, and
  - strengthening of domestic security countermeasures by bolstering the National Security Law and imposing restrictions on freedom of speech and assembly.

- Establish trade barriers to protect noncompetitive industries.
- Reduce the ability of regulatory agencies such as the Korea Fair Trade Commission and Financial Supervisory Commission to identify and prosecute wrongdoing.

- Revert to behavior mired in moral hazard, questionable loans, corruption, and crime increase consistent with a return to crony capitalism.
- Protect domestic markets, causing Korean firms to become less competitive, lose labor flexibility, and reduce access to capital for some firms.
- Cope with trading partners that increasingly challenge the ROK government to remove trade barriers or threaten to retaliate, establishing another vicious cycle of decline.
- Face GDP growth that stagnates or declines.
- Placate workers who are unhappy due to low wages and their inability to work in companies that have increasingly progressive corporate climates that empower them in ways not possible under the rigid corporate culture of the Korea Inc. model.
- Adjust government practices to account for a citizenry—including news media and university students—that increasingly demands improvements in democracy, including making the National Assembly an independent branch of government, empowering citizens to help select political party candidates to public office, and holding both elected and appointed officials accountable for laws enacted. The government regards such demands as subversive and implements countermeasures to maintain social order.
- Cope with declining public confidence in government as Koreans react with surprise to the extent of reversion to Korea Inc. practices and over time become dismayed at their inability to improve prosperity, democracy, and/or sense of personal security.
- Consider increasingly stronger government countermeasures to restore order as social tension increases, which alarms the military.

Scenario Four: Military Coup d'État

More than 70 percent of Koreans in 1999 considered the military to be the most trustworthy of six political institutions. Most Koreans distrusted ROK government civil servants, the police, National

Assembly, and political parties, with fewer than one Korean in four trusting the National Assembly and political parties. However, fewer than one in ten Koreans wanted a return of military government and none wanted a complete dictatorship.[2] Well over 80 percent of Koreans wanted their country to be an increasingly prosperous democracy although they seemed to assign a higher value to prosperity than to democracy.

A military coup d'état appeared to be a remote option in 2001; however, Scenario Four takes precedent into account[3] and considers the possibility of a coup under extreme conditions that could be created by Scenarios Two and Three.

Scenario Four assumes Scenarios Two and Three will have failed to improve prosperity and democracy, prompting public outrage. To reestablish order, the government imposes countermeasures that infuriate the general population and incite widespread strikes and demonstrations. Senior military officers worry that the government's failure to maintain order will further degrade constructive efforts to improve the economy and prompt more virulent civil disorder. ROK officers become increasingly concerned that North Korea might seek to take advantage of South Korea's deteriorating situation and attack. Military officers exaggerate public affection for former President Park Chung-hee, who became president through a military coup in 1961, and conclude that the future of the nation demands that they patriotically assume power, if only for the brief time required to install a new civilian president.

The situation that military coup leaders would face in the twenty-first century would be quite different from what Park Chung-hee faced in the early 1960s. Then, Koreans had no experience in an industrialized economy, much less the knowledge-based global economy. They fully subscribed to Confucian values that prize loyalty to government and seniors. They had no experience with democracy. What Koreans in the 1960s and Koreans in the first decade of the twenty-first century could have in common is disapproval of an inept government that fails to improve economic performance and whose policies create a vicious downward cycle of failure. The experiences and expectations of twenty-first-century Koreans, especially netizens, are vastly different from those of the early 1960s.

In addition, the knowledge, attitudes, and skills required to manage government affairs, including Korea's large multifaceted economy, in the twenty-first century are far more complex than in the 1960s. Outside of the military, relatively few Koreans in the 1960s had the management skills to plan and orchestrate the industrialization process. The situation in the twenty-first century is much different.

Scenario Four envisions a period of martial law and a mixture of measures previously outlined under Scenarios Two and Three. Military coup leaders are unlikely to implement the empowering measures of Scenario One. The military's role will be to restore order. The sooner it can implement an exit strategy under which Koreans can elect a new government, the better. While Koreans might be relieved in the near term by the restoration of order, they will soon demand actions to improve the economy and some groups will also clamor for a return of democratic liberties. The military leaders will be challenged to meet these demands deftly and constructively.

Foreign creditors, investors, and trading partners will likely respond to a military coup with greater alarm than Scenarios Two and Three. Capital flight should be expected, further damaging the prospects for prompt economic recovery.

The United States in particular will likely protest the coup in the strongest possible terms, especially if ROK military units under the peacetime operational control of the ROK-U.S. Combined Forces Command are used in the coup, because such employment would implicitly make the United States an unwitting accessory. The U.S. government would likely demand coup leaders promptly take measures to restore civilian government, with the U.S. Congress threatening extreme measures to pressure Korean compliance.

Indicators of Scenario Four: Military Coup d'État

Scenario Four is an extreme case, reflecting a mixture of certain external factors and a widespread loss of confidence in the ROK government's ability to govern. External and domestic factors that might prompt the ROK military to act are outlined below.

Domestic factors

- Unemployment increases to an unacceptable level as the government and the financial sector refuse or become unable to bail out noncompetitive Korean firms.
- GDP growth stagnates or declines for an unacceptable period of time owing in part to a significant drop in the competitiveness of Korean products.
- Anxiety among ordinary Koreans increases, fueled by government failure to assuage their concerns.
- Ordinary Koreans—workers, unemployed, and family members—join students and labor union leaders in public demonstrations calling for government action to improve the economy and social welfare assistance.
- The government fails to address demonstrators' concerns and increasingly uses force to disperse the demonstrators.
- The demonstrations become riots.
- The government reveals an inability to govern.

External factors

- South Korean exports become less competitive and decline, a situation perhaps exacerbated by trade barriers imposed to retaliate against Korean import barriers.
- North Korea

  - expresses support for South Korean demonstrators, encouraging more unrest,
  - criticizes the ROK government as a puppet government whose authorities are failing to meet the needs of South Korean workers,
  - increases its public diplomacy to emphasize that its system is the appropriate one for all Koreans, and
  - increases military training and unit deployments.

- In response to North Korea, the ROK military increasingly expresses concern about

  - the threat of hostile North Korean action,
  - public demonstrations and riots,
  - ROK government inability to maintain public order, and

- the importance of the nation returning to proven traditional values and the days of Park Chung-hee.

A military coup seemed to be a very remote scenario in early 2001 but cannot be wholly ruled out given Korea's history.

Summary

Koreans at the turn of the twenty-first century were carrying out Scenario One to achieve economic prosperity and stronger democracy. Some reforms date back to the early 1990s under President Kim Young-sam, Korea's first truly civilian president in more than 30 years. Kim Young-sam made a determined effort following his inauguration in February 1993 to implement major reforms in the financial, social welfare, and corporate sectors. Efforts to reform *chaebol* at that time were problematic as the grip of Korea Inc. was still too strong. The 1997 financial crisis demonstrated the shortcomings of the Korea Inc. model and provided impetus for more comprehensive reforms, which most Koreans accepted.

Scenario One is the only one of the four that promotes each person's ability to contribute to making Korea a better place for all human activity—a virtuous cycle of development. The other scenarios promise short-term relief from difficulties inherent in Korea's turbulent transition to the knowledge era, but ultimately they are reactionary and hark back to an earlier age when empowerment was neither the norm nor the goal. The increasingly competitive global economy that rewards those possessing knowledge-era skills and attitudes—just those attributes that Scenarios Two, Three, and Four reject—could very well propel Korea into a vicious cycle of decline.

Notes

1. Former speaker of the U.S. House of Representatives Thomas P. O'Neill.
2. Shin and Rose, "1999 New Korea Barometer Survey," 28.
3. Two precedents for a military coup d'état are the military coup of 1961 that installed Maj. Gen. Park Chung-hee as president, and the "rolling coup" of 1979–1980 that installed Maj. Gen. Chun Doo-hwan as president.

8 ■
The Knowledge Era and Korea

> There is nothing more difficult to take in hand, more perilous to conduct, or more uncertain in its success, than to take the lead in the introduction of a new order of things.
>
> —Niccolò Machiavelli
> *The Prince*

Elements of national culture change very slowly over time, if at all. Korea, although it became a republic in the twentieth century, is also a culture that has survived exceptional challenges throughout its 4,000-year history. Its well-established social values, institutions, and authorities have given the Korean people great cohesion. Like most people, Koreans did not move to a new land to develop a new society; instead they accommodated the engines of change through the lengthy process of adapting their established institutions, traditions, and authorities. However, the extensive, rapid changes in Korea's transition from an agrarian society, through the industrial age, to the brink of the knowledge era in one 30-year generation have placed unprecedented and sometimes unbearable demands on Korea's ancient traditions and authorities.

Global Trends

The CSIS Global Trends analysis, of which this Korea study is a part, broadly concludes that the dominant trends of the knowledge era are hopeful: empowering, democratizing, egalitarian, and environmentally healthy. The knowledge era provides the information, social institutions, and technologies to realize the trends. Powerful, well-established forces within a society can thwart or completely prevent a society's transition to the knowledge era, however. A society's ability to shape its transformation to achieve the promise of the knowledge era demands new social values, new institutions, and new authorities. Most important to a free society's transition are education, a "renewed capitalism," moral values and social responsibility, and democracy.

Education plays a decisive role because it equips people for success in the knowledge era. Korea has a strong education system, but it requires reform to provide students with the intellectual agility essential for flexible, creative problem solving.

Korea's effort to implement free-market capitalism is in progress through the four-sector reforms. However, unbridled capitalism does not automatically nurture community, mercy, equality, justice, or the environment. "Renewed capitalism" acknowledges the importance of tempering capitalism to address moral and humanitarian issues.

Moral values and social responsibility are essential for the conduct of all human activities that seek to empower and produce growth. Corruption and crime thrive amid immorality, but what constitutes immorality can vary among societies. Democracy and free-market economics require standards of behavior—morals—that are quite different from those found in autocracies and managed economies. Democracy includes the rule of law established with the consent of the governed; it is sometimes enforced by autonomous institutions that check and balance the abuse of power by organizations and individuals. Free speech is essential. Without a vigorous sense of the values that underpin effective public policy in a free-market democracy, leaders and members of the society might be unable to make or follow appropriate decisions to accomplish the society's objectives.

Democracy—government of the people, by the people, for the people—is essential for the empowerment of people in a free, knowledge-era society. It is unlikely that such people will accept any government that they cannot influence. The Global Trends analysis recognizes that citizens of free societies en route to the knowledge era insist on democracy, as is increasingly evident in Korea.

Korea's Unique Challenges

One great challenge for Korea is to reconcile its traditional institutions, authorities, and values with the vastly different concepts, institutions, and authorities inherent in democracy and free-market economics. President Park Chung-hee used to tell Western critics of his authoritarian rule that his style of democracy was appropriate for Korea (*Minju-juei-hwa Hankuk-shikouro*). Modern Koreans know he was wrong: democracy is not top-down; it is bottom-up. Koreans at the beginning of the twenty-first century understand that governments exist to carry out the will of the people. Empowered with this understanding and their knowledge-era tools, Koreans changed the course of the 16th general election for the National Assembly in 2000. The four-sector reforms are helping Koreans replace Korea Inc.'s managed economy with capitalist, free-market principles and practices. To weaken the grip of corrupting personal relationships and adapt democracy and free-enterprise concepts, Koreans need greater devolution of government power, institutional checks and balances to prevent the abuse of power, and stronger respect for the rule of law throughout the society.

A second great challenge is to resist the temptations of the quick fix—*Han-Tang Ju-yee*. It takes time to lay a solid foundation for the new knowledge-era society with its empowering institutions. Under firm leadership, Koreans mobilized their resources in the 1960s and developed an industrial nation in impressively quick fashion, using the Korea Inc. development model. That model served well in the early years but outgrew its usefulness. Koreans must now patiently lay a solid foundation for growth in the third millennium. Properly accomplished, Korea could bring about another "miracle on the Han" and again become an international model for development. More important, they could position themselves to move closer to becoming the self-actualized people they imagine.

The third great challenge is to develop a national vision that empowers each person to pass from Korea's traditional culture to the knowledge era, especially if times become difficult. Many Koreans can generally envision a prosperous democracy; however, individual Koreans—assembly-line workers, housewives, software designers, company managers, students, entry-level workers, and government officials, for example—need to understand their roles as individuals to achieve that vision. Once Koreans understand the vision, the obstacles and solutions before them, and their roles, they will be empowered to succeed.

However, success cannot be assumed. The scenarios in chapter 7 map the different routes to 2010.

The route to 2010 that is most consistent with knowledge-era trends is the Scenario One path on which Koreans are currently traveling to implement and build on the four-sector reforms. The strength of Korea's traditional social values, institutions, and authorities is so strong, however, that success could be elusive. Sustaining Scenario One will be problematic if, for example, Koreans place a higher value on achieving social harmony than on personal empowerment. Initial success in meeting the challenges of transition will help Koreans work through obstacles and disappointments in the future, but leadership and a sense of destiny are crucial to stay on course.

Scenario Two envisions Koreans embracing temporary adjustments, and in Scenario Three they consciously reject reform. Decisions to apply temporary adjustments would retard Korea's transition but not necessarily halt it. On the other hand, decisions to give up on the reforms and return to some version of Korea Inc. would likely prevent Korea from becoming a prosperous, knowledge-era democracy in the foreseeable future.

Scenario Four envisions perceptions of a growing external threat to national security and internal social turbulence of such magnitude that the military would seize control. While imagining such a desperate situation is difficult, the scenario cannot be discounted in light of Korea's relatively recent past.

Only one of these four scenarios presents Korea with a bright outlook for continuing growth. The liberalizing and empowering Scenario One promotes sustainable growth compatible with knowledge-era trends. The other three scenarios lay the foundation for eventual decline relative to competitors in the global economy and could prevent Korea from quickly becoming a prosperous, knowledge-era democracy.

To achieve the hopeful future of the knowledge era, Korea must surmount intense challenges to the very social concepts, institutions, and authorities that enabled it to survive a difficult history and become an industrialized nation in record time. People and organizations do not readily change the behavior that made them successful, but the 1997 financial crisis was a significant emotional event that provided an impetus for change. Korea seized the opportunity and has made significant progress although much more needs to be accomplished.

Sustaining reform will likely be increasingly difficult over the 2001–2010 decade, particularly if unemployment should become unacceptably high, GDP growth unacceptably low, and people perceive their quality of life to be worse than they recall before 1998. Vested interests will resist changes that reduce their authority in this ancient culture while Koreans wrestle to define who they want to be in the twenty-first century. And yet, we know Koreans—in the spirit of *Ha myun dwen da!*—can accomplish what they set their minds to. This knowledge inspires hope that Korea can persevere to become a prosperous, empowered, knowledge-era democracy.

Index

About the Author

PAUL F. CHAMBERLIN, a Korea specialist since the early 1970s, has served in business, management, diplomatic, intelligence, operational, and policy planning positions in the United States and in South Korea. He is currently vice president of International Technology and Trade Associates (ITTA) and an adjunct fellow at the Center for Strategic and International Studies (CSIS). He formerly held positions on the U.S. Joint Staff, at the U.S. embassy in Seoul, with the U.S. Defense Intelligence Agency, ROK-U.S. Combined Forces Command, UN Command, and U.S. Forces Korea.

He was the principal political-military policy planner for Korean affairs and an adviser to the chairman of the Joint Chiefs of Staff, assisting in development of U.S. policy regarding the Korean peninsula. In recognition of his contributions to enhancing South Korean security, he was awarded the Korean national security medal (Samil), approved by the president of the Republic of Korea.

He holds a bachelor's degree and a master's degree and is an honor graduate of the U.S. Defense Language Institute's Korean language course. He has written extensively on business, security, and social topics regarding Korea and the U.S.-Korea relationship, including *High Technology Development in Korea: A Comparison of the Use of Capital Markets in Korea and the United States*, published by CSIS.

.769   15

Korea 2010: The Challenges of the New Millennium
Paul F. Chamberlin, with a foreword by Kim Kihwan

"*Korea 2010* provides an in-depth analysis of contemporary Korea and alternative visions of its future. It features a rich, lucid, up-to-date, and balanced analysis . . . [an] innovative book."

Chung-in Moon, Dean, Graduate School of International Studies, Yonsei University

"Paul Chamberlin is extraordinarily well qualified to explain a traditional Korea in a changing world. His research is meticulous and balanced . . . an important book."

James R. Lilley, U.S. Ambassador to the Republic of Korea (1986–1989) and to the People's Republic of China (1989–1991)

"*Korea 2010* is a must read for anyone interested in or involved with Korea. Chamberlin provides an informative analysis of the social, political, and economic institutions in Korea and the challenges that must be overcome for Korea to reach the next plateau."

Jeffrey D. Jones, President, American Chamber of Commerce in Korea

"*Korea 2010* is a vivid portrayal of the extraordinary challenges ahead for a country already in the midst of much greater change than is generally recognized. This useful work demonstrates that quite apart from the struggle with the North, South Korea faces a complex and difficult future."

Don Oberdorfer, author of *Two Koreas* and former *Washington Post* diplomatic correspondent

"With growth come challenges, and anyone contemplating Korean investments, operations, or alliances needs to be well informed. You'll find in this book a solid overview of Korea today, and a thoughtful analysis of its outlook for tomorrow."

Richard D. McCormick, President, International Chamber of Commerce

Paul F. Chamberlin is vice president of International Technology and Trade Associates, Inc., and a former military attaché at the U.S. embassy in Seoul.

The Center for Strategic and International Studies
Washington, D.C.
September 2001

ISBN 0-89206-390-4

9 780892 063901